Mitchell Symons was born in 1957 in London and educated at Mill Hill School and the LSE where he studied just enough Law to get a Third. Since leaving BBC TV, where he was a researcher and then a director, he has worked as a writer, broadcaster and journalist. He was a principal writer of early editions of the board game Trivial Pursuit and has devised many television formats. Currently, he writes an award-winning weekly column for the *Daily Express* and, when he really can't avoid it, his third novel.

Also by Mitchell Symons

Non-fiction:
Forfeit!
The Equation Book of Sports Crosswords
The Equation Book of Movie Crosswords
The You Magazine Book of Journolists (co-author)
Movielists (co-author)
The Sunday Magazine Book of Crosswords
The Hello! Magazine Book of Crosswords
How To Be Fat: The Chip And Fry Diet (co-author)
The Book of Criminal Records
The Book of Lists
The Book of Celebrity Lists
The Book of Celebrity Sex Lists
The Bill Clinton Joke Book
National Lottery Big Draw 2000 (co-author)

Fiction:
All In
The Lot

THAT
BOOK

THAT
BOOK

MITCHELL SYMONS

BANTAM PRESS

LONDON · NEW YORK · TORONTO · SYDNEY · AUCKLAND

TRANSWORLD PUBLISHERS
61–63 Uxbridge Road, London W5 5SA
a division of The Random House Group Ltd

RANDOM HOUSE AUSTRALIA (PTY) LTD
20 Alfred Street, Milsons Point, Sydney,
New South Wales 2061, Australia

RANDOM HOUSE NEW ZEALAND LTD
18 Poland Road, Glenfield, Auckland 10, New Zealand

RANDOM HOUSE SOUTH AFRICA (PTY) LTD
Endulini, 5a Jubilee Road, Parktown 2193, South Africa

Published 2003 by Bantam Press
a division of Transworld Publishers

A catalogue record for this book is available from the British Library.
ISBN 0593 052404

Printed by Mackays of Chatham, Chatham, Kent

10 9 8 7 6 5 4 3 2 1

Papers used by Transworld Publishers are natural, recyclable products made
from wood grown in sustainable forests. The manufacturing processes
conform to the environmental regulations of the country of origin.

To my darling wife, Penny,
and to our wonderful sons,
Jack and Charlie

'There is much pleasure to be gained from useless knowledge'

BERTRAND RUSSELL

FATHERS

Uma Thurman's father was the first American to be ordained a Buddhist monk

Nicholas Parsons's GP father delivered Margaret Thatcher

Stephen King's father went out for a packet of cigarettes and never returned

Julianna Margulies's father wrote the 'plop, plop, fizz, fizz' jingle for Alka-Seltzer

Laura Dern was bullied at school because her father – Bruce Dern – was 'the only person to kill John Wayne in the movies'

Rachel Weisz's father invented the artificial respirator

Vic Reeves's father and grandfather share his birthday – and his real name of Jim Moir

Dame Helen Mirren's father was a Russian aristocrat who was stranded in London after the 1917 Russian Revolution

Bob Marley had a white Liverpudlian father

Elvis Costello's father sang the 'I'm A Secret Lemonade Drinker' jingle for R. White's lemonade

Eminem, Eartha Kitt, Lance Armstrong, Sir Charlie Chaplin, Bill Clinton, Evander Holyfield (whose father had 27 children), Vanilla Ice, Eric Clapton, Naomi Campbell and Mike Tyson never knew their fathers

The fathers of Peter O'Toole, Sir Albert Finney, Mel Smith and Frances Barber were all bookmakers, while Sir Jimmy Savile's father was a bookmaker's clerk

The fathers of George Michael and Yusuf Islam (Cat Stevens) were both Greek restaurateurs

The fathers of Sir Roger Moore, Selina Scott, Julian Clary, Burt Reynolds, Terry Waite, Queen Latifah, Ross Kemp, Arnold Schwarzenegger and Eddie Murphy were all policemen

The fathers of Gordon Brown, Otis Redding, Jane Austen, Sir David Frost, Alice Cooper, John Hurt, Ike Turner, Denzel Washington, Rita Coolidge, Aretha Franklin, Lord Laurence Olivier, Tori Amos, Nina Simone, Frances McDormand and Jessica Simpson were all clergymen

The fathers of Fred Perry, Sir James Goldsmith, Emma Soames, Captain Marryat, Bertrand Russell, Malcolm Muggeridge, Lord Montagu of Beaulieu, Susie Orbach and Elizabeth David were all MPs

The fathers of Harry Houdini, Erich Segal, Jackie Mason and Isaac Asimov were all rabbis

The fathers of Gil Scott-Heron, Ian McShane, Colin Farrell, Steve Harley and Jimmy Nail were all professional footballers

The fathers of Glenn Close, Roger Black, Pamela Stephenson, Katharine Hepburn, Mike Oldfield, Jacqueline Bisset, Brian de Palma, Tony Blackburn, Jane Seymour, Bill Pullman, Edvard Munch, William Roache, Willem Dafoe, Kate Bush, W.H. Auden, Mike Leigh, Dame Judi Dench, Sir Nigel Hawthorne, Sir Tom Stoppard, Humphrey Bogart, Stephen Hawking, Sir Ben Kingsley, Hillary Clinton and Gavin Rossdale were all doctors

Lucy Davis (Jasper Carrott), Emilio Estevez (Martin Sheen), Jennifer Jason Leigh (Vic Morrow) and Norah Jones (Ravi Shankar) all have/had famous fathers but found fame themselves with different surnames

People whose fathers died in World War One: Dame Barbara Cartland, Alfred Shaughnessy, David Niven, Lord Killanin, Lord Longford, Dame Ninette de Valois, Albert Camus

People whose fathers died in World War Two: Bill Cash, Norman Stone, Leslie Thomas, Nick Raynsford, Sir Ludovic Kennedy, Dame Norma Major, Henry Cecil, Tim Rathbone, Roy Walker, John Phillips, Leonard Rossiter, John Ehrlichman, Robert Kilroy-Silk, Screaming Lord Sutch, The Duke of Kent, Gerhard Schroeder, Roger Waters

The fathers of Ricky Gervais, Julie Walters, Jean Shrimpton, Glenda Jackson, Bill Wyman and Boy George all worked in the building trade

The fathers of David Bailey, Harvey Goldsmith, Edwina Currie and Steve Wright were all tailors

The fathers of Michael Parkinson, Gareth Edwards and Robson Green were all miners while Bryan Ferry's father tended pit ponies

The fathers of Melvyn Bragg, Malcolm McDowell and Jamie Oliver were all publicans

The fathers of Dennis Waterman, Alexei Sayle, Dudley Moore and Paul Merton all worked on the railways

The fathers of Jim Carrey and Jeremy Irons were both accountants

The fathers of Barbara Windsor and George Harrison were both bus drivers

The fathers of Alan Bennett and George Cole were both butchers

The fathers of Jerry Hall, Sir Sean Connery and Zandra Rhodes were all lorry drivers

The fathers of Faye Dunaway and Christina Aguilera were both US Army sergeants

The fathers of Rupert Everett and Elizabeth Hurley were both British Army majors

The fathers of Mick Jagger and Ewan McGregor were both PE teachers

The fathers of Robert Redford, Sting and Emma Bunton were all milkmen

The fathers of Sarah Lancashire and Victoria Wood were both writers who wrote episodes of *Coronation Street*

The fathers of Russell Crowe and Patricia Hodge were both hoteliers

The fathers of Olivia Newton-John and Noel Edmonds were both headmasters

The fathers of Robert Duvall and Jim Morrison were admirals in the US Navy while Kris Kristofferson's father was a US Air Force general

Rufus Sewell's father was an animator who worked on *Yellow Submarine*

Anthony Quinn (81), Sir Charlie Chaplin (73), Clint Eastwood (66), Sir John Mortimer (61), Cary Grant (62), Yves Montand (67), Marlon Brando (65), Pablo Picasso (68), Arthur English (61), Francisco de

Goya (68), Saul Bellow (84), Lord Snowdon (68), James Doohan (80), David Jason (61) and James Brown (67) all became fathers past the age of 60

Sylvia Plath, Charlotte Brontë and Gloria Vanderbilt all had father fixations

The fathers of Judy Garland, Jacqueline Onassis, Liza Minnelli and Anne Heche were all gay

The fathers of Sir Michael Redgrave, Lord Jeffrey Archer and Patrick Mower were all bigamists

'To be a successful father there's one absolute rule: when you have a kid, don't look at it for the first two years' (Ernest Hemingway); 'Fathers should neither be seen nor heard. That is the only proper basis for family life' (Oscar Wilde); 'The most important thing a father can do for his children is to love their mother' (Theodore Hesburgh); 'The fundamental defect of fathers is that they want their children to be a credit to them' (Bertrand Russell)

'My father told me all about the birds and the bees. The liar – I went steady with a woodpecker till I was 21.' (Bob Hope)

'It's a wonderful feeling when your father becomes not a god but a whole man. When he comes down from the mountain and you see this man with weaknesses. And you love him as this whole being – not just a figurehead.' (Robin Williams)

'When I was a boy of fourteen, my father was so ignorant I could hardly stand to have the old man around. But when I got to twenty-one, I was astonished at how much he had learned in seven years.' (Mark Twain)

'My dad was always there for me and I want my kids to have the same.' (Kevin Costner)

'My dad is a lot smarter than I am and his line of integrity is to a fault.' (George Clooney)

'My father was frightened of his mother. I was frightened of my father and I'm damned well going to make sure that my children are frightened of me.' (King George V)

'I looked up to my father too much to really open my heart to him. We were almost formal. I did not tell him I loved him. All I can do is hope that he would have known.' (Hugh Laurie)

'My father was the great influence on me. At home he was always building something and we'd always be down with him in his workshop at night. He encouraged me to use my hands and eyes – to be observant and inquisitive. He taught me about beautiful objects.' (Viscount Linley)

'My father made me feel I could do anything a boy could do.' (Esther Rantzen)

'I knocked on his door and was told to wait so I stood around for a while and eventually my father came down and told me to go away. I said, "If I do, I will never see you again," and he said that was what he wanted. So I did go away and I never saw him again.' (Sir Norman Wisdom)

MOTHERS

Eric Clapton, Jack Nicholson and Bobby Darin had mothers whom the rest of the world thought were their sisters; indeed, Darin was 32 before he discovered that his 'mother' was actually his grandmother and that his 'sister' was his mother

Charlton Heston's mother's maiden name was Charlton

When Sir Michael Caine was a child, his mother pasted his ears to his head to stop them sticking out

Victoria Principal's mother's maiden name was Ree Veal

Jarvis Cocker's mother made him wear lederhosen at school, which caused the other children to laugh at him

Jeremy Clarkson's mother made her fortune from Paddington Bear merchandise

David Schwimmer's mother is the attorney who handled Roseanne's first divorce

Telly Savalas and Tommy Lee both had mothers who won the Miss Greece beauty contest

Ryan Giggs, Shirley Maclaine, Marilyn Monroe, Sally Jessy Raphael, Jean Harlow, Lauren Bacall, Pablo Picasso, Shelley Winters and Catherine Deneuve all used their mother's maiden name instead of their father's surname

Priscilla Presley and Claudia Cardinale both became mothers again after becoming grandmothers

Uma Thurman's mother had been married to Timothy Leary before marrying Uma's father

Baroness Shirley Williams (Vera Brittain), Liza Minnelli (Judy Garland), Caron Keating (Gloria Hunniford), Joely Richardson (Vanessa Redgrave), Emma Forbes (Nanette Newman), Mia Farrow (Maureen O'Sullivan), Jennifer Ehle (Rosemary Harris), Carrie Fisher (Debbie Reynolds), Melanie Griffith (Tippi Hedren), Gaynor Faye (Kay Mellor), Kate Hudson (Goldie Hawn) and Sophie Ellis-Bextor (Janet Ellis) all have/had famous mothers but found fame themselves with different surnames

James Cagney, Adolf Hitler, D.H. Lawrence, Marcel Proust, Liberace, Gustav Mahler, Sir J.M. Barrie, Sigmund Freud, Elvis Presley, Peter Tchaikovsky, Harry Houdini, Frank Lloyd Wright and Sir Isaac Newton all had mother fixations

The mothers of Oscar Wilde, Peter O'Toole, Ernest Hemingway, General Douglas MacArthur, Bill Tilden and Franklin D. Roosevelt dressed their sons as girls for the first few years of their lives

The mothers of Sarah Bernhardt and Clara Bow were both prostitutes

The mothers of Patrick Macnee and Jodie Foster were both lesbians

Dame Cleo Laine's mother was a bigamist

'My mother was an incredible character who was very funny and would outride any storm.' (Sir Michael Caine)

'My mother was consumed with her own interest, which was gambling. She was really very self-centred.' (Michael Winner)

'I look so much like my mum, especially when I dress up as a woman.' (Terry Jones)

'The mother is the one who tells you you are beautiful. The mother is the one who keeps reassuring you during those times of insecurity, who keeps your chin up. And I didn't have that.' (Mick Hucknall, whose mother left when he was three)

'My mother is a wonderful, eccentric lady who has no concept whatever of interior monologue. We'll be driving along in the car and she'll suddenly say, "Ants don't like cucumbers, you know. And roaches don't like cinnamon. Do you want some cheese, Michael? Rembrandt was the Lord of the day."' (Mike Myers)

'My mother's death was the most painful thing, because I was so close to her. When you lose someone dear it really encourages you to seize every day, you know, because no one knows how long they've got.' (Ronan Keating)

'There are only two things a child will share willingly – communicable diseases and his mother's age.' (Benjamin Spock)

'My mother loved children – she would have given anything if I had been one.' (Groucho Marx)

'I modelled Tootsie on my mother who was a great character. Sadly she didn't live to see it as she died while I was making the movie but she's in it.' (Dustin Hoffman)

'When I told my mother I was going to marry a Catholic, she couldn't hear me because her head was in the oven.' (Mel Brooks)

'My mum was a great feminist and always said, "Hold your head high – no matter what happens. It's fine, as long as you know you've conducted yourself properly."' (Nicole Kidman)

'My mother gave me two pieces of advice: "Never talk about the movies you didn't do and never talk specifically about men."' (Gwyneth Paltrow)

'My mother's best advice to me was: "To thine own self be true." She often thought Polonius was much maligned. She is the smartest woman I know, with a mind like a steel trap.' (Ben Affleck)

'My mom's a tough bird and one of my best friends in the world. She told me when I was very young, "Don't ever take any crap off anybody, ever." All through my teens and to this day, I don't.' (Johnny Depp)

'My life has been a whirlwind but my mother always helps me to put things in perspective.' (Claire Sweeney)

'There's nothing I won't tell my mother. Nothing. We talk every day on the telephone.' (Claudia Schiffer)

'When I was growing up, the biggest influence in my life was my mother. She made great sacrifices to send me to private school and I will always be grateful for that.' (Naomi Campbell)

Stewardesses is the longest word that is typed with only the left hand

WORDS

The only 15-letter word that can be spelled without repeating a letter is uncopyrightable

Hull City is the only British league football team that hasn't got any letters you can fill in with a biro

If you mouth the word 'colourful' to someone, it looks like you are saying, 'I love you'

'Knightsbridge' is the place with the most consonants in a row

There is no Albanian word for headache

Just 1,000 words make up 90 percent of all writing

No word in the English language rhymes with orange, silver or month

The Hawaiian alphabet has only 12 letters

'Dreamt' is the only English word that ends in the letters 'mt'

The Frying Squad, The Cod Father, Codswallop, Fryer Tuck, Flash in the Pan, Our Plaice and Rock & Sole are all genuine names of fish and chip restaurants

Hairport, Fringe Benefits, Cutting Time, The Clip Joint, Short & Curlers, Power Cuts, Hairs & Graces and Millionhairs are all genuine names of hairdressing salons

Queue is the only word in the English language to be pronounced the same way even if the last four letters are removed

Zenith, tariff, sherbet, algebra, carafe, syrup, cotton, mattress and alcohol are all derived from Arabic

The following words are rarely used in the singular: trivia (trivium), paparazzi (paparazzo), assizes (assize), auspices (auspice), timpani (timpano), minutiae (minutia), grafitti (grafitto), scampi (scampo), scruples (scruple), measles (measle)

The following words are rarely used in the positive: advertent, maculate, clement, consolate, delible, feckful, furl, sipid, speakable, kempt, corrigible, placable, effable, nocuous, pervious, expurgated, peccable, evitable

The expression 'rule of thumb' derives from the old English law that said you couldn't beat your wife with anything wider than your thumb

The name 'jeep' came from the abbreviation 'GP', used in the army for general-purpose vehicle

The word 'chunder' comes from convict ships bound for Australia: when people were going to vomit they used to shout, 'Watch under!'

The word 'bigwig' takes its name from King Louis IV of France who used to wear big wigs

There are only two words in the English language ending in -gry: hungry and angry

Shakespeare invented more than 1,700 words (including 'assassination' and 'bump')

Tom Cruise, Leslie Ash, Susan Hampshire, Cher, Henry Winkler, Sarah Miles, Jackie Stewart, Anthea Turner, Walt Disney, Whoopi Goldberg, Thomas Edison, Leonardo da Vinci, Sir Richard Branson, Noel Gallagher, Ruby Wax, Guy Ritchie, Tommy Hilfiger, Liv Tyler and Robbie Williams have all suffered from dyslexia

Gerard Depardieu, Bill Clinton and Bill Gates have photographic memories

THE NAMES OF THINGS YOU DIDN'T KNOW HAD NAMES

Rowel: **the revolving star on the back of a cowboy's spurs**

Columella: the bottom part of the nose that separates the nostrils

Saddle: **the rounded part on the top of a book of matches**

Ophyron: the space between your eyebrows

Rasceta: **the creases on the inside of your wrist**

Purlicue: the space between the extended thumb and index finger

Nittles: **the punctuation marks designed to denote swear words in comics**

Ferrule: the metal band on the top of a pencil that holds the rubber in place

Peen: **on a hammer, the end opposite the striking face**

Obdormition: when an arm or a leg goes to 'sleep' as a result of numbness caused by pressure on a nerve

Keeper: **the loop on a belt that holds the end in place after it has passed through the buckle**

Armsate: the hole in a shirt or a jumper through which you put your hand and arm

SOME EXPLANATIONS OF BRAND NAMES

Babycham: an abbreviation of 'baby chamois', which is the goat-like antelope used in the TV commercials

Harpic: from the first three letters of the first name and surname of the man who developed it – Harry Pickup

Vim: from the Latin word meaning 'with strength'

Quink: from the words 'quick-drying ink'

Ryvita: from the word 'rye' and the Latin for life, 'vita'

Findus: from the words 'fruit industries' (i.e. F and Indus)

7-Up: named by the inventor who had already rejected six names for his product

Mazda: named after the Persian god of light

Hovis: derives its name from the Latin words 'hominis vis' meaning 'man's strength'

Lego: from the Danish words 'leg godt' meaning 'play well'

THINGS THAT ARE NOT WHAT THEY SEEM

Rice paper contains not a grain of rice

French fries originated in Belgium not France

Great Danes come from Germany not Denmark

10-gallon hats hold only about six pints of water

Koala bears aren't bears, they're marsupials

Mountain goats aren't goats, they're small antelopes

Fireflies aren't flies, they're beetles

The funny bone isn't a bone, it's a nerve

Jackrabbits aren't rabbits, they're hares

Shooting stars are meteors

Prairie dogs aren't dogs, they're rodents

Guinea pigs aren't pigs and nor are they from Guinea: they're South American rodents

Catgut isn't made from cats, it's made from sheep

Lead pencils contain no lead, they contain only graphite

Glow-worms aren't worms, they're beetles

The horned toad isn't a toad, it's a lizard

Bombay duck isn't duck, it's dried fish

Turkish baths originated in Ancient Rome, not in Turkey

Silkworms aren't worms, they're caterpillars

Peanuts aren't nuts, they're legumes

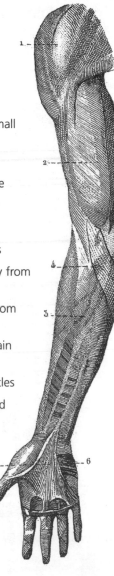

SPOONERISMS

'Kinquering congs their titles take'

'Let us drink to the queer old dean'

'The Lord is a shoving leopard'

'That is just a half-warmed fish'

'The cat popped on its drawers'

'Is the bean dizzy?'

'Please sew me to another sheet'

'You will leave by the next town drain'

THE HUMAN CONDITION

Only one person in two billion will live to be 116 or older

The human body grows the equivalent of a new skeleton every seven years

A newborn baby's heart beats twice as fast as an adult's

The average person's heart beats 36 million times a year

Adult humans have 206 bones. At birth, an infant has 350 bones. As the child grows, many bones fuse with other bones

A quarter of the 206 bones in the human body are in the feet

As a child grows, the body part that grows least is the eye. While the rest of an adult body is 20 times bigger than it was at birth, the eye is only three and a quarter times bigger

Women get more migraines than men

The average person is a quarter of an inch taller at night

Fingernails grow four times faster than toenails

The average person sleeps for about 220,000 hours (or just over 25 years) in a lifetime

It takes just one minute for blood to travel through the whole human body

People who live in the city have longer, thicker nose hairs than people who live in the country

The first of the five senses to go with age is smell

More boys than girls are born during the day; more girls are born at night

Your stomach has to produce a new layer of mucus every two weeks otherwise it will digest itself

The human sneeze travels at 600mph

The strongest muscle in the body is the tongue

You can't kill yourself by holding your breath

Right-handed people live, on average, nine years longer than left-handed people do

Humans are the only animals that cry

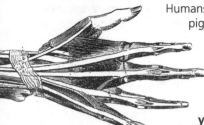

Humans are the only primates that don't have pigment in the palms of their hands

Men get more ulcers than women

Children have more taste buds than adults

Your tongueprint is as unique as your fingerprints

If you yelled for eight years, seven months and six days, you would have produced enough sound energy to heat one cup of coffee

The human heart creates enough pressure while pumping to squirt blood 30 feet

Banging your head against a wall uses 150 calories an hour

We shed an average of 40 pounds of dead skin in a lifetime

The average person laughs 15 times a day

Pain travels through our bodies at a speed of 350 feet a second

When we blush, our stomach lining also turns red

Our eyes don't freeze in very cold weather because of the salt in our tears

Women blink nearly twice as often as men

We get goose bumps where our ancestors used to have hair

Humans are the only animals to sleep on their backs

The brain weighs three pounds but uses some 20 percent of the body's blood and oxygen

The average person has 100,000 hairs on his or her head – but redheads have fewer and blondes have more

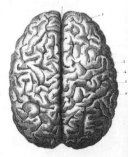

On one square inch of our skin there are 20 million microscopic animals

 The average human eats eight spiders in his or her lifetime at night

Babies are born without kneecaps. They don't appear until the child reaches 2–6 years of age

If you farted continuously for six years and nine months, enough wind would be produced to equal the energy of an atomic bomb

Science

The microwave was invented after a researcher walked by a radar tube and a chocolate bar melted in his pocket

Grapes explode when you put them in the microwave

There are more than 1,000 chemicals in a cup of coffee; of these, only 26 have been tested, and half of them caused cancer in rats

A rainbow can occur only when the sun is 40 degrees or less above the horizon

Cut an onion in half, rub it on the sole of your foot and an hour later you'll taste onion in your mouth

In ten minutes, a hurricane releases more energy than all the world's nuclear weapons combined

Britney Spears and Anna Kournikova have both had computer viruses named after them

AROUND THE WORLD

Disneyworld is bigger than the world's five smallest countries

The Danish flag – dating back to the thirteenth century – is the world's oldest unchanged national flag

Italy's national flag was designed by Napoleon

There is a city called Rome in every continent

There are three American towns named Santa Claus

Istanbul is the only city in the world to be in two continents (Europe and Asia)

Los Angeles's full name is: 'El Pueblo de Nuestra Señora la Reina de los Angeles de Poriuncula' and can be abbreviated to 3.63 percent of its size: 'LA'

Mongolians put salt in their tea instead of sugar

Americans on average eat 18 acres of pizza every day

All the continents are wider in the north than in the south

You could drive a car round the world four times with the amount of fuel in a jumbo jet

If the population of China walked past you in single file, the line would never end because of the rate of reproduction

China has more English speakers than the United States

Ten percent of the Russian government's income comes from the sale of vodka

The glue on Israeli postage stamps is certified kosher

The highest point in Pennsylvania is lower than the lowest point in Colorado

The Dead Sea is really a lake

'Q' is the only letter that doesn't appear in the names of any of the fifty states of the US

There isn't a (real) river in the whole of Saudi Arabia

If all the Antarctic ice melted, the ocean level would rise nearly 250 feet, and 25 percent of the world's land surface would be flooded

Antarctica is the only continent without snakes or reptiles

ESSENTIAL FACTS

There are 293 ways to make change for a dollar

Nutmeg is extremely poisonous if injected intravenously

$111,111,111 \times 111,111,111 = 12,345,678,987,654,321$

Pearls melt in vinegar

No former American president has ever died in the month of May

If 20-a-day smokers inhaled a week's worth of nicotine they would die instantly

The buttons on a man's jacket cuff were originally intended to stop manservants from wiping their noses on the sleeves of their uniforms

Watching TV uses up 50 percent more calories than sleeping

20 percent of the people in the whole history of mankind who have lived beyond the age of 65 are alive today

Volleyball is the most popular sport at nudist camps

On average, a drop of Heinz tomato ketchup leaves the bottle at a speed of 25 miles per year

At any given moment, there are some 1,800 thunderstorms somewhere on the planet earth

Tuesday Weld was born on a Friday

Six out of seven gynaecologists are men

The Bible is the most shoplifted book in the US

Strawberries have more vitamin C than oranges

Pollen lasts for ever

If Barbie – whose full name is Barbara Millicent Roberts – were lifesize, her measurements would be 39–23–33, she would stand 7 feet 2 inches tall and she would have a neck twice the length of a normal human's neck

No piece of paper can be folded in half more than 7 times

ANIMALS

There isn't a single reference to a cat in the Bible

Nearly all polar bears are left-handed

A newborn panda is smaller than a mouse

The heads of a freak two-headed snake will fight over food – despite sharing the same stomach

There are no furry animals native to Antarctica

The armadillo is the only animal – apart from man – that can catch leprosy

The elephant is the only animal with four knees

Some snakes can live up to a year without eating

A beaver can chop down more than 200 trees in a year

Besides humans, the only animal that can suffer sunburn is the pig

Giraffes can live without water for longer than camels can

The average rabbit takes 18 naps a day

Besides humans, the only animal which can stand on its head is the elephant

The Basenji is the only dog that doesn't bark

A pig's orgasm lasts for 30 minutes

It takes a male horse only 14 seconds to copulate

The elephant is the only mammal that can't jump

A skunk will not bite and throw its scent at the same time

Cats have over one hundred vocal sounds; dogs have only about ten

The female nutria, a furry rodent, is the only mammal with nipples along its backbone

A donkey will sink in quicksand but a mule won't

Pigs can become alcoholics

Tigers have striped skin, not just striped fur

The reindeer is the only female animal with antlers

Polar bears can smell a human being from 20 miles away

Most dinosaurs were no bigger than chickens

Wombats can run up to 40kph and stop dead in half a stride. They kill their prey this way – the prey runs into the wombat's bum-bone and smashes its face

When hippopotamuses get upset, their sweat turns red

Of all the mammal species in the world, almost a quarter are bats

No new animals have been domesticated in the last 4,000 years

The world's biggest frog is bigger than the world's smallest antelope

An angry gorilla pokes its tongue out

Sir Anthony Hopkins (black-footed penguin), Marie Helvin (black rhino), Steve Davis (camel) and Rolf Harris (koala bear) have all 'adopted' animals at London Zoo

Insects etc

A male spider's reproductive organ is located at the end of one of his legs

The average caterpillar has 2,000 muscles in its body (we humans have 656)

Tarantulas can go for up to two years without eating

Anteaters can stick out their tongues up to 160 times a minute

Mother tarantulas kill 99 percent of the babies they hatch

Queen bees only ever use their stingers to kill other queen bees

Queen termites can live for up to 100 years

The most poisonous spider is not the black widow but the wingless daddy longlegs – but its fangs can't pierce human skin and so it poses no threat

A cockroach can live for several weeks after being decapitated

The snail is the only insect with retractable antennae

Gram for gram, a bumblebee is 150 times stronger than an elephant

An ant can survive for two weeks underwater

The house fly hums in the middle octave key of F

Hmmmmmmmm

The male gypsy moth can 'smell' the virgin female gypsy moth from 1.8 miles

Snails can sleep for three years without eating

The ant can lift 50 times its own weight and can pull 30 times its own weight

The praying mantis is the only insect that can turn its head without moving its body

A bee is more likely to sting you on a windy day

The flea can jump 350 times its body length

Fish etc

Starfish don't have brains

The catfish has over 27,000 taste buds (more than any other creature on the planet)

Goldfish kept in a darkened room eventually turn white

The baby blue whale gains ten pounds in weight per hour

Whale songs rhyme

The male rather than the female seahorse carries the eggs

The starfish is the only creature on the planet that can turn its stomach inside out

A goldfish has a memory span of three seconds

The giant squid has the largest eyes in the world

A pregnant goldfish is called a twit

The oldest recorded age reached by a goldfish is 41

The white shark is the only sea creature with no natural enemies

Dolphins sleep with one eye open

A blue whale's tongue weighs more than an elephant

BIRDS ETC

The longest recorded flight of a chicken is thirteen seconds

Female canaries can't sing

The ptarmigan turns completely white in the winter

The average ostrich's eye is the size of a tennis ball and bigger than its brain

There is the same number of chickens in the world as humans

The waste produced by one chicken in its lifetime could supply enough electricity to run a 100-watt bulb for five hours

A duck's quack doesn't echo and no one knows why

The most common bird in the world is the starling

The hummingbird is the only bird that can fly backwards

The average lifespan of a parrot is 120 years

The golden eagle can spot a rabbit from nearly two miles away

The penguin is the only bird that walks upright (it is also the only bird that can swim but not fly)

Ostriches yawn in groups before going to sleep

Owls are the only birds that can see the colour blue

Pigeons are the only birds that can drink water without having to raise their heads to swallow

Flamingoes can only eat with their heads upside down

HISTORY

Each king in a deck of playing cards represents a great king from history: Spades – King David; Clubs – Alexander the Great; Hearts – Charlemagne; Diamonds – Julius Caesar

The only painting Vincent Van Gogh sold in his lifetime was *The Red Vineyard*

The Roman Emperor Nero 'married' his male slave Scotus

Michelangelo's cook was illiterate so he drew her a shopping list – which today is priceless

Spiral staircases in medieval castles ran clockwise so that attacking knights climbing the stairs couldn't use their right hands – their sword hands – while the defending knights coming down could. And left-handed men, believed to descend from the devil, couldn't become knights

The shortest war in history was between Zanzibar and England in 1896: Zanzibar surrendered after 38 minutes

February 1865 is the only month in recorded history not to have a full moon

Pirates wore earrings in the belief that it improved their eyesight

The architect who built the Kremlin had his eyes gouged out by Ivan The Terrible so that he'd never be able to design another building like it

In Ancient Egypt, priests plucked every hair from their bodies, including their eyebrows and eyelashes

PEOPLE WHO WOULD HAVE TURNED 100 IN 2004

Graham Greene, writer

Nancy Mitford, writer

Irene Dunne, actress

Dame Anna Neagle, actress

Moss Hart, playwright

Harold Larwood, cricketer

Dick Powell, actor

Sir Harold Hobson, theatre critic

Max Factor, cosmetician

Deng Xiaoping, politician

Christopher Isherwood, writer

Vladimir Horowitz, musician

George Balanchine, choreographer

Ray Bolger, actor

Cary Grant, actor

Cecil Beaton, photographer and designer

Alexei Kosygin, politician

William Shirer, writer and historian

Isaac Bashevis Singer, writer

George Formby, entertainer

Johnny Weissmuller, actor

Ralph Bellamy, actor

Harold Acton, aesthete

Salvador Dalí, artist

Jean Gabin, actor

Robert Montgomery, actor

Fats Waller, jazz musician

Sir John Gielgud, actor

Bruce Cabot, actor

Robert Oppenheimer, physicist

C. Day Lewis, poet

Bing Crosby, singer and actor

Sir Gordon Richards, jockey

John Snagge, sports commentator

Jimmy Dorsey, bandleader

Dr Seuss, children's writer

Glenn Miller, bandleader

George Brent, actor

Ward Bond, actor

People who turn 80 in 2004

Lord Brian Rix, actor and charity head

Sidney Poitier, actor

Ron Moody, actor

Tony Britton, actor

George Bush, politician

Jimmy Carter, politician

Charlton Heston, actor

Leslie Phillips, actor

Charles Aznavour, singer and actor

Dennis Weaver, actor

Marlon Brando, actor

Doris Day, actress

Sir John Harvey-Jones, industrialist

Henry Mancini, composer

PEOPLE WHO TURN 70 IN 2004

Dame Maggie Smith, actress

Dame Judi Dench, actress

Brigitte Bardot, actress

Sophia Loren, actress

Leonard Cohen, singer/songwriter and poet

Nanette Newman, actress

Jackie Mason, comedian

Giorgio Armani, fashion designer

Dame Eileen Atkins, actress

Wendy Craig, actress

Jamie Farr, actor

Jean Marsh, actress

Sydney Pollack, director and actor

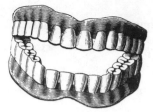

Colin Welland, actor and writer

Louise Fletcher, actress

Millicent Martin, singer and actress

Sir Alan Bates, actor

Barry Humphries, actor, comedian and writer

Rue McClanahan, actress

Jean Chrétien, politician

Shirley MacLaine, actress

Sir Henry Cooper, boxer

Alan Bennett, writer and actor

Sian Phillips, actress

Mary Quant, fashion designer

Timothy West, actor

Charles Manson, murderer

Billy Paul, singer

George Segal, actor

Gloria Steinem, feminist

Alan Arkin, actor

Shirley Jones, actress

Norman Schwarzkopf, general

PEOPLE WHO TURN 60 IN 2004

Michael Douglas, actor

Anne Robinson, TV presenter and journalist

Duke of Gloucester

Roger Waters, pop/rock star

Danny DeVito, actor

Harold Ramis, actor and director

Ralph McTell, pop/rock star

Neil Innes, pop/rock star

Booker T. Jones, pop/rock star

Jane Lapotaire, actress

Clive Lloyd, cricketer

John Simpson, TV news reporter

Jacqueline Bisset, actress

David Soul, actor and singer

Bobbie Gentry, pop/rock star

Mary Robinson, stateswoman

John Newcombe, tennis player

Roger Rees, actor

Joe Cocker, pop/rock star

Robert Powell, actor

Gladys Knight, pop/rock star

Marvin Hamlisch, composer

Michelle Phillips, singer and actress

Boz Scaggs, pop/rock star

Helmut Berger, actor

Sly Stone, pop/rock star

John Sebastian, pop/rock star

Diana Ross, pop/rock star

Mary Wilson, pop/rock star

Richard O'Sullivan, actor

George Lucas, film director

Dave Edmunds, pop/rock star

Daniel Galvin, designer

Jill Clayburgh, actress

Rita Coolidge, pop/rock star

Dame Kiri Te Kanawa, singer

Christine McVie, pop/rock star

Loretta Swit, actress

Kinky Friedman, pop/rock star

Sir Tim Rice, lyricist

Erno Rubik, puzzle setter

Geraldine Chaplin, actress

Jonathan Dimbleby, broadcaster

Ray Davies, pop/rock star

Klaus Maria Brandauer, actor

Jeff Beck, pop/rock star

Arthur Brown, pop/rock star

Robbie Robertson, pop/rock star

Tony Jacklin, golfer

Glenys Kinnock, politician

Roger Daltrey, pop/rock star

Peter Tork, pop/rock star

Jerry Springer, TV presenter

Stockard Channing, actress

Sir Alan Parker, film director

Scott Mackenzie, pop/rock star

Patti Labelle, pop/rock star

Angela Rippon, TV presenter

Roger Taylor, tennis player

David Trimble, politician

Dennis Franz, actor

Carl Bernstein, journalist

Scott Walker (Engel), pop/rock star

Jimmy Page, pop/rock star

Joe Frazier, boxer

Rutger Hauer, actor

Françoise Hardy, pop/rock star

PEOPLE WHO TURN 50 IN 2004

Annie Lennox, pop/rock star

Denzel Washington, actor

Christie Brinkley, model

Matt Groening, creator of *The Simpsons*

James Cameron, film director

Joe Jackson, pop/rock star

Elvis Costello, pop/rock star

John Lloyd, tennis player

Anne Diamond, TV presenter

Bertie Ahern, politician

Rickie Lee Jones, pop/rock star

Adam Ant, pop/rock star

Chris Difford, pop/rock star

Yanni, pop/rock star

Cherie Blair, wife of Tony Blair

Bob Geldof, pop/rock star

**Jermaine Jackson,
pop/rock star**

Chris Evert,
tennis player

**Marvin Hagler,
boxer**

Jim Belushi, actor

**Kathleen Turner,
actress**

Anne Kirkbride, actress

Neil Tennant, pop/rock star

Rick Moranis, actor

Captain Sensible, pop/rock star

Jerry Seinfeld, comedian

Ray Parker Jr, pop/rock star

Rene Russo, actress

Lesley-Anne Down, actress

Iain Duncan-Smith, politician

Ellen Barkin, actress

Dennis Quaid, actor

Jackie Chan, actor

Robert Carradine, actor

John Travolta, actor

Oprah Winfrey, TV presenter

Howard Stern, broadcaster

Ron Howard, actor and director

PEOPLE WHO TURN 40 IN 2004

Keanu Reeves, actor

Tracy Chapman, pop/rock star

Russell Crowe, actor

Lisa Kudrow, actress

Jean Alesi, racing driver

Kathy Burke, actress

Courteney Cox, actress

Johnny Herbert, motor racing driver

Courtney Love, actress and singer

Yasmin Le Bon, model

Calista Flockhart, actress

Liza Tarbuck, TV presenter and actress

Robin Givens, actress

Marisa Tomei, actress

Beatrice Dalle, actress

Patrick Marber, playwright and actor

Janeane Garofalo, actress

Harry Hill, comedian

Sarah Lancashire, actress

Yvonne Murray, athlete

Teri Hatcher, actress

Matt Dillon, actor

Lee Evans, comedian and actor

Famke Janssen, actress

John Leguizamo, actor

Jürgen Klinsmann, footballer

Nicolas Cage, actor

Jane Horrocks, actress

Bridget Fonda, actress

Linus Roache, actor

Juliette Binoche, actress

Prince Edward, Duke of Wessex

Neneh Cherry, pop/rock star

Rob Lowe, actor

Bonnie Blair, actress

Courtney Pine, jazz musician

Elle Macpherson, model

Yeardley Smith, actress

Tori Amos, pop/rock star

Mats Wilander, tennis player

Joanne Whalley, actress

Jason Priestley, actor

Davis Love III, golfer

Diana Krall, singer and jazz musician

Hank Azaria, actor

Lady Helen Taylor (née Windsor)

Lady Sarah Chatto (née Armstrong Jones)

John Parrott, snooker player

Earl Spencer, brother of Diana, Princess of Wales

Liz McColgan, athlete

David Baddiel, comedian and writer

Butch Reynolds, athlete

PEOPLE WHO TURN 30 IN 2004

Leonardo DiCaprio, actor

Penelope Cruz, actress

Melanie Chisholm (Mel C), pop/rock star

Denise Van Outen, TV presenter and actress

Kate Moss, model

Christian Bale, actor

Prince Naseem Hamed, boxer

Robbie Williams, pop/rock star

Melanie Blatt, pop/rock star

Andrea Corr, pop/rock star

Victoria Beckham, pop/rock star

Tony McCoy, jockey

Jewel, pop/rock star

Alanis Morissette, pop/rock star

Dani Behr, TV presenter

Maurice Greene, athlete

Hilary Swank, actress

Natasha Henstridge, actress

Tim Henman, tennis player

Keith Duffy, pop/rock star

Joaquin Phoenix, actor

Chloe Sevigny, actress

Vanessa Paradis, singer and actress

People who turn 25 in 2004

Sophie Ellis-Bextor, pop/rock star

Brandy Norwood, singer and actress

Mena Suvari, actress

Jennifer Love Hewitt, actress

Shola Ama, pop/rock star

Norah Jones, pop/rock star

Natasha Lyonne, actress

Heath Ledger, actor

Keshia Knight Pulliam, actress

Claire Danes, actress

Kate Hudson, actress

Lance Bass, pop/rock star

Jonny Wilkinson, rugby union player

Shane Filan, pop/rock star

Donna Air, TV presenter

Tiffany Chapman, actress

Sophie Dahl, model

Kelly Brook, model and TV presenter

Michael Owen, footballer

THINGS THAT STARTED IN THE 1950S

Rock 'n' roll, X-certificate films, the singles charts, CND, nuclear submarines, telephone weather forecasting service, the Planetarium at Madame Tussaud's, televising of Rugby League matches, credit cards, the EEC, NATO, duty-free booze for holidaymakers, the Mini, the Miss World contest, Angry Young Men (in literature and in the theatre), kitchen-sink dramas, Teddy Boys, *This Is Your Life*, teabags, the frisbee, *Carry On* films, Wimpy Bars, ABTA, Luncheon Vouchers, *Andy Pandy*, tranquillizers, parking meters, Disneyland, *The Guinness Book of Records*, space travel, fluoride toothpaste, Lego, transistor hearing aids, ITV (and, therefore, TV commercials), Cinemascope, diet soft drinks (no-cal ginger ale), the Eurovision Song Contest, Yellow Pages, Barbie dolls, comprehensive schools, fishfingers, automatic electric kettles, television detector vans, TV situation comedies, heart pacemakers, yellow no-parking lines, typewriter correction fluid, microwave ovens, the hovercraft, TV party political broadcasts, the Velcro fastener, *Blue Peter*, zebra crossings, Premium Bonds, *The Mousetrap*, Polyfilla, British motorways, trunk calls, life peers, postcodes, non-stick saucepans, Club Med, the Moonies, supermarket chains, go-karts, polio vaccines, Beatniks, kidney transplants, roll-on deodorants, boutiques, Legal Aid, disposable nappies

WINNERS OF THE *SPECTATOR* PARLIAMENTARIAN OF THE YEAR AWARD

2002: Tony Blair

2001: David Trimble

2000: Tony Benn and
Sir Edward Heath

1999: John Major

1998: William Hague

1997: Gordon Brown

1996: Michael Forsyth

1995: James Molyneaux

1994: Richard Shepherd

**1993: George Robertson
and Geoffrey Hoon**

1992: Betty Boothroyd

1991: Robin Cook

1990: Douglas Hurd

1989: John Smith

1988: Sir Edward
Heath

1987: Nigel Lawson

1986: John Smith

1985: John Biffen

1984: Dr David Owen

THE ODDS AGAINST VARIOUS EVENTUALITIES

Being struck by lightning: one in 10 million

Being killed by a bee sting: one in 6 million

Giving birth to quintuplets: one in 57 million births – without fertility treatment

Hitting two holes-in-one during the same round of golf: one in 8 million

Dying during a football knockabout: one in 25,000

Being hijacked on a plane by terrorists twice in the same year: one in 150 million

Every match in a full Premier League programme finishing in a 0–0 draw: one in 60 million

Being hit by a meteorite: one in 200 million

A woman being colour blind: one in 1,000 (women are ten times less likely than men to suffer from colour blindness)

An adult catching head lice in any given year: one in 100

Dying in an aeroplane crash: one in 2.2 million

A male being impotent between the ages of 20 and 30: one in 124

Winning first prize – not shared – on the National Lottery: one in 14 million

Choking to death on food: one in 250,000

Getting killed in a road accident: one in 15,800

Going into a permanent vegetative state following a head injury: one in one million

Getting kidney stones in any year: one in 100

Your unborn child getting a stutter: one in 400

Flying on an aeroplane with the same flight number as a plane that crashed: zero (flight numbers are always eliminated after a crash)

Becoming an alcoholic if you drink regularly: one in ten

Maniacs

Kleptomaniac (person obsessed with stealing)

Chionomaniac (snow)

Ablutomaniac (bathing)

Timbromaniac (stamps)

Pyromaniac (fire)

Nudomaniac (nudity)

Cynomaniac (dogs)

Ailuromaniac (cats)

Ichthyomaniac (fish)

Oniomaniac (buying)

Arithomaniac (counting)

Philopatridomaniac (homesickness)

Bruxomaniac (grinding teeth)

Klazomaniac (shouting)

Catapedamaniac (jumping from high places)

Onychotillomaniac (picking nails)

Cresomaniac (personal wealth)

Phagomaniac (food)

Titillomaniac (scratching)

Erythromaniac (blushing)

Dromomaniac (travelling)

THINGS THAT MONEY CAN'T BUY

Membership of the MCC or Glyndebourne (long waiting-lists that you can't leapfrog no matter how rich you are)

The affection of a dog (they either love you or they don't – irrespective of how wealthy you are)

A handgun (at least not legally)

A swan (all swans are owned by the Queen)

Any freehold property in Grosvenor Square (the Duke of Westminster owns Grosvenor Square and they have a policy of never selling freeholds)

An entry in *Who's Who*

An Aztec bar (Cadbury's don't make them any more)

A full driving licence

The *Mona Lisa* (like all paintings kept in museums, it's simply not for sale)

Entry to the Royal Enclosure at Royal Ascot

A cure for a cold

A new Citroën 2CV car

The skeleton of the Elephant Man (it's in the London Hospital, from whom Michael Jackson tried to buy it – offering millions – to no avail)

'Rude' number plates

A place at a British university

A private beach in mainland England (you can buy a private road giving you private access to the shore but you can't buy the beach itself)

Fellowship of the Royal Society

Immunity from the law

A Cuban Red Macaw (the last one disappeared in 1894)

A ticket for a PanAm flight (at least not since 3 December 1991)

Entry to a British Playboy Club (the last one closed in 1988)

A planet (there's an international agreement which prohibits any country or individual from buying one)

A Nobel prize

Money can't buy a wild donkey (no such animal now exists)

MURPHY'S LAW

Anything that can go wrong will go wrong

The first place to look for something is the last place you would expect to find it

When someone says, 'It's not the money, it's the principle', nine times out of ten it's the money

Whenever you make a journey by bicycle, it's always more uphill than downhill

As soon as you mention something:
a) if it's good, it goes away;
b) if it's bad, it happens

You never find something until you replace it

When the train you are on is late, the bus to take you home from the station will be on time

If an experiment works, something has gone wrong

It always rains when you've just washed your car but washing your car to make it rain won't work

When you dial a wrong number, it's never engaged

Cheques get lost in the post but bills never do

In a supermarket, the other queues always move faster than yours

Illnesses always start on a Friday evening ... but end on a Monday morning

Friends come and go but enemies accumulate

The odds of the bread falling butter-side down are directly proportional to the value of the carpet

The severity of an itch is inversely proportional to how easy it is to scratch

If during a month only three enjoyable social activities take place, they will all happen on the same evening

The only way to get a bank loan is to prove you don't need one

SINGULAR PEOPLE

Samuel L. Jackson was Bill Cosby's stand-in for three years on *The Cosby Show*

Kate Beckinsale won the W.H. Smith Young Writers Competition for prose and poetry – two years running

Chuck Berry invented his duck walk initially to hide the creases in his suit

John Wayne once won the dog Lassie from its owner in a poker game

Jack Nicholson was in detention every day for a whole school year

Olivia Newton-John is president of the Isle of Man Basking Sharks Society

Mariah Carey's vocal range spans five octaves

Nick Nolte ate real dog food in the film *Down And Out In Beverly Hills* (when he was showing the dog how to eat from a dog bowl)

When Paul Gambaccini was at Oxford at the same time as Bill Clinton, it was he who was voted The American Most Likely To Succeed

Melissa Joan Hart can recite the mathematical expression 'pi' to 400 decimal places

Nicolas Cage ate a live cockroach for *Vampire's Kiss*

Sir Winston Churchill smoked an estimated 300,000 cigars in his lifetime

Tom Cruise has saved three lives – in Santa Monica, off the island of Capri and in London

Ben Stiller was taught how to swim by The Pips (as in Gladys Knight & the Pips)

Amanda Peet can recite all the lines from *Tootsie* and *A Chorus Line*

Richard Gere never swears. Any visitor who swears in his home is asked to leave

Pierce Brosnan bought the typewriter of James Bond creator Ian Fleming for £52,800

When he was a teenager, Colin Farrell put Smarties under his pillow in an attempt to bring Marilyn Monroe back from the dead

Isaac Asimov is the only author to have a book in every Dewey-decimal category

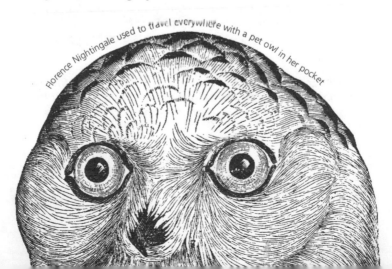

Florence Nightingale used to travel everywhere with a pet owl in her pocket

ALL THE GOLDEN RASPBERRY AWARDS (OR RAZZIES) FOR WORST FILM, WORST ACTOR AND WORST ACTRESS

For 2002 (awarded in 2003): *Swept Away*; Roberto Benigni (*Pinocchio*); Madonna (*Swept Away*) tied with Britney Spears (*Crossroads*)

For 2001: *Freddy Got Fingered*; Tom Green (*Freddy Got Fingered*); Mariah Carey (*Glitter*)

For 2000: *Battlefield Earth*; John Travolta (*Battlefield Earth* and *Lucky Numbers*); Madonna (*The Next Best Thing*)

For 1999: *Wild Wild West*; Adam Sandler (*Big Daddy*); Heather Donahue (*The Blair Witch Project*)

For 1998: *Burn, Hollywood, Burn!*; Bruce Willis (*Armageddon*, *Mercury Rising* and *The Siege*); The Spice Girls (*Spiceworld The Movie*)

For 1997: *The Postman*; Kevin Costner (*The Postman*); Demi Moore (*G.I. Jane*)

For 1996: *Striptease*; Tom Arnold (*Big Bully*, *Carpool* and *The Stupids*); Demi Moore (*The Juror* and *Striptease*)

For 1995: *Showgirls*; Pauly Shore (*Jury Duty*); Elizabeth Berkley (*Showgirls*)

For 1994: *Color of Night*; Kevin Costner (*Wyatt Earp*); Sharon Stone (*Intersection* and *The Specialist*)

For 1993: *Indecent Proposal*; Burt Reynolds (*Cop And A Half*); Madonna (*Body of Evidence*)

For 1992: *Shining Through*; Sylvester Stallone (*Stop! Or My Mom Will Shoot*); Melanie Griffith (*Shining Through* and *A Stranger Among Us*)

For 1991: *Hudson Hawk*; Kevin Costner (*Robin Hood, Prince of Thieves*); Sean Young (*A Kiss Before Dying*)

For 1990: *Adventures of Ford Fairline* tied with *Ghosts Can't Do It*; Andrew Dice Clay (*Adventures of Ford Fairline*); Bo Derek (*Ghosts Can't Do It*)

For 1989: *Star Trek V*; William Shatner (*Star Trek V*); Heather Locklear (*Return of The Swamp Thing*)

For 1988: *Cocktail*; Sylvester Stallone (*Rambo III*); Liza Minnelli (*Arthur 2: On The Rocks* and *Rent-A-Cop*)

For 1987: *Leonard: Part 6*; Bill Cosby (*Leonard: Part 6*); Madonna (*Who's That Girl?*)

For 1986: *Howard The Duck* tied with *Under The Cherry Moon*; Prince (*Under The Cherry Moon*); Madonna (*Shanghai Surprise*)

For 1985: *Rambo: First Blood Part II*; Sylvester Stallone (*Rambo: First Blood Part II* and *Rocky IV*); Linda Blair (*Night Patrol, Savage Island* and *Savage Streets*)

For 1984: *Bolero*; Sylvester Stallone (*Rhinestone*); Bo Derek (*Bolero*)

For 1983: *The Lonely Lady*; Christopher Atkins (*A Night In Heaven*); Pia Zadora (*The Lonely Lady*)

For 1982: *Inchon!*; Laurence Olivier (*Inchon!*); Pia Zadora (*Butterfly*)

For 1981: *Mommie Dearest*; Klinton Spillsbury (*Legend of The Lone Ranger*); Bo Derek (*Tarzan, The Ape Man*) tied with Faye Dunaway (*Mommie Dearest*)

For 1980: *Can't Stop The Music*; Neil Diamond (*The Jazz Singer*); Brooke Shields (*The Blue Lagoon*)

THE BRITISH ASSOCIATION OF TOY RETAILERS' TOY OF THE YEAR

2002/2003: Beyblades

2001/2002: Bionicle by Lego

2000/2001: Teksta

1999/2000: Furby Babies

1998: Furby

1997: Teletubbies

1996: Barbie

1995: POGS

1994: Power Rangers

1993: Thunderbirds Tracey Island

1992: WWF Wrestlers

1991: Nintendo Game Boy

1990: Teenage Mutant Ninja Turtles

1989: Sylvanian Families

1988: Sylvanian Families

1987: Sylvanian Families

1986: Transformers (Optimus Prime)

1985: Transformers (Optimus Prime)

1984: Masters of the Universe

1983: Star Wars toys

1982: Star Wars

1981: Rubik's Cube

1980: Rubik's Cube

1979: Legoland Space kits

1978: Combine Harvester (Britains)

1977: Playmobil Playpeople

1976: Peter Powell kites

1975: Lego Basic set

1974: Lego Family set

1973: Mastermind – board game

1972: Plasticraft modelling kits

1971: Katie Kopykat writing doll

1970: Sindy

1969: Hot Wheels cars

1968: Sindy

1967: Spirograph

1966: Action Man

1965: James Bond Aston Martin die-cast car

ALL THE BRITISH FORMULA 1 WORLD MOTOR RACING CHAMPIONS

Mike Hawthorn (1958)

Graham Hill (1962 and 1968)

Jim Clark (1963 and 1965)

John Surtees (1964)

Jackie Stewart (1969, 1971 and 1973)

James Hunt (1976)

Nigel Mansell (1992)

Damon Hill (1996)

THE LANGUAGE OF THE NOTTING HILL CARNIVAL

Cease and sekkle! – Stop everything and relax!

Come dung – Come down, get ready (prepare to play a tune)

Cool runnings – A greeting; things are going smoothly

Darkers – Sunglasses

Duns, Dunsa, Funds – Money

Feel no way – Don't take offence, don't be sorry, don't worry

Irie – Powerful and pleasing

Laba-laba – To chat, gossip

(Too) Likky-likky – Used to describe those who like to eat any food they encounter, without discretion

Skin your teeth – Smile

Wanga-gut – Hungry-belly

(Don) Gorgon – Outstanding dreadlocks, a person who is respected

Shake out – Leave without haste

ALL THE REARS OF THE YEAR

As awarded by the British jeans industry

2003: Natasha Hamilton and Ronan Keating

2002: Charlotte Church and Scott Wright

2001: Claire Sweeney and John Altman

2000: Jane Danson and Graham Norton

1999: Denise Van Outen and Robbie Williams

1998: Carol Smillie and Frank Skinner

1997: Melinda Messenger and Gary Barlow

1996: Tracy Shaw

1995: No award

1994: Mandy Smith and Richard Fairbrass

1993: Sarah Lancashire

1992: Ulrika Jonsson

1990, 1991: No awards

1989: Marina Ogilvy

1988: Su Pollard

1987: Anita Dobson

1986: Anneka Rice and Michael Barrymore

1985: Lynsey de Paul

1984: Elaine Paige

1983: Lulu

1982: Suzi Quatro

1981: Felicity Kendal

1976: Barbara Windsor (it was a one-off award; the next one wasn't until five years later)

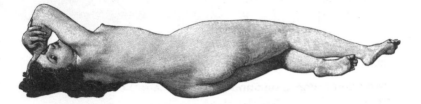

DUMB THINGS PEOPLE HAVE SAID

'Go back to Liverpool, Mr Epstein, groups with guitars are out.' (Dick Rowe of Decca, rejecting The Beatles)

'Get rid of the lunatic who says he's got a machine for seeing by wireless.' (The then editor of the *Daily Express* refusing to meet John Logie Baird – the man who invented television)

'Iran is an island of stability in one of the most volatile parts of the world.' (President Jimmy Carter, speaking just before the Shah was booted out and Iran went pear-shaped)

'We will make them grovel.' (Tony Greig, the then captain of the England cricket team, on what he and his men were going to do to the West Indies in 1976. In the event, the West Indies won the series 3–0)

'This picture is going to be one of the biggest white elephants of all time.' (Victor Fleming, the director of *Gone With The Wind*, assessing its likely prospects at the box office)

'I'm astounded by people who take 18 years to write something. That's how long it took that guy to write *Madame Bovary* and was that ever on the bestseller list?' (Sylvester Stallone)

'Come, come – why, they couldn't hit an elephant at this dist—' (John Sedgwick, American Civil War general, just before he was shot dead)

'Yes, the Great Fire of London. It started in a baker's shop in Pudding Lane in 1666. I wonder if it's still there?' (Dave Lee Travis)

'I must apologize to the deaf for the loss of subtitles.' (Angela Rippon)

'And don't forget, on Sunday you can hear the two-minute silence on Radio One.' (DJ Steve Wright)

'Who could take that scruffy arrogant buffoon seriously?' (Eddie Fisher on Richard Burton – just before Burton ran off with Dame Elizabeth Taylor, Fisher's wife)

'China is a big country, inhabited by many Chinese.' (French President Charles de Gaulle)

'Smoking kills. If you're killed, you've lost a very important part of your life.' (Brooke Shields)

THE WORKER'S PRAYER

'Grant me the serenity to accept the things I cannot change, the courage to change the things I cannot accept and the wisdom to hide the bodies of those people I had to kill today because they pissed me off, and also help me to be careful of the toes I step on today as they may be connected to the butt that I might have to kiss tomorrow.'

FRIDAY THE 13TH

The fear of the number 13 – or 'triskaidekaphobia' as it's technically known – goes back a long way. According to Scandinavian mythology, there was a banquet in Valhalla into which Loki (the God of Strife) intruded – thereby making thirteen guests – where Balder (the God of Light) was murdered. In Christian countries, this superstition was confirmed by the Last Supper.

Meanwhile, Friday is considered unlucky because it was the day of the Crucifixion and because Adam and Eve ate the forbidden fruit on a Friday and also died on a Friday. Some Buddhists and Brahmins (high caste Hindus) also consider Friday to be unlucky. In combining superstitions about both Friday and the number thirteen, Friday the 13th is feared as being twice as frightful.

Sir Winston Churchill, the former British Prime Minister, never travelled on a Friday the 13th unless it was absolutely essential.

Graham Chapman, the late member of the Monty Python team, actually *liked* Friday the 13ths. Indeed, he arranged to be buried on the 13th hour of Friday, 13th October 1989.

Good things that have happened on a Friday the 13th include: John Betjeman was knighted (June 1969), *The Third Man* (one of the greatest films of all time) received its premiere (January 1950), the Allies recaptured Tobruk (November 1942) and Alfred Dreyfus was restored to the French army and promoted to major (July 1906).

Notable things that have happened on a Friday the 13th include: the first condom commercial was screened by the BBC (November 1987), Viv Richards took his score to 291 against England at the Oval (August 1976) and Harold Macmillan dismissed a third of his Cabinet (July 1962).

Bad things that have happened on a Friday the 13th include: a violent earthquake in Turkey killed more than a thousand people (March 1992), a hurricane in Britain left nine people dead (January 1984) and a plane crash left survivors stranded in the Andes without food and compelled to turn to cannibalism to stay alive (October 1972).

Months that begin on a Sunday will always have a Friday the 13th.

People who were born on a Friday the 13th include Steve Buscemi, Sara Cox, Zoe Wanamaker, Peter Scudamore, Suggs, Howard Keel, Christopher Plummer and Robin Smith.

People who have died on a Friday the 13th include Benny Goodman, Sir Henry Irving and former US Vice-President Hubert Humphrey.

BEDS AND SLEEP

We spend something like a third of our lives in bed

An adult sleeping with another adult in a standard bed – 4 foot 6 inches wide and 6 foot 2 inches long – has less personal space than a baby in a cot

When the Hays Office censored Hollywood films, there was a series of rules concerning what could and could not be shown on screen: for example, couples – even married couples – could not be shown in a bed together unless both the man and the woman had at least one foot on the floor

Sian Phillips solved the problem of sharing a bed: 'In the past I had an arrangement where I had a large double bed and my partner had a single bed.'

When the playwright Kay Mellor was first married, she and her husband Anthony lived in his mother's home in a single bed

Gary Barlow, the singer and songwriter, lost his virginity at the age of 14 in a single bed; Shane Richie, the TV presenter and actor, lost his virginity at the age of 12 in a single bed

Hans Christian Andersen, the Danish writer of fairytales, died falling out of bed (actuarially, the chances of dying by falling out of bed are one in two million in a year)

In Tallin, Estonia, couples are not allowed to play chess in bed while making love

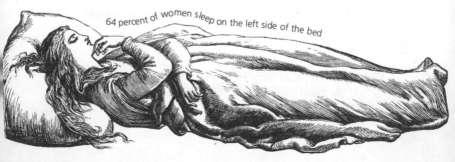

64 percent of women sleep on the left side of the bed

Not only is homosexuality banned in Albania, but two people of the same sex are also banned from sharing a bed – even if they're not homosexual

A bed is the third most popular luxury chosen by castaways on the radio programme *Desert Island Discs* (a piano is first and 'writing materials' are second)

The expression 'to get out of bed on the wrong side' comes from the nineteenth-century superstition that there was a 'right' side (the right) for getting out of bed and a 'wrong' side (the left), based, of course, on the traditional fear of anything 'left' ('sinister' being the Latin word for left)

King Louis XI of France started the practice of French kings receiving their courtiers and ministers in bed by introducing *lit de justice* (bed of justice), a ceremonial appearance before his parliament of the king lying in bed, with his princes on stools, and with great officials standing and lesser ones kneeling

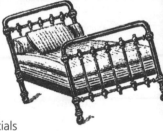

Mark Twain wrote large parts of *Huckleberry Finn* and *The Adventures of Tom Sawyer* in bed, though he pointed out that working in bed must be very dangerous as so many deaths occur there

Mae West did all her writing in bed, remarking, 'Everybody knows I do my best work in bed.'

Robert Louis Stevenson wrote most of *Kidnapped* in bed

Sir Winston Churchill habitually dictated letters and went through his red boxes in bed

Thomas Hobbes, the philosopher, and the writers Edith Wharton, F. Scott Fitzgerald and Marcel Proust all worked in their beds

W.C. Fields's cure for insomnia was: 'Get plenty of sleep.'

When John Denver lost his temper with his then wife, Annie (made famous in *Annie's Song*), he sawed their bed in half

Peter Stringfellow, the nightclub owner, shared a single bed with his three younger brothers when he was growing up

More than 600,000 Americans each year are injured on beds and chairs

The shortest recorded time taken by one person to make a bed is 28.2 seconds by Wendy Wall of Sydney, Australia in 1978; the record time for two people to make a bed is 14 seconds by Sister Sharon Stringer and Nurse Michelle Benkel at London's Royal Masonic Hospital at the launch of the 1994 edition of *The Guinness Book of Records*

George Burns once said: 'You have to have something to get you out of bed. I can't do anything in bed anyway.'

The United States has many sleepy towns: Sleepy Eye (Minnesota), Sleepy Creek (Oregon), Sleeping Beauty Peak (Arizona), Sleepers Bend (California)

According to the philosopher Friedrich Nietzsche: 'Sleeping is no mean art. For its sake one must stay awake all day.'

Max Kauffmann reckoned that 'the amount of sleep required by the average person is about five minutes more', while Fran Lebowitz decided: 'Sleep is death without the responsibility.'

Insomnia is defined as 'a chronic inability to fall asleep or to enjoy uninterrupted sleep' and it affects nearly everyone at some stage. Worse than insomnia is the extremely rare condition chronic colestites, a form of total insomnia that renders its victims incapable of definable sleep – sometimes for years.

Famous insomniacs include David Baddiel, Dame Elizabeth Taylor, Winona Ryder, Baroness Margaret Thatcher, Robbie Williams, Gwyneth Paltrow, Daryl Hannah, Renée Zellweger, Hillary Clinton, Mariah Carey (who claims that she sleeps for just three hours a night) and Michelle Pfeiffer (who can't sleep at all some nights)

Famous people in history who were insomniacs include Samuel Beckett, Abraham Lincoln, Marilyn Monroe, Spencer Tracy, Vincent Van Gogh, Napoleon Bonaparte, Charles Dickens, Cary Grant, Caligula, Joseph Conrad, Marlene Dietrich, W.C. Fields, F. Scott Fitzgerald, Galileo, Hermann Goering and Rudyard Kipling

Sleepwalking, or somnambulism, is no joke. In 1987, an 11-year-old American boy, Michael Dixon, was found 100 miles away from his home after sleepwalking to a freight train and travelling on it from Illinois to Indiana

Snoring is also no joke – especially for the sleeping partners of sufferers. Great snorers in history have included Beau Brummell, Abraham Lincoln, King George II and Benito Mussolini. 'Laugh and the world laughs with you; snore and you sleep alone,' declared Anthony Burgess, while Mark Twain wondered why 'there ain't no way to find out why a snorer can't hear himself snore'.

St Valentine's Day

St Valentine was a Bishop of Terni who was martyred in Rome in the year 270 but is now omitted from the calendar of Saints' Days as 'probably non-existent'

In 1477, one Margery Brews sent a letter to a man named John Paston addressed 'To my right welbelovyd Voluntyne'; this is reckoned to be the oldest known Valentine card in existence

The British send more Valentine cards than any other country

People who were born on St Valentine's Day include Carl Bernstein, Gregory Hines, Kevin Keegan, Meg Tilly, Helen Baxendale, Dean Gaffney and Sir Alan Parker

People who died on St Valentine's Day include Captain James Cook, Sir P.G. Wodehouse and the composer of *My Fair Lady* Frederick Loewe

Things that have happened on St Valentine's Day include Torvill and Dean getting maximum points for 'artistic expression' in the 1984 Winter Olympics, the opening night of Oscar Wilde's *The Importance of Being Earnest* in 1895 and, of course, the St Valentine's Day massacre in 1929

DOCTORS

Throughout the UK, the average number of patients per doctor is 2,000

About 388 million diagnoses are made annually by GPs in the UK – which works out as an average of 6.93 diagnoses per person per year

The leading UK diagnosis is 'neurosis' (an annual diagnosis rate of 355 per thousand population)

British GPs prescribe an average of 6.3 items per person per year

Doctors are three times more likely than the rest of the general population to commit suicide or become alcoholics, and are also above average when it comes to divorce, drug addiction and mental illness

Louis XIII's doctors administered 212 enemas, 215 purgations and 47 bleedings to him in the course of just one year

ACRONYMS USED BY DOCTORS AND NURSES

TMB – Too Many Birthdays

NFN – Normal for Norfolk

GOK – God Only Knows

GROLIES – Guardian Reader Of Limited Intelligence In Ethnic Skirt

SIG – Stroppy Ignorant Girl

TEETH – Tried Everything Else, Try Homoeopathy

TFBUNDY – Totally Fucked But Unfortunately Not Dead Yet

PFO – Pissed and Fell Over

TUBE – Totally Unnecessary Breast Examination

FLK, FLP – Funny Looking Kid, Funny Looking Parents

FORD – Found On Road Drunk

FTF – Failure To Fly (of attempted suicide)

ADASTW – Arrived Dead And Stayed That Way

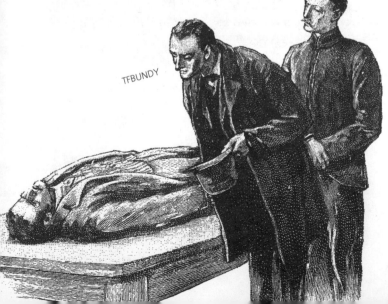

TFBUNDY

WOFTAM – Waste of Fucking Time And Money

OAP – Over-Anxious Patient

LTBB – Lucky To Be Breathing

OTHER MEDICAL EXPRESSIONS USED IN HOSPITALS

Ash Cash – money paid for signing cremation forms

Ash Point – where you collect the Ash Cash

Code Brown – incontinence-related emergency

Cold Tea Sign – the several cups of cold tea on the bedside cabinet beside a geriatric patient indicating that he/she is deceased

Crumblie – a geriatric patient

Departure Lounge – geriatric ward

Digging For Worms – varicose vein surgery

Eternal Care – intensive care

Guessing Tube – stethoscope

Handbag Positive – an old lady lying in her hospital bed clutching her handbag, indicating that she's confused and disorientated

House Red – blood

Sieve – a doctor who admits every patient he sees

Treat 'n' Street – quick patient turnaround

Wall – a doctor who resists admitting patients at all costs

HONOURS

Winston Churchill turned down the Order of the Garter after losing the 1945 General Election, saying, 'I could not accept the Order of the Garter from my sovereign when I have received the order of the boot from the people,' but he did accept it eventually

Graham Greene turned down a knighthood: apparently he read the letter offering him one, passed it to his secretary and asked her to 'refuse in the normal way'

Other men who rejected knighthoods include Alastair Sim, J.B. Priestley, Augustus John, Henry Moore, Francis Bacon, T.S. Eliot, Michael Faraday, E.M. Forster and Paul Scofield (twice)

George Bernard Shaw turned down an earldom as well as a knighthood, saying, 'Being Bernard Shaw is sufficient honour for any man – anyway, if I want to satirise the Establishment and all of its rituals, I must be free to do so.' He also said, 'Titles distinguish the mediocre, embarrass the superior and are disgraced by the inferior.'

John Lennon returned his MBE in 1969 citing three reasons: the UK's involvement in Vietnam, the war in Biafra and because *Cold Turkey* (his latest record) was slipping down the charts

Men who were stripped of their honours for committing crimes include Sir Roger Casement (before being hanged for treason in 1916), Lester Piggott (his OBE, after being sent to prison for tax evasion in 1988) and Lord Michael Spens (his MBE, after being jailed for theft in 1975)

Other men who were stripped of their honours include the Italian dictator, Benito Mussolini (Order of the Bath in 1940), and the spies

Kim Philby (OBE in 1965) and Anthony Blunt (Knight Commander of the Royal Victorian Order in 1979)

Pele (1997), Henry Kissinger (1995), Norman Schwarzkopf (1991), Kurt Waldheim (1969), J. Edgar Hoover (1947), Sidney Poitier (1974), André Previn (1996), Colin Powell (1993), President Mitterrand (1984), Alistair Cooke (1973), Magnus Magnusson (1989), Bob Geldof (1986), Douglas Fairbanks Jr (1949), Lech Walesa (1991), Steven Spielberg (2001), Spike Milligan (2001), James Galway (2001) and Rudolph Giuliani (2002) are among the people who have received honorary knighthoods (as non-British citizens they can't put 'Sir' before their name)

As everyone knows, honours are handed out to civil servants with, so to speak, their payslips. Within the Civil Service certain honours are known by these initials: CMG (Call Me God); KCMG (Kindly Call Me God) and GCMG (God Calls Me God)

People who have been honoured with university doctorates include Liam Neeson (Ulster), Mark Knopfler (Leeds), Joanna Lumley (Kent), Dame Kiri Te Kanawa (Durham), Sting (Northumbria), Sean Bean (Sheffield Hallam), Sir Alex Ferguson (Robert Gordon University in Aberdeen), Paul Scofield (Sussex), Sir David Attenborough (Bristol), Victoria Wood (Lancaster), Sir Sean Connery (Heriot-Watt), Kenneth Branagh (Belfast), Dame Maggie Smith (London), Sir Anthony Hopkins (University of Wales), Dame Judi Dench (Oxford), J.K. Rowling (D. Litt, Exeter), Delia Smith (John Moores and East Anglia), Lulu (Westminster), Robson Green (Newcastle), Lennox Lewis (North London University), Geena Davis (Boston), Matt Damon (Harvard), Arnold Schwarzenegger (Wisconsin), Tom Selleck (Pepperdine, Malibu), Robert De Niro (New York)

Tony Blair is an honorary member of the Dennis the Menace Fan Club

Johnny Vaughan is an honorary Butlin's Redcoat

THE FUNNIEST JOKE IN THE WORLD?

In 2002, after much research, British scientists identified what they called 'The Funniest Joke in the World'. Here it is:

A couple of New Jersey hunters are out in the woods when one of them falls to the ground. He doesn't seem to be breathing; his eyes are rolled back in his head. The other guy whips out his cell phone and calls the emergency services. He gasps to the operator: 'My friend is dead! What can I do?' The operator, in a calm, soothing voice, says: 'Just take it easy. I can help. First, let's make sure he's dead.' There is a silence, then a shot is heard. The guy's voice comes back on the line. He says: 'OK, now what?'

STAR TREK

In all its different incarnations, *Star Trek* has become the most popular form of entertainment of all time. As a result of the different TV series – including *Star Trek: The Next Generation* and a cartoon series – and seven films, *Star Trek* has become a billion-dollar industry, with more merchandise (books, comics, clothes, etc.) sold than any other film or TV series. It is now estimated that an episode of *Star Trek* is transmitted somewhere on earth 24 hours a day, 365 days of the year.

Given that the original TV series wasn't such a hit – after every season, the programme's future was in doubt – there weren't many famous guest stars. One exception to this was Joan Collins, who played Edith Keller in *City On The Edge of Forever*. This was the one in which Kirk fell in love with a woman (Joan) on earth in the past but was forced to watch her die in a road accident.

City On The Edge of Forever and *The Trouble With Tribbles* (the one with all the little furry animals) are acknowledged by most Trekkers to be the best two episodes of *Star Trek*. It is also generally accepted that *Spock's Brain* – in which the great man has his brain stolen – is the most stupid episode.

There were 79 *Star Trek* episodes but William Shatner appeared in only 78 of them. In the pilot, *The Cage*, the Captain (Captain Pike) was played by Jeffrey Hunter. When the TV series got the go-ahead, Hunter declined to be in it (rumour has it that his wife advised him against it) and William Shatner was picked instead.

In *Star Trek*, the Klingons are the enemy. The Klingons have their own language and only upper-class Klingons (those serving in the highest levels of the government or the military) speak English. Incredibly, there are now American universities where you can study Klingon, and more people in the world speak Klingon than speak the international language, Esperanto.

Like Leonard Nimoy (Spock), William Shatner was born in 1931, but his character, Captain Kirk, was born in the year 2233. Even if William Shatner lives to the age of 300, he still won't have been 'born'.

Just as Humphrey Bogart never said, 'Play it again, Sam' and James Cagney never said, 'You dirty rat', so Captain Kirk never said, 'Beam me up, Scottie'. He did say, 'Beam me up, Mr Scott' and 'Two to beam up, Mr Scott' but never the most famous (mis)quote from the series.

James Doohan, who played Scottie, was Canadian by birth. The actor was a captain in the Royal Canadian Artillery during World War Two and, along with DeForest Kelley (Dr McCoy), was the oldest of the *Star Trek* regulars – both having been born in 1920.

Nichelle Nichols, who played Lieutenant Uhura, broke new ground in US television – simply by being a black actress on screen as an equal with white actors. Nevertheless, she almost quit because her role was limited to a couple of lines per show (e.g. 'Getting no reply, Captain' and 'Hailing frequencies open, Captain'). She was persuaded to stay by the great civil rights leader, Dr Martin Luther King.

CLASSIC MOVIES THAT DIDN'T WIN A SINGLE OSCAR BETWEEN THEM

Bad Day At Black Rock (1955)

The Sixth Sense (1999)

Taxi Driver (1976)

Four Weddings And A Funeral (1994)

Awakenings (1990)

The Elephant Man (1980)

Being John Malkovich (1999)

Brief Encounter (1946)

The Talented Mr Ripley (1999)

To Be Or Not To Be (1942)

Deliverance (1972)

The Magnificent Ambersons (1942)

I Am A Fugitive From A Chain Gang (1932)

The Shawshank Redemption (1994)

Quiz Show (1994)

The Great Escape (1963)

American Graffiti (1973)

A Clockwork Orange (1971)

Top Hat (1935)

Dr Strangelove (Or How I Learned To Stop Worrying And Love The Bomb) (1964)

Psycho (1960)

It's A Wonderful Life (1946)

12 Angry Men (1957)

The Green Mile (1999)

Vertigo (1958)

Odd Man Out (1947)

Ninotchka (1939)

The Maltese Falcon (1941)

Lenny (1974)

Field of Dreams (1989)

The Player (1992)

Rebel Without A Cause (1955)

The Caine Mutiny (1954)

The Great Dictator (1940)

Fatal Attraction (1987)

The China Syndrome (1979)

When Harry Met Sally (1989)

Cat On A Hot Tin Roof (1958)

Rear Window (1954)

Ace In The Hole (1951)

A Star Is Born (1954)

Alfie (1966)

Pretty Woman (1990)

North By Northwest (1959)

Full Metal Jacket (1987)

The Wild Bunch (1969)

A Few Good Men (1992)

Singin' In The Rain (1952)

Amelie (2001)

Serpico (1973)

CLASSIC MOVIES THAT DIDN'T WIN A SINGLE OSCAR NOMINATION BETWEEN THEM

The Wild One (1953)

Oliver Twist (1948)

His Girl Friday (1940)

Reservoir Dogs (1992)

The Night Of The Hunter (1955)

The Searchers (1956)

Dirty Harry (1971)

The Postman Always Rings Twice (1946)

The 39 Steps (1935)

The Big Sleep (1946)

Sweet Smell Of Success (1957)

This Is Spinal Tap (1984)

Kind Hearts And Coronets (1948)

King Kong (1933)

Mean Streets (1973)

A Night At The Opera (1934)

Bringing Up Baby (1938)

Paths of Glory (1957)

Modern Times (1936)

The Lady Vanishes (1939)

Once Upon A Time In America (1984)

ALL OF *TIME* MAGAZINE'S
MAN OF THE YEAR WINNERS

2002: The Whistleblowers

2001: Rudolph Giuliani

2000: George W. Bush

1999: Jeff Bezos

1998: Bill Clinton and Kenneth Starr

1997: Andy Grove

1996: Dr David Ho

1995: Newt Gingrich

1994: Pope John Paul II

1993: The Peacemakers

1992: Bill Clinton

1991: Ted Turner

1990: The Two George Bushes

1989: Mikhail Gorbachev

1988: Endangered Earth

1987: Mikhail Gorbachev

1986: Corazon Aquino

1985: Deng Xiaoping

1984: Peter Ueberroth

1983: Ronald Reagan and Yuri Andropov

1982: The Computer

1981: Lech Walesa

1980: Ronald Reagan

1979: Ayatollah Khomeini

1978: Teng Hsiao-P'ing

1977: Anwar Sadat

1976: Jimmy Carter

1975: American Women

1974: King Faisal

1973: John Sirica

1972: Richard Nixon and Henry Kissinger

1971: Richard Nixon

1970: Willy Brandt

1969: The Middle Americans

1968: Astronauts Anders, Borman and Lovell

1967: Lyndon Johnson

1966: Twenty-Five and Under

1965: General William Westmoreland

1964: Lyndon Johnson

1963: Martin Luther King Jr

1962: Pope John XXIII

1961: John Kennedy

1960: US Scientists

1959: Dwight Eisenhower

1958: Charles de Gaulle

1957: Nikita Krushchev

1956: Hungarian Freedom Fighter

1955: Harlow Curtice

1954: John Foster Dulles

1953: Konrad Adenauer

1952: Queen Elizabeth II

1951: Mohammed Mossadegh

1950: American Fighting-Man

1949: Winston Churchill

1948: Harry Truman

1947: George Marshall

1946: James Byrnes

1945: Harry Truman

1944: Dwight Eisenhower

1943: George Marshall

1942: Joseph Stalin

1941: Franklin Roosevelt

1940: Winston Churchill

1939: Joseph Stalin

1938: Adolf Hitler

1937: Generalissimo and Madame Chiang Kai-Shek

1936: Wallis Simpson

1935: Haile Selassie

1934: Franklin Roosevelt

1933: Hugh Johnson

1932: Franklin Roosevelt

1931: Pierre Laval

1930: Mohandas Gandhi

1929: Owen Young

1928: Walter Chrysler

1927: Charles Lindbergh

ALL THE PERRIER AWARD WINNERS AT THE EDINBURGH FESTIVAL

2002: Daniel Kitson (Best Newcomer: The Consultants)

2001: Garth Marenghi's Netherhead (Best Newcomer: Let's Have a Shambles)

2000: Rich Hall as Otis Lee Crenshaw (Best Newcomer: Noble and Silver)

1999: Al Murray (Best Newcomer: Ben 'n' Arn)

1998: Tommy Tiernan (Best Newcomer: The Mighty Boosh)

1997: The League of Gentlemen (Best Newcomer: Arj Barker)

1996: Dylan Moran (Best Newcomer: Milton Jones)

1995: Jenny Eclair (Best Newcomer: Tim Vine)

1994: Lano and Woodley (Best Newcomer: Scott Capurro)

1993: Lee Evans (Best Newcomer: Dominic Holland)

1992: Steve Coogan In Character With John Thomson (Best Newcomer: Harry Hill)

1991: Frank Skinner

1990: Sean Hughes

1989: Simon Fanshawe

1988: Jeremy Hardy

1987: Brown Blues

1986: Ben Keaton

1985: Theatre de Complicité

1984: The Brass Band

1983: Los Trios Ringbarkus

1982: Writers Inc

1981: Cambridge Footlights (including Stephen Fry, Hugh Laurie, Tony Slattery and Emma Thompson)

The following are among those nominated without (so far) ever winning: Fascinating Aida, Hank Wangford Band, Nick Revell, Dillie Keane, Jack Dee, Eddie Izzard, Lily Savage, Jo Brand, Donna McPhail, Greg Proops, Alan Davies, Bill Bailey, Graham Norton, Johnny Vegas, Ed Byrne, Peter Kay, Ross Noble and Dave Gorman

BANNED BOOKS

Catcher In The Rye (J.D. Salinger): banned in Boron, California in 1989 because of the word 'goddamn'. It was also banned in another US state because of the words 'hell' and 'for Chrissake'. This is probably the most famous work of fiction never to have been turned into a feature film.

The Adventures of Tom Sawyer (Mark Twain): banned by several London libraries (in politically correct Labour-controlled boroughs) in the mid-1980s on account of the book's 'racism' and 'sexism'.

Black Beauty (Anna Sewell): banned by the African country Namibia in the 1970s because the government took offence at the 'racist' title.

The Scarlet Pimpernel (Baroness Orczy): banned by the Nazis – not because of its language or its theme (though Leslie Howard starred in an anti-Nazi film entitled *Pimpernel Smith*) – but because Baroness Orczy was Jewish. Other authors banned by the Nazis for the same reason included Erich Maria Remarque, Thomas Mann, Sigmund Freud and Marcel Proust. Authors banned by the Nazis because of their political sentiments included Ernest Hemingway, Upton Sinclair and Jack London.

Noddy (Enid Blyton): banned by several British libraries in the 1960s – along with other Enid Blyton books – because they weren't thought to be 'good' for children.

The Grapes of Wrath **(John Steinbeck): banned from schools in Iowa, USA in 1980 after a parent complained that the classic novel – by the Nobel Prize-winner – was 'vulgar and obscene'. Steinbeck's other famous novel, *Of Mice And Men*, has also been banned in other US states for similar reasons.**

The Joy of Sex (Alex Comfort): banned in Ireland from its publication until 1989 on account of the book's uninhibited approach to sex and relationships. The Irish have done more than their share of banning: All of Steinbeck and Zola's novels were banned in Ireland in 1953 for being 'subversive' and/or 'immoral'. Other books once banned by the Irish include *Brave New World* (Aldous Huxley), *Elmer Gantry* (Sinclair Lewis) and *The Sun Also Rises* (Ernest Hemingway).

Billy Bunter **books (Frank Richards): banned from British libraries in the 1970s in case it led children to tease overweight schoolmates. In more recent years, other politically correct institutions have banned the books because of the black character, Hurree Ramset Jam Singh, known to all his pals as 'Inky'.**

On The Origin of Species (Charles Darwin): banned in several US states (especially in the Christian Fundamentalist South) through the years – but particularly before World War Two – owing to the fact that Darwin didn't accept the Bible's account of Creation. Incredibly, Desmond Morris's *The Naked Ape* has been banned from one or two US libraries on the same basis. Darwin's book was also banned by the USSR because it was 'immoral'.

My Friend Flicka **(Mary O'Hara): banned from schoolchildren's reading lists in Clay County, Florida in 1990 because the book contains the word 'bitch' to describe 'a female dog'.**

LOSING US PRESIDENTIAL AND VICE-PRESIDENTIAL CANDIDATES

Year:	Presidential Candidate	Vice-Presidential Candidate
2000:	Al Gore	Joseph Lieberman
1996:	**Robert Dole**	**Jack Kemp**
1992:	George Bush	Dan Quayle
1988:	**Michael Dukakis**	**Lloyd Bentsen**
1984:	Walter Mondale	Geraldine Ferraro
1980:	**Jimmy Carter**	**Walter Mondale**
1976:	Gerald Ford	Robert Dole
1972:	**George McGovern**	**Sargent Shriver**
1968:	Hubert Humphrey	Edmund Muskie
1964:	**Barry Goldwater**	**William Miller**
1960:	Richard Nixon	Henry Cabot Lodge

THE LEADER OF THE PARTY THAT CAME SECOND IN GENERAL ELECTIONS

William Hague (Conservative; 2001)

John Major (Conservative; 1997)

Neil Kinnock (Labour; 1992)

Neil Kinnock (Labour; 1987)

Michael Foot (Labour; 1983)

James Callaghan (Labour; 1979)

Edward Heath (Conservative; October 1974)

Edward Heath (Conservative; February 1974)

Harold Wilson (Labour; 1970)

Edward Heath (Conservative; 1966)

Sir Alec Douglas-Home (Conservative; 1964)

Hugh Gaitskell (Labour; 1959)

NUMBER-ONE RECORDS AT THE TIME OF ALL GENERAL ELECTIONS SINCE RECORD CHARTS BEGAN

7 June 2001: 'Do You Really Like It' (DJ Pied Piper and the Master of Ceremonies)

1 May 1997: 'I Believe I Can Fly' (R Kelly)

9 April 1992: 'Stay' (Shakespear's Sister)

11 June 1987: 'I Wanna Dance With Somebody (Who Loves Me)' (Whitney Houston)

9 June 1983: 'Every Breath You Take' (The Police)

3 May 1979: 'Bright Eyes' (Art Garfunkel)

10 October 1974: 'Kung Fu Fighting' (Carl Douglas)

28 February 1974: 'Devil Gate Drive' (Suzi Quatro)

18 June 1970: 'In The Summertime' (Mungo Jerry)

31 March 1966: 'The Sun Ain't Gonna Shine Anymore' (The Walker Brothers)

15 October 1964: 'Oh Pretty Woman' (Roy Orbison)

8 October 1959: 'Only Sixteen' (Craig Douglas)

26 May 1955: 'Stranger In Paradise' (Tony Bennett)

THINGS FROM ABROAD

Danish pastry, German measles, Brazil nuts, Mexican stand-off, Dutch elm disease, Chinese whispers, Russian salad, Indian gift, French leave, Russian roulette, Swiss roll, Hong Kong flu, Cuban heels, Mexican wave, Greek urn, Singapore sling, Dutch uncle, Turkish delight, Indian tonic water, French bread, Maltese cross, Italian vermouth, Panama hat, Spanish omelette

THINGS THAT ARE BRAND NAMES

Tannoy, Li-Lo, Jiffy Bag, Optic, Plasticine, Biro, Crimplene, Hoover, Fibreglass, Babygro, Sellotape, Cellophane, Portakabin, Catseyes, Rawlplug, Jacuzzi, Spam, Perspex, Calor Gas, Formica, Yo-Yo, Tarmac

THE LAST WORDS OF MEN ABOUT TO BE EXECUTED

GEORGE APPEL (1928) As Appel was being strapped into the electric chair, he said to the witnesses, 'Well, folks, you'll soon see a baked Appel.'

THOMAS GRASSO (1995) Before he was given his lethal injection, he complained, 'I did not get my Spaghetti-O's, I got spaghetti. I want the press to know this.'

SIR WALTER RALEIGH (1618) 'So the heart be right, it is no matter which way the head lieth.' And then he was beheaded.

JAMES FRENCH (1966) On his way to the chair, he said to a newspaper reporter, 'I have a terrific headline for you in the morning: "French Fries".'

FRANCIS CROWLEY (1931) 'You sons of bitches. Give my love to Mother.' Then he was electrocuted.

NEVILLE HEATH (1946) Just before being hanged, his last request was for a whisky. 'In the circumstances,' he added, 'you might make that a double.'

JOHNNY FRANK GARRETT (1992) Before being lethally injected, he said, 'I'd like to thank my family for loving me and taking care of me. And the rest of the world can kiss my ass.'

ERSKINE CHILDERS (1922) He called out to the firing squad, 'Take a step forward, lads. It will be easier that way.'

ROBERT DREW (1994) Before being given his lethal injection, he said, 'Remember, the death penalty is murder.'

FREDERICK WOOD (1963) When Wood was in the electric chair, he said to the assembled company, 'Gentlemen, you are about to see the effects of electricity upon wood.'

NED KELLY (1880) The notorious Australian bushwacker's last words as he stood on the scaffold awaiting his hanging were: 'Ah well, I suppose it had to come to this. Such is life.'

JIMMY GLASS (1987) said, 'I'd rather be fishing.' Then he was electrocuted.

GERALD CHAPMAN (1926) Just before he was hanged, he said, 'Death itself isn't dreadful, but hanging seems an awkward way of entering the adventure.'

GARY GILMORE (1977) Having campaigned for the right to die, he just said, 'Let's do it!' – and the firing squad duly did.

ROBERT ALTON HARRIS (1992) Before being gassed, he said, 'You can be a king or a street sweeper, but everyone dances with the Grim Reaper.'

DR WILLIAM PALMER (1856) The British serial killer stood on the gallows and asked the officials, 'Are you sure this thing is safe?'

SCRABBLE

Scrabble was invented in 1931 by Alfred Butts, an unemployed American architect. Butts (who wasn't himself a good Scrabble player and admitted that the game should have had fewer 'i's) originally called the game 'Lexico'. However, both the format and the name were changed many times – later names included 'Alpha' and 'Criss Cross Words' – before the current format was established with the name Scrabble in 1948. The game wasn't commercially successful until 1952 when the chairman of the New York department store Macy's became addicted to it on holiday. He placed a large order for the game and did a huge promotional campaign. The rest is history.

In 1954, the game took off in Britain – selling a phenomenal 4.5 million sets. Today, an estimated 53 percent of homes in Britain have a set. Scrabble is currently produced in 30 different languages – from Afrikaans to Hebrew, from Japanese and English to Malaysian. In total, more than 100 million games have been sold in 121 countries.

Celebrity Scrabble fans include Brad Pitt, Jennifer Aniston, Will Smith, Robbie Williams, Dame Elizabeth Taylor, Kylie Minogue, Madonna, Sting and Mel Gibson.

The highest number of points that can be achieved on the first go (when there are no other letters on the board) is 126 – using the word QUARTZY or the word SQUEEZY. Don't forget that there is a 50-point bonus for using all seven letters in one go.

The highest score achieved for one word in a competition (i.e. when other people were watching) was 392 for CAZIQUES down two triple word scores, by Dr Karl Khoshnaw from Twickenham.

As all good Scrabble players know, there are 109 permissible two-letter words.

These include 'Jo' (a northern sweetheart), 'Ka' (an attendant spirit), 'Xi' (a letter in the Greek alphabet) and 'Qi' (derived from Chinese – means life force).

THE MOST VALUABLE WORDS YOU CAN MAKE AT SCRABBLE

Word	Meaning	Score (+ bonus of 50 for using all 7 letters)
QUIZZIFY*	To cause to look odd	31

(NB If this were stretched across two triple word scores, it would total 419 points – including the 50-point bonus and the double letter bonus for the Z)

Word	Meaning	Score
WHIPJACK	A whining beggar who pretends to be a sailor	29
HIGHJACK	Alternative spelling of hijack	28
JUMBOIZE	To enlarge a ship by adding a prefabricated section	28
BEZIQUES	Plural of card game	28
CAZIQUES	West Indian chiefs	28
QUIZZERY*	Collection of quizzes or information pertaining to quizzes	28
TZADDIQS	In Judaism, leaders or persons of extraordinary piety	28
VIZCACHA	S. American burrowing rodent of heavy build	27
ZAMBUCKS	New Zealand or Australian colloquial term for members of St John's Ambulance Brigade	27

* indicates that the second Z is a blank

CHARACTERS FROM GILBERT & SULLIVAN

Captain Fitzbattleaxe: *Utopia Limited*

Ernest Dummkopf: *The Grand Duke*

Don Alhambra del Bolero: *The Gondoliers*

Sir Marmaduke Pointdextre: *The Sorcerer*

Dick Deadeye: *HMS Pinafore*

Richard Dauntless: *Ruddigore*

Lady Psyche: *Princess Ida*

King Paramount the First: *Utopia Limited*

Sir Despard Murgatroyd:
Ruddigore

Stupidas: *Thespis*

BEATLES SONGS AND WHO OR WHAT INSPIRED THEM

'A Hard Day's Night'

Although the title was inspired by a comment from Ringo (as indeed was 'Eight Days A Week'), John wrote the song for Julian, his baby son ('But when I get home to you, I find the things that you do, will make me feel all right'). It was for Julian, of course, that Paul wrote 'Hey Jude' – to cheer the lad up when his parents split up.

'Eleanor Rigby'

Paul claimed that he made up the story and the name, but there is a gravestone of a woman named Eleanor Rigby ('Died 10th Oct. 1939 Aged 44 Years. Asleep') in St Peter's, Woolton – where Paul first met John at a church fête. Could be one of the greatest coincidences of all time.

'Something'

Written by George for his wife Patti. 'Something in the way she moves, attracts me like no other lover.' Unfortunately, she had the same effect on Eric Clapton, who wrote 'Layla' for her and then married her.

'Lucy In The Sky With Diamonds'

Long after it wouldn't have mattered anyhow, John always insisted that this song had nothing to do with the drug LSD but rather was inspired by a picture painted by a schoolfriend of his son Julian.

'A Day In The Life'

This song was about lots of things but the line 'He blew his mind out in a car' was inspired by the death in a car of Tara Browne, an Irish heir (he was male, despite the name) who was related to the Guinness family. Browne was friendly with Paul and other members of the rock aristocracy.

'Things We Said Today'

Written by Paul for Jane Asher. 'We'll go on and on.' Alas not.

'We Can Work It Out'

Once again for Jane Asher. 'Try to see it my way,' begged Paul, but she wouldn't.

'You've Got To Hide Your Love Away'

Supposedly written by John 'for' Brian Epstein. The love that Epstein had to hide was, of course, his homosexuality.

'She's Leaving Home'

Paul read a story in the papers about teenage runaway Melanie Coe. Her father was quoted as saying, 'I cannot imagine why she should run away. She has everything here,' which has its echo in Paul's line: 'We gave her everything money could buy.' Amazing coincidence: unknown to Paul, he had actually met the young girl when he had presented her with a competition prize on *Ready Steady Go* four years earlier.

'She Said She Said'

Written by John during his acid phase. John got the line 'I know what it's like to be dead' when he overheard the actor Peter Fonda talking to George about a near-death childhood experience.

'I Saw Her Standing There'

Like the girl in the song, Iris Caldwell was just 17 when Paul met her while she was dancing in a nightclub. Iris, whose brother was Liverpool musician Rory Storm, went out with Paul for two years.

'Sexy Sadie'

Famously written by John for the Maharishi Mahesh Yogi, who, John reckons, 'made a fool of everyone' by pretending to be pure when really he was a bit of a lech.

'Dear Prudence'

Written to encourage Prudence Farrow (Mia Farrow's younger sister) to stop meditating so much – 'won't you come out to play?' – during The Beatles' time in India.

HOW THE RECORD FOR THE MILE HAS BEEN BETTERED SINCE ROGER BANNISTER BROKE THE FOUR-MINUTE BARRIER

3:59.4	**Roger Bannister (Great Britain)**	**Oxford, UK (06.05.1954)**
3:58.0	John Landy (Australia)	Turku, Finland (21.06.1954)
3:57.2	**Derek Ibbotson (Great Britain)**	**London, UK (19.07.1957)**
3:54.5	Herb Elliott (Australia)	Dublin, Ireland (06.08.1958)
3:54.4	**Peter Snell (New Zealand)**	**Wanganui, New Zealand (27.01.1962)**

3:54.1	Peter Snell	Auckland, New Zealand (17.11.1964)
3:53.6	**Michel Jazy (France)**	**Rennes, France (09.06.1965)**
3:51.3	Jim Ryun (USA)	Berkeley, USA (17.07.1966)
3:51.1	**Jim Ryun**	**Bakersfield, USA (23.07.1967)**
3:51.0	Filbert Bayi (Tanzania)	Kingston, Jamaica (17.05.1975)
3:49.4	**John Walker (New Zealand)**	**Gothenburg, Sweden (12.08.1975)**
3:49.0	Sebastian Coe (Great Britain)	Oslo, Norway (17.07.1979)
3:48.8	**Steve Ovett (Great Britain)**	**Oslo, Norway (01.07.1980)**
3:48.53	Sebastian Coe	Zurich, Switzerland (19.08.1981)
3:48.40	**Steve Ovett**	**Koblenz, Germany (25.08.1981)**
3:47.33	Sebastian Coe	Brussels, Belgium (28.08.1981)
3:46.32	**Steve Cram (Great Britain)**	**Oslo, Norway (27.07.1985)**
3:44.39	Noureddine Morceli (Algeria)	Rieti, Italy (05.09.1993)
3:43.13	**Hicham El Guerrouj (Morocco)**	**Rome, Italy (07.07.1999)**

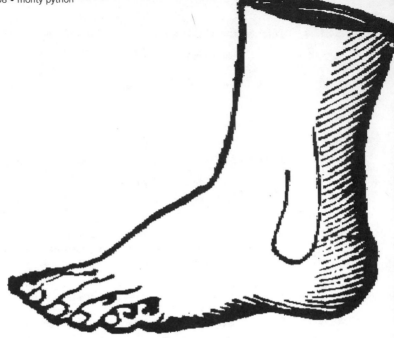

THE TITLES OF ALL *MONTY PYTHON'S FLYING CIRCUS* TV PROGRAMMES

SEASON 1 (first shown 5 October 1969 to 11 January 1970)

1. Whither Canada?

2. Sex And Violence

3. How To Recognize Different Types Of Tree From Quite A Long Way Away

4. Owl-Stretching Time

5. Man's Crisis Of Identity In The Latter Half Of The Twentieth Century

6. The BBC Entry To The Zinc Stoat Of Budapest

7. You're No Fun Any More

8. Full Frontal Nudity

9. The Ant, An Introduction

10. Untitled

11. The Royal Philharmonic Orchestra Goes To The Bathroom

12. The Naked Ant

13. Intermission

SEASON 2 (first shown 15 September 1970 to 22 December 1970)

1. Dinsdale

2. The Spanish Inquisition

3. Show 5

4. The Buzz Aldrin Show

5. Live From The Grill-o-Mat Snack Bar

6. School Prizes

7. The Attila The Hun Show

8. Archaeology Today

9. How To Recognize Different Parts Of The Body

10. Scott of The Antarctic

11. How Not To Be Seen

12. Spam

13. Royal Episode 13

SEASON 3 (first shown 19 October 1972 to 18 January 1973)

1. Whicker's World

2. Mr & Mrs Brian Norris's Ford Popular

3. The Money Programme

4. Blood, Devastation, Death, War, And Horror

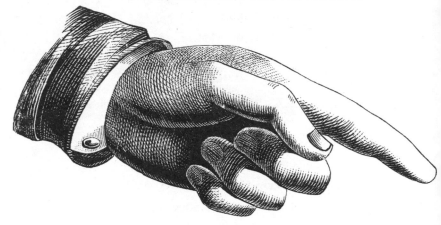

5. The All-England Summarize Proust Competition

6. The War Against Pornography

7. Salad Days

8. The Cycling Tour

9. The Nude Man

10. E. Henry Tripshaw's Disease

11. Dennis Moore

12. A Book At Bedtime

13. Grandstand

SEASON 4 (first shown 31 October 1974 to 5 December 1974)

1. The Golden Age of Ballooning
2. Michael Ellis
3. Light Entertainment War
4. Hamlet
5. Mr Neutron
6. Party Political Broadcast

TITLES CONSIDERED INSTEAD OF *MONTY PYTHON'S FLYING CIRCUS* FOR *MONTY PYTHON'S FLYING CIRCUS*

It's ...

A Horse, a Bucket and a Spoon

A Toad-Elevating Moment

Bun, Whackett, Buzzard, Stubble and Boot

Sex and Violence

Owl-Stretching Time

1 2 3

Vaseline Parade

The Horrible Earnest Megapode

The Plastic Mac Show

The Venus De Milo Panic Show

The Year of the Stoat

The Nose Show

ITEMS OF *DOCTOR WHO* MEMORABILIA

Doctor Who and the Daleks Sweet Cigarettes, 'I'm Gonna Spend My Christmas With A Dalek' (1964 record), Dalek's Death Ray Ice-Lolly, Dalek Slippers, TARDIS Toffee, Doctor Who Aim 'n' Shoot Bagatelle Game, Doctor Who Invisible Ink, Doctor Who Give-A-Show Projector, Dalek Meteorite Storm, Doctor Who and the Daleks – The Great Escape Game

NAMES WALT DISNEY CONSIDERED AND REJECTED FOR SNOW WHITE'S DWARFS

Gloomy, Wheezy, Shirty, Sniffy, Woeful, Weepy, Lazy, Snoopy, Puffy, Shorty, Baldy, Biggo-Ego, Burpy, Gabby, Jumpy, Nifty, Stubby, Stuffy

SOUVENIRS FROM THE JAMES BOND FILMS

James Bond Children's Pink Slippers (1979), James Bond Underpants (1983), James Bond Thermos Flask (1965), James Bond Bumper Boots (1981), James Bond Soap (1985), James Bond Moon Buggy (1971), James Bond Lunch Box (1965), James Bond Socks (1988), James Bond Pencil Box (1985), James Bond Spear Gun (1965)

THE FIRST EUROPEAN COUNTRIES TO HAVE MCDONALD'S

Germany (Munich 1971)

Holland (Voorburg 1972)

Sweden (Stockholm 1973)

UK (Woolwich, London 1974)

Switzerland (Geneva 1975)

Ireland (Dublin 1977)

Austria (Vienna 1977)

Belgium (Brussels 1978)

France (Strasbourg 1979)

Spain (Madrid 1981)

COUPLES WHO DIVORCED AND THEN REMARRIED

Dame Elizabeth Taylor & Richard Burton

Melanie Griffith & Don Johnson

Elliott Gould & Jenny Bogart

Sarah Miles & Robert Bolt

Robert Wagner & Natalie Wood

Dorothy Parker & Alan Campbell

George Peppard & Elizabeth Ashley

Jane Wyman & Fred Karger

Dionne Warwick & Bill Elliott

Paul Hogan & Noelene Edwards

Kurt Weill & Lotte Lenya

José Ferrer & Rosemary Clooney

George C. Scott & Colleen Dewhurst

Dennis Wilson & Karen Lamm

Milton Berle & Joyce Matthews

Billy Rose & Joyce Matthews

Neil & Diane Simon

Andy & Kate Summers

Note also: Cher's parents married and divorced each other three times

MEN WHO FELL IN LOVE WITH THEIR WIFE'S SISTER

Stavros Niarchos, Charles Dickens, George Sanders (after divorcing
Zsa Zsa Gabor he married her sister Magda), Peter Paul Rubens (did it
the other way round – marrying the sister, Helena, of Suzanne, his
former mistress), Peter Bogdanovich (also did it the other way round
– marrying the sister, Louise, of his murdered lover Dorothy Stratton),
King Henry VIII (also did it the other way round – marrying the sister,
Anne Boleyn, of his erstwhile lover Mary), Wolfgang Mozart,
Sigmund Freud, Robert Southey

PEOPLE WHO MARRIED
THEIR COUSIN

**James Boswell, Franklin D. Roosevelt, Albert Einstein, Lewis
Carroll, Mary, Queen of Scots, Queen Victoria, Satyajit Ray,
Charles Darwin, Saddam Hussein, King Olav V of Norway,
Karen Blixen, Catherine the Great, André Gide, H.G. Wells,
Rose Tremain, Edgar Allan Poe (whose bride was just 13), Jerry
Lee Lewis (whose bride was also just 13)**

PEOPLE WHO WERE BETROTHED VERY QUICKLY

Muhammad Ali – in 1964 he met Sonji Roi and proposed to her on
the same day; they married 42 days later

**Michael Douglas – in 1977 he met Diandra Luker at Jimmy
Carter's presidential inauguration. They spent two days in his
Washington hotel room, he proposed after nine days and they
married six weeks later**

Peter Noone – in 1967 he married Mireille six weeks after they met

**Marco Pierre White – in 1992 he proposed to Lisa Butcher three
weeks after they met**

Pamela Anderson – in 1995 she and Tommy Lee decided to marry after a five-day courtship

Leslie Ash – in 1982 she married Jonathan Weston after a two-week courtship

Charlie Sheen – in 1995 he married Donna Peele after a six-week courtship

Julia Roberts – in 1993 she married Lyle Lovett after a three-week romance

Kate Jackson – in 1978 she married Andrew Stevens after a six-week courtship

Drew Barrymore – in 1994 she married Jeremy Thomas after a six-week courtship

Shannen Doherty – in 1993 she married Ashley Hamilton after a two-week romance

John Major – in 1970 he and Norma Wagstaff decided to marry after just three weeks

Lord David Owen – in 1968 he and Debbie Schabert were married after a 26-day courtship

Jim Davidson – he and Alison Holloway were married after a three-week courtship

Judy Geeson – in 1985 she and Kristoffer Tabori were married eight weeks after they met

Raine, Countess Spencer – in 1993 she was proposed to by Count Jean-François de Chambrun 33 days after they met

Mike Oldfield – in 1978 he married Diana Fuller who ran the Exegesis course he'd been on; the marriage lasted one month

COUPLES WHO HAD OPEN MARRIAGES

Aneurin Bevan & Jennie Lee

Harold & Grace Robbins

Bertrand Russell & Dora Black

Carl & Emma Jung

John F. & Jacqueline Kennedy

Leonard & Virginia Woolf

William & Jane Morris

Salvador & Gala Dalí

Lord Louis & Lady Edwina Mountbatten

Dmitri & Nina Shostakovich

Gary & Veronica (Rocky) Cooper

Sir William & Lady Emma Hamilton

Horatio & Fanny Nelson

Marlene Dietrich & Rudolf Sieber

Lyndon & Lady Bird Johnson

PEOPLE WHO COMMITTED BIGAMY

Rudolph Valentino, George Gissing, King George III, Anaïs Nin, Judy Garland (unwittingly married Mark Herron in 1964 when she was still married to Sid Luft) and Sidney Reilly (the Ace of Spies)

It is also claimed that John F. Kennedy married a Palm Beach socialite in 1947 and was still married to her in 1953 when he married Jacqueline Bouvier

MEN WHO MARRIED THEIR SECRETARY

Bertrand Russell, Jorge Luis Borges, Lord Hailsham, T.S. Eliot, Burt Lancaster, Lord Douglas Hurd, Fyodor Dostoevsky, Robin Cook, Lord Woodrow Wyatt, Sir James Goldsmith, Thomas Hardy, Sir Peter Hall, Jimmy Hill, Sir Henry Wood, Bryan Gould, John Stonehouse, Lord John Wakeham

PEOPLE WHO NEVER MARRIED

Greta Garbo, Sir Isaac Newton, Florence Nightingale, Ludwig van Beethoven, Cecil Rhodes, Frederic Chopin, Dame Flora Robson, Queen Elizabeth I, Henri de Toulouse-Lautrec, Jane Austen, Louisa May Alcott, Christabel Pankhurst, Giacomo Casanova, Alma Cogan, Alexander Pope, Lillian Gish, P.L. Travers, George Gershwin, Juan Fangio, Tessie O'Shea, Lilian Baylis, Helene Hanff, David Hume, John Locke, Jean-Paul Sartre, Rene Descartes, Immanuel Kant, Friedrich Nietzsche, Philip Larkin, Patricia Highsmith, Adam Smith, A.L. Rowse, Edgar Degas, Rory Gallagher, Maria Montessori, Edward Lear, Benny Hill, Stendhal, Johannes Brahms, Rupert Brooke, Voltaire, Mack Sennett, Coco Chanel, Vitas Gerulaitis, Stephane Grappelli, Frank Richards, Screaming Lord Sutch

PEOPLE WHO MARRIED NINE TIMES

Mike Love, Pancho Villa, Zsa Zsa Gabor

PEOPLE WHO MARRIED EIGHT TIMES

Dame Elizabeth Taylor (twice to the same man), Marie
McDonald, Mickey Rooney, Alan Jay Lerner, Artie Shaw

PEOPLE WHO MARRIED SEVEN TIMES

Lana Turner, Richard Pryor, Barbara Hutton, Claude Rains, Stan Laurel
(three times to the same woman), Jennifer O'Neill

PEOPLE WHO MARRIED SIX TIMES

Sir Rex Harrison, Johnny Weissmuller, Gloria Swanson, Hedy Lamarr,
Norman Mailer, King Henry VIII, Larry King, Harold Robbins, Steve
Earle, Jerry Lee Lewis, David Merrick (twice to the same woman)

PEOPLE WHO MARRIED FIVE TIMES

Tony Curtis, Danielle Steel, James Cameron, Billy Bob Thornton,
Martin Scorsese, Jan Leeming, Joan Collins, Stavros Niarchos,
David Lean, Ernest Borgnine, George C. Scott (twice to the same
woman), George Peppard (twice to the same woman), John Huston,
J. Paul Getty I, Roy Boulting, Ginger Rogers, Rue McClanahan, Victor
Mature, Eva Gabor, Judy Garland, Henry Fonda, Jane Wyman (twice
to the same man), George Foreman, Rita Hayworth, Ingmar Bergman,
Tammy Wynette, Clark Gable, Veronica Lake, Dick Emery, Richard
Burton (twice to the same woman), John Osborne

PEOPLE WHO MARRIED FOUR TIMES

Frank Sinatra, Stockard Channing, Jason Robards, Ethel Merman, Doris Day, André Previn, Jim Davidson, Merle Oberon, Keith Floyd, Dennis Hopper, Janet Leigh, Ernest Hemingway, Barry Humphries, John Derek, David Soul, Donald Pleasence, Liza Minnelli, Bertrand Russell, Sir Peter Hall, Sir Charlie Chaplin, George Sanders, Paulette Goddard, Peggy Lee, Bette Davis, Al Jolson, Jane Seymour, Michael Crichton, Peter Sellers, Christina Onassis, Lawrence Durrell, Kim Philby, Yul Brynner, Leslie Charteris, Bertolt Brecht, Lionel Barrymore, Melanie Griffith (twice to the same man), Joan Fontaine, Erica Jong, Humphrey Bogart, Cary Grant, Christie Brinkley, Madeleine Carroll, William Shatner, Andy McNab, Joan Crawford, Connie Francis, Mao Tse-Tung, Lindsay Wagner, Dinah Sheridan, Brigitte Bardot, Dudley Moore, David Bailey, Eddie Fisher, Burgess Meredith, Janet Street-Porter

MEN WHO MARRIED OLDER WOMEN

Robert Browning (his wife, Elizabeth Barrett, was 6 years older than him)

Raymond Chandler (his wife, Pearl Bowen, was 17 years older than him)

Clark Gable (his first wife Josephine Dillon was 17 years older)

Benjamin Disraeli (his wife, Mary Wyndham Lewis, was 12 years older than him)

William Shakespeare (his wife, Anne Hathaway, was 7 years older than him)

Sir Roger Moore (his second wife, Dorothy Squires, was 12 years older than him)

WOMEN WHO MARRIED YOUNGER MEN

Sarah Bernhardt (her only husband was 11 years younger than her)

Martha Raye (married a man, Mark Harris, 23 years younger than her)

Colette (her third husband was 17 years younger than her)

Dame Elizabeth Taylor (married a man, Larry Fortensky, 20 years younger than her)

Edith Piaf (married a man, Theo Sarapo, 20 years younger than her)

Merle Oberon (married a man, Robert Wolders, 25 years younger than her)

Jennie Churchill (married George Cornwallis-West who was 20 years younger than her and Montagu Porch who was 23 years younger than her)

Marti Webb (married Tim Flavin who was 15 years younger than her and Tom Button who is 23 years younger than her)

Sian Phillips (married Robin Sachs who is 17 years younger than her)

Jenny Lind (married Otto Goldschmidt who was 9 years younger than her)

Kate Jackson (she twice married men who were 6 years younger than her)

Joanna Lumley (her husband Stephen Barlow is 8 years younger than her)

Ruth Gordon (her husband, Garson Kanin, was 16 years younger than her)

Isadora Duncan (her husband, Sergei Esenin, was 17 years younger than her)

Janet Street-Porter (her fourth husband, David Solkin, was 22 years younger than her)

Millicent Martin (her second husband, Norman Eshley, was 11 years younger than her)

Helena Rubenstein (her husband, Prince Artchil Gourielli-Tchkonia, was 20 years younger than her)

Kate O'Mara (her husband, Richard Willis, was 18 years younger than her)

Vivienne Westwood (her husband Andreas Kronthoaler is 25 years younger than her)

Joan Collins (her husband Percy Gibson is 32 years younger than her)

PEOPLE WHO MARRIED AT THE AGE OF 13

Josephine Baker, Loretta Lynn, Mahatma Gandhi, June Havoc

PEOPLE WHO MARRIED AT THE AGE OF 14

Marie Antoinette, Jerry Lee Lewis, Janet Leigh (eloped – the marriage was later annulled)

PEOPLE WHO MARRIED AT THE AGE OF 15

Mary, Queen of Scots, Eva Bartok, Annie Oakley, Fanny Brice

PEOPLE WHO MARRIED AT THE AGE OF 16

Dolores del Rio, Sophie Tucker, Marti Caine, Kay Mellor, Placido Domingo, Marilyn Monroe, Catherine The Great, Ellen Terry, Beverley Callard, Joan Bennett, Sandra Dee, Tom Jones, Doris Day, Linda Thorson

COUPLES WHO MARRIED IN LAS VEGAS

Ursula Andress & John Derek

John & Bo Derek

Melanie Griffith & Don Johnson (the first time)

Samantha Janus & Mauro Mantovani

Noel Gallagher & Meg Mathews

Sheena Easton & Tim Delarm

George Clooney & Talia Balsam (by an Elvis impersonator)

Paul Newman & Joanne Woodward

Clint Eastwood & Dina Ruiz

Paula Yates & Bob Geldof

Caroline Aherne & Peter Hook

Jason Connery & Mia Sara

Ruby Wax & Trevor Walton

Frank Sinatra & Mia Farrow

Natasha Henstridge & Damian Chapa

Ross Boatman & Sophie Camara

Sir Michael Caine & Shakira Baksh

Nicolas Cage & Patricia Arquette

Joan Collins & Peter Holm

Richard Gere & Cindy Crawford

Demi Moore & Bruce Willis

Caroline Goodall & Derek Hoxby

Dinah Sheridan & Aubrey Ison

Gabriel Byrne & Ellen Barkin

Sylvia Kristel & Alan Turner

Dudley Moore & Brogan Lane

Elvis Presley & Priscilla Beaulieu (but not by an Elvis impersonator)

Jonathan Ross & Jane Goldman

Richard & Sally Burton

Brigitte Bardot & Gunther Sachs

Jane Russell & Robert Waterfield

Milla Jovovich & Luc Besson

Bette Midler & Martin Von Haselburg (by an Elvis impersonator)

Chris Evans & Billie Piper

Angelina Jolie & Billy Bob Thornton

ENGAGEMENTS THAT DIDN'T LEAD TO MARRIAGE

Brad Pitt & Gwyneth Paltrow

Audrey Hepburn & Lord James Hanson

Jimmy Connors & Chris Evert

Lauren Bacall & Frank Sinatra

Julia Roberts & Kiefer Sutherland

Sir David Frost & Diahann Carroll

Lucille Ball & Broderick Crawford

King George V (when he was Duke of York) &
Hon. Julia Stonor (because she was a Catholic)

Naomi Campbell & Adam Clayton

Greta Garbo & John Gilbert (the engagement ended on the wedding
day – she stood him up at the altar)

Sir Paul McCartney & Jane Asher

Brian Cox & Irina Brook

Claudia Schiffer & David Copperfield

Johnny Depp & Winona Ryder

Liza Minnelli & Desi Arnaz Jnr

Roger Vadim & Catherine Deneuve

Bryan Ferry & Jerry Hall

Ruthie Henshall & John Gordon Sinclair

Scott Baio & Pamela Anderson

Ben Stiller & Jeanne Tripplehorn

Alyssa Milano & Scott Wolf

Cameron Diaz & Jared Leto

Demi Moore & Emilio Estevez

Sean Penn & Elizabeth McGovern

Sela Ward & Peter Weller

Laura Dern & Jeff Goldblum

Minnie Driver & Josh Brolin

Marriage proposals that were turned down

Ernest Hemingway's proposal to Gertrude Stein

The Duke of Westminster's proposal to Coco Chanel

Howard Hughes's proposal to Susan Hayward

James Stewart's proposal to Olivia de Havilland

Kenneth Williams's proposal for a celibate marriage to Joan Sims

MARRIAGES THAT LASTED LESS THAN SIX MONTHS

Eva Bartok & William Wordsworth (less than one day – after the wedding ceremony)

Giuseppe Garibaldi & Giuseppina Raimondi (less than one day)

Julie Goodyear & Tony Rudman (one day – he walked out on her during the wedding reception saying that he didn't like the idea of living in the spotlight)

Jean Arthur & Julian Anker (one day)

Katherine Mansfield & George Mansfield (one day)

Rudolph Valentino & Jean Acker (one day)

Adolf Hitler & Eva Braun (one day)

Robin Givens & Svetozar Marinkovic (one day)

Fanny Brice & Frank White (three days)

John Heard & Margot Kidder (six days)

Dennis Hopper & Michelle Phillips (one week)

Cher & Gregg Allman (nine days)

Catherine Oxenberg & Robert Evans (twelve days)

Patty Duke & Michael Tell (two weeks)

Carole Landis & Irving Wheeler (three weeks)

Germaine Greer & Paul du Feu (three weeks)

Katharine Hepburn & Ludlow Ogden Smith (three weeks)

Shannen Doherty & Ashley Hamilton (three weeks)

Gloria Swanson & Wallace Beery (three weeks)

Roger Taylor & Dominique Beyrand (25 days)

**John Milton & Mary Powell
(one month)**

Mike Oldfield & Diana Fuller (one month)

Jane Wyman & Eugene Wyman (one month)

Greer Garson & Edward Snelson (five weeks)

George Brent & Constance Worth (five weeks)

Jean Peters & Stuart Cramer (five weeks)

Drew Barrymore & Jeremy Thomas (six weeks)

Derek Fowlds & Lesley Judd (two months)

Leslie Ash & Jonathan Weston (three months)

Nicolas Cage & Lisa Marie Presley (three months)

P.J. O'Rourke & Amy Lumet (three months)

Tracy Edwards & Simon Lawrence (three months)

Frank Lloyd Wright & Miriam Noel (three months)

Halle Berry & Eric Benet (three months)

Davina McCall & Andrew Leggett (three months)

Joanna Lumley & Jeremy Lloyd (four months)

Colin Farrell & Amelia Warner (four months)

Marco Pierre White & Lisa Butcher (four months)

Charlie Sheen & Donna Peele (five months)

Carole Landis & Willie Hunts Jr (five months)

Sylvia Kristel & Alan Turner (five months)

PEOPLE WHO MARRIED THEIR EX-SPOUSE'S RELATION

Cleopatra married Ptolemy XIII and then when he died his brother Ptolemy XIV

George Sanders married the Gabor sisters, Zsa Zsa and Magda

Dame Barbara Cartland married the McCorquodale cousins

Gloria Grahame's second husband was the film director Nicholas Ray; her fourth husband was his son, Tony

Joseph Chamberlain married the Kenrick cousins, Harriet and Florence

MEN WHO WERE VIRGINS ON THEIR WEDDING DAY

Victor Hugo (did it nine times on his wedding night), Tiny Tim, Jonathan Edwards, Lord Laurence Olivier, Terry Wogan, Sir Alfred Hitchcock, George S. Kaufman, Dr Benjamin Spock, Ronan Keating

THE UK ENTRIES IN THE EUROVISION SONG CONTEST — AND WHERE THEY FINISHED

2003: 'Cry Baby' by Jemini (last with nul points)

2002: 'Come Back' by Jessica Garlick (3rd)

2001: 'No Dream Impossible' by Lindsay D (15th)

2000: 'Don't Play That Song Again' by Nikki French (16th)

1999: 'Say It Again' by Precious (12th)

1998: 'Where Are You' by Imaani (2nd)

1997: 'Love Shine A Light' by Katrina & The Waves (1st)

1996: 'Ooh Aah Just A Little Bit' by Gina G (8th)

1995: 'Love City Groove' by Love City Groove (joint 10th)

1994: 'Lonely Symphony' by Frances Ruffelle (10th)

1993: 'Better The Devil You Know' by Sonia (2nd)

1992: 'One Step At A Time' by Michael Ball (2nd)

1991: 'A Message To Your Heart' by Samantha Janus (10th)

1990: 'Give A Little Love Back To The World' by Emma Booth (6th)

1989: 'Why Do I Always Get It Wrong?' by Live Report (2nd)

1988: 'Go' by Scott Fitzgerald (2nd)

1987: 'Only The Light' by Rikki (13th)

1986: 'Runner In The Night' by Ryder (7th)

1985: 'Love Is' by Vikki Watson (4th)

1984: 'Love Games' by Belle and the Devotions (7th)

1983: 'I'm Never Giving Up' by Sweet Dreams (6th)

1982: 'One Step Further' by Bardo (7th)

1981: 'Making Your Mind Up' by Bucks Fizz (1st)

1980: 'Love Enough For Two' by Prima Donna (3rd)

1979: 'Mary Anne' by Black Lace (7th)

1978: 'Bad Old Days' by CoCo (11th)

1977: 'Rock Bottom' by Lynsey de Paul and Mike Moran (2nd)

1976: 'Save Your Kisses For Me' by The Brotherhood of Man (1st)

1975: 'Let Me Be The One' by The Shadows (2nd)

1974: 'Long Live Love' by Olivia Newton-John (4th)

1973: 'Power To All My Friends' by Cliff Richard (4th)

1972: 'Beg, Steal Or Borrow' by The New Seekers (2nd)

1971: 'Jack In The Box' by Clodagh Rodgers (4th)

1970: 'Knock, Knock, Who's There?' by Mary Hopkin (2nd)

1969: 'Boom Bang A Bang' by Lulu (Joint 1st)

1968: 'Congratulations' by Cliff Richard (2nd)

1967: 'Puppet On A String' by Sandie Shaw (1st)

1966: 'A Man Without Love' by Kenneth McKellar (7th)

1965: 'I Belong' by Kathy Kirby (2nd)

1964: 'I Love The Little Things' by Matt Monro (2nd)

1963: 'Say Wonderful Things' by Ronnie Carroll (4th)

1962: 'Ring A Ding Girl' by Ronnie Carroll (4th)

1961: 'Are You Sure' by The Allisons (2nd)

1960: 'Looking High High High' by Bryan Johnson (2nd)

1959: 'Sing Little Birdie' by Pearl Carr and Teddy Johnson (2nd)

1958: No UK entry

1957: 'All' by Patricia Bredin (finished 7th)

The contest started in 1956 but the UK didn't participate that year

THE AGE THEY WOULD HAVE REACHED IN 2004 IF THEY WERE STILL ALIVE

Diana, Princess of Wales – 43 (died 1997)

James Dean – 73 (died 1955)

River Phoenix – 34 (died 1993)

Marilyn Monroe – 78 (died 1962)

Les Dawson – 68 (died 1993)

John Lennon – 64 (died 1980)

Marc Bolan – 57 (died 1977)

Jill Dando – 43 (died 1999)

Elvis Presley – 69 (died 1977)

Jimi Hendrix – 62 (died 1970)

Anne Frank – 75 (died 1945)

Dr Martin Luther King – 75 (died 1968)

James Hunt – 57 (died 1993)

THE THREE GERMAN REICHS

The First Reich was The Holy Roman Empire (962–1806)

The Second Reich was The German Empire (1871–1918)

The Third Reich was The Nazi Empire (1933–1945)

WAYS IN WHICH BRITAIN IS ON TOP OF THE WORLD

Highest (joint) percentage of the population that is literate

Highest proportionate number of botanical gardens and zoos in the world

In Queen Victoria, the longest-reigning queen the world has ever known

Top Air Ace of World War One (Edward Mannock – 73 kills)

More public lending libraries than any other country in the world

The three most published authors of all time are British: William Shakespeare, Charles Dickens and Sir Walter Scott

The busiest international airport in the world in London Heathrow

London has the longest underground railway network in the world

We publish more books than any other country in the world

Highest (joint) percentage of the population that has access to sanitation services

The longest-running show in the world – *The Mousetrap*, since 1952

THINGS THAT BRITAIN GAVE TO THE WORLD

The Mariner's Compass (1187)

The Slide Rule (1621)

The Pressure Cooker (1679)

The Match (1680)

The Kitchen Range (seventeenth century)

Vasectomy (seventeenth century)

The Machine-Gun (1718)

The Chronometer (1735)

The Sandwich (1760)

Modern Flush Toilet (1775)

The Power Loom (1785)

Gas Lighting (1792)

The Piggy Bank (eighteenth century)

Clothes Washer and Dryer (1800s)

The Locomotive (1804)

Photographic Lens (1812)

The Electromagnet (1824)

Modern Rainwear (1830)

The Lawn Mower (1830)

The Computer (1835)

Photography (on paper) (1838)

The Postage Stamp (1840)

The Bicycle (1840)

The Travel Agency (1841)

Ship's Metal Hull and Propeller (1844)

The Pneumatic Tyre (for coaches) (1845)

The Glider (1853)

Steel (Production) (1854)

The Refrigerator (1855)

Linoleum (1860)

Colour Photography (1861)

The Telegraph (Transatlantic Cable) (1866)

The Stapler (1868)

The Electric Light (1878)

The Vending Machine (1883)

The Pneumatic Tyre (for bicycles) (1888)

The Thermos (1892)

The Loudspeaker (1900)

The Electric Vacuum Cleaner (1901)

Car Disc Brakes (1902)

The Telephone Booth (1903)

The Geiger Counter (1908)

Stainless Steel (1913)

The Tank (1916)

The Turbojet (1928)

The Decompression Chamber (1929)

The Food Processor (1947)

The Integrated Circuit (1952)

The Hovercraft (1955)

Acrylic Paint (1964)

The CAT Scanner (1972)

Test-Tube Babies (1978)

Genetic Fingerprinting (1987)

Note also: Football, the Railway, Tennis, Sell-by Dates on food, the Disposable Nappy, Airline Meals, the Underground, the custom of embracing under the mistletoe, Package Tours, Garden Cities, the Hearse, Christmas Cards, the Mini-Skirt, Punk Rock, Cricket

THINGS INVENTED BY THE FRENCH

The suit (eighteenth century), the tie (seventeenth century), aluminium ware (early nineteenth century), aspirin (1853), the coffee pot (1800), the handkerchief (fifteenth century), the Christmas cracker (nineteenth century), the sewing machine (1830), Teflon utensils (1954), wallpaper (fifteenth century)

GENUINE PRODUCTS

Sor Bits (Danish mints), Krapp (Scandinavian toilet paper), Grand Dick (French red wine), Nora Knackers (Norwegian biscuits), Moron (Italian wine), Mukki (Italian yoghurt), Cock (French deodorant), Plopp (Swedish toffee bar), Bum (Turkish biscuits), Donkee Basterd Suker (Dutch sugar), Zit (Greek fizzy drink), Bimbo Bread (South America), Craps Chocolate (France), Darkie Toothpaste (Taiwan), Pschitt (French fizzy drink), Homo-Milk (Canada)

UNINTENTIONALLY FUNNY (GENUINE) NEWSPAPER HEADLINES

CAUSE OF AIDS FOUND – SCIENTISTS

LAWYERS GIVE POOR FREE LEGAL ADVICE

MAN FOUND BEATEN, ROBBED BY POLICE

JUVENILE COURT TO TRY SHOOTING DEFENDANT

TRAFFIC DEAD RISE SLOWLY

SHOT OFF WOMAN'S LEG HELPS NICKLAUS TO 66

SQUAD HELPS DOG BITE VICTIM

DRUNK GETS NINE MONTHS IN VIOLIN CASE

DOCTOR TESTIFIES IN HORSE SUIT

THUGS EAT THEN ROB PROPRIETOR

CITY MAY IMPOSE MANDATORY TIME FOR PROSTITUTION

ENRAGED COW INJURES FARMER WITH AXE

GRANDMOTHER OF EIGHT MAKES HOLE IN ONE

FARMER BILL DIES IN HOUSE

DEFENDANT'S SPEECH ENDS IN LONG SENTENCE

WHY YOU WANT SEX CHANGES WITH AGE

AMERICAN SHIPS HEAD TO LIBYA

NEW VACCINE MAY CONTAIN RABIES

BLIND WOMAN GETS NEW KIDNEY FROM DAD SHE HASN'T SEEN IN YEARS

HOSPITALS SUED BY SEVEN FOOT DOCTORS

KICKING BABY CONSIDERED TO BE HEALTHY

DEADLINE PASSES FOR STRIKING POLICE

BOYS CAUSE AS MANY PREGNANCIES AS GIRLS

SUDDEN RUSH TO HELP PEOPLE OUT OF WORK

SAFETY EXPERTS SAY SCHOOL BUS PASSENGERS SHOULD BE BELTED

CEMETERY ALLOWS PEOPLE TO BE BURIED BY THEIR PETS

ANTIQUE STRIPPER TO DEMONSTRATE WARES AT STORE

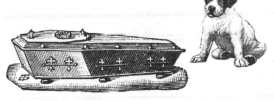

ALEXANDER HOPING PAST IS BEHIND HIM

FLAMING TOILET SEAT CAUSES EVACUATION AT HIGH SCHOOL

MINERS REFUSE TO WORK AFTER DEATH

LUNG CANCER IN WOMEN MUSHROOMS

GENETIC ENGINEERING SPLITS SCIENTISTS

HALF OF ALL CHILDREN TESTED SCORED BELOW AVERAGE

LIVING TOGETHER LINKED TO DIVORCE

STOLEN PAINTING FOUND BY TREE

MAN HELD OVER GIANT L.A. BRUSH FIRE

KIDS MAKE NUTRITIOUS SNACKS

DENTIST RECEIVES PLAQUE

MAN ROBS, THEN KILLS HIMSELF

PROSTITUTES APPEAL TO POPE

POLICE SEARCH FOR WITNESSES TO ASSAULT

FIRSTS

The world's **first** traffic island was installed – at his own expense – by Colonel Pierrepoint outside his London club; he was killed crossing over to it

The **first** ready-to-eat breakfast cereal was Shredded Wheat in 1893 (it beat Kellogg's Corn Flakes by just five years)

The **first** scientifically planned slimming diet was devised in 1862 by Dr Harvey, an ear specialist, for an overweight undertaker (incidentally, dieting was initially something that only men tended to do – women didn't start to do it until they stopped wearing figure-altering corsets)

The **first** dry cleaning was in 1849 by a Monsieur Jolly-Bellin of France, who discovered the process by mistake when he upset a lamp over a newly laundered tablecloth and found that the part that was covered with spirit from the lamp was cleaner than the rest

The **first** ice lolly dates back to 1923 when lemonade salesman Frank Epperson left a glass of lemonade with a spoon in it on a windowsill one very cold night: the next morning, the ice lolly was born

The **first** ever guest on *This Is Your Life* – in Britain – was Eamonn Andrews (and, of course, he went on to host the show)

Paddy Ashdown's grandfather was the **first** man in Ireland to buy a car

Steven Seagal was the **first** non-Asian to successfully open a martial arts academy in Japan

Groucho Marx ate his **first** bagel at the age of 81

Steven Spielberg directed the very **first** episode of *Columbo*

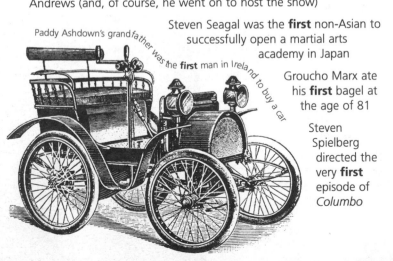

The **first** presenter of *A Question of Sport* (in 1970) wasn't David Coleman but David Vine

Courteney Cox was the **first** person on US TV ever to use the word 'period' – in an ad for Tampax

Harry Houdini was the **first** man to fly a plane in Australia – in 1910

Jimmy Carter was the **first** president to have been born in a hospital

The **first** man to fly over the North Pole – and indeed the South Pole – was called Dickie Byrd

The **first** Englishman to be killed in an aviation accident was Mr Rolls of Rolls-Royce fame

Soft toilet paper was sold for the **first** time in Britain in 1947 and was only available in Harrods

Gustav Mahler composed his **first** piece of music at the age of four, Sergei Prokofiev composed his **first** piece of music aged five and Wolfgang Mozart was just eight when he composed his **first** symphony

The **first** song Bruce Springsteen ever learned to play on the guitar was The Rolling Stones's 'It's All Over Now'

The **first** person in Britain to own a video phone was Jeremy Beadle (the second was Alan Minter)

Peter Snow and Peter Hobday co-presented the **first** edition of *Newsnight* in 1980

Barbra Streisand's **first** performance was as a chocolate chip cookie

Peter Sellers was the **first** male to feature on the cover of *Playboy*; he also provided the voices for the **first** PG Tips chimps ad – for which he was paid £25

The **first** duplicating machine was invented by James Watt, the inventor of the steam engine, in 1778 (patented in 1780) to help him with all the copying he had to do for his steam-engine business

Britain's **first** National Lottery was in 1567 to pay for public works. There were 400,000 tickets at ten shillings each (though these could be subdivided 'for the convenience of the poorer classes'). The top prize was £5,000, of which £3,000 was paid in cash, £700 in plate and the rest in good tapestry, etc.

Humphrey Bogart was the **first** Gerber baby (for Gerber Baby Foods)

The **first** member of the Royal Family ever to leave home for a haircut was the Queen: it was in Malta back in the days when she was a princess and she is said to have enjoyed the experience

Cuba Gooding Jr's **first** job was as a dancer for Lionel Richie at the 1984 Los Angeles Olympics

Harrison Ford's **first** film role was as a bellboy in the 1966 film *Dead Heat On A Merry-Go-Round* and he had to say, 'Paging Mr Ellis' (Ellis being James Coburn)

PROVERBS THAT ARE CLEARLY NOT TRUE

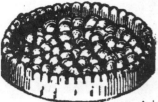

An apple a day keeps the doctor away

You can't judge a book by its cover

You can't have your cake and eat it

The best things in life are free

Every cloud has a silver lining

Ask no questions and you will be told no lies

Barking dogs seldom bite

There is no accounting for taste

The race is not to the swift

It never rains but it pours

PEOPLE WHO WERE BORN ON SIGNIFICANT DAYS IN HISTORY

Grandmaster Flash – the day that the EEC came into being

Cuba Gooding Jr – the day that Christiaan Barnard performed his second heart transplant

Barry John – the day that the Battle of the Bulge ended

Mark Lamarr – the day of the first transmission of the first episode of *The Forsyte Saga*

Michael Crawford – the day that Burma was invaded by the Japanese

Stefan Edberg – the day that Indira Gandhi became Indian Prime Minister

Emma Bunton – the day that Concorde made its first commercial flight (to Bahrain)

Frank Skinner – the day that Prince Charles started prep school

Jean Simmons – the day that Leon Trotsky was expelled from the USSR

Terry Jones – the day that Vidkun Quisling became Prime Minister of Norway

Alice Cooper – the day that Ceylon gained its independence

Natalie Imbruglia – the day that Edward Heath resigned as leader of the Conservative Party

Carole King – the day that soap rationing began in Britain

Robbie Williams – the day that Alexander Solzhenitsyn was expelled from the USSR

John McEnroe – the day that Fidel Castro became Prime Minister of Cuba

Seal – the day that the USSR stood down in the Cuban Missile Crisis

Alan Rickman – the day that the Indian navy mutinied

Lee Evans – the day that Muhammad Ali first became world heavyweight champion

Sir Peter O'Sullevan – the day that Germany and Russia signed the Treaty of Brest-Litovsk

Lord Douglas Hurd – the day that Mahatma Gandhi began his campaign of civil disobedience

Mickey Spillane – the day that Moscow became the capital of Russia

Patti Boyd – the day that the US defeated Japan in the Battle of Iwo Jima

Gary Oldman – the day that the London Planetarium opened

Ayrton Senna – the day that the Sharpeville massacre took place in South Africa

Gail Porter – the day that Bangladesh proclaimed its independence from Pakistan

Sir David Frost – the day that Italy invaded Albania

Neil Kinnock – the day that British commandos raided St Nazaire

Marc Overmars – the day that the last US troops left Vietnam

Janice Long – the day that Sir Winston Churchill resigned as PM

Sharon Corr – the day that Sir Henry Cooper regained the British heavyweight boxing title

John McCririck – the day that Yugoslavia surrendered to Germany

Hayley Mills – the day that the International Court of Justice was opened in The Hague

Sue Barker – the day that Prince Rainier married Grace Kelly

Bianca Jagger – the day that the Germans surrendered in World War Two

Brian Lara – the day the *QE2* sailed from Southampton on her maiden voyage

Lance Bass – the day that Margaret Thatcher became PM

George Clooney – the day that Spurs won the FA Cup to achieve the Double

Billy Joel – the day that Britain's first launderette opened

Dr Miriam Stoppard – the day of King George VI's coronation

Ayatollah Khomeini – the day that the Siege of Mafeking was relieved

Naomi Campbell – the day that the South African cricket tour of England was cancelled

Bob Dylan – the day that the *Bismarck* sunk the *Hood*

Stevie Nicks – the day that apartheid began in South Africa

Helena Bonham Carter – the day that Guyana became independent

Charlie Watts – the day that clothes rationing began in the UK

Craig Stadler – the day that Queen Elizabeth II was crowned

Ice Cube – the day that Georges Pompidou was elected French President

Joshua Nkomo – the day that the Royal Family adopted the surname Windsor

Esther Rantzen – the day that France signed an armistice with Germany

Mike Tyson – the day that US bombs hit Hanoi for the first time

Olivia de Havilland – the day that the first Battle of the Somme began

Pamela Anderson – the day that BBC2 began regular colour broadcasts

Kenneth Clarke – the day that the Vichy Government was set up in France

Tom Cruise – the day that French rule in Algeria ended

Shane Lynch – the day that Israeli commandos rescued hostages in a raid on Entebbe airport

O J Simpson – the day that Princess Elizabeth's engagement to Prince Philip was announced

Gaby Roslin – the day that the communications satellite *Telstar* was launched

Nelson Mandela – the day that the second Battle of the Marne was fought

Raymond Chandler – the day that John Dunlop applied to patent a pneumatic tyre

Salvador Allende – the day that the FBI was created

Dame Helen Mirren – the day that the Labour Party came to power in the 1945 General Election

Geri Halliwell – the day that Idi Amin ordered the expulsion of 50,000 Asians from Uganda

Steve Martin – the day that Japan surrendered (VJ Day)

Jenny Hanley – the day that India and Pakistan both achieved independence

Lily Tomlin – the day that Germany invaded Poland

Siegfried Sassoon – the day that Johannesburg was founded

Kate Adie – the day that William Joyce was sentenced to death

Larry Hagman – the day that Britain abandoned the Gold Standard

Keith Duffy – the day that the Watergate trial started

Anneka Rice – the day that the first transatlantic jet service started

Vaclav Havel – the day that the Jarrow Hunger March started

Kate Winslet – the day that Niki Lauda became world motor racing champion

Matthew Pinsent – the day that Fiji became independent

Eminem – the day that the Queen made the first ever visit by a British monarch to a communist state (Yugoslavia)

Joan Plowright – the day of the Wall Street Crash

Yasmin Le Bon – the day that Tanganyika and Zanzibar combined to make Tanzania

Tom O'Connor – the day that the Battle of Britain ended

Stubby Kaye – the day that World War One ended

Leonardo DiCaprio – the day that the new Covent Garden fruit market opened at Nine Elms

Imran Khan – the day that *The Mousetrap* opened in London

Sir Geoff Hurst – the day that the US and Britain declared war on Japan

Frank Sinatra – the day that the Germans built the first all-metal aeroplane

ALL THE WINNERS OF THE LIFETIME ACHIEVEMENT AWARD AT THE BRITISH COMEDY AWARDS

2002: Michael Palin

2001: David Jason

2000: Alan Bennett

1999: Barry Humphries; The Two Ronnies

1998: Dame Thora Hird; Denis Norden and Frank Muir (posthumously) won the Writers' Guild of Great Britain lifetime achievement award

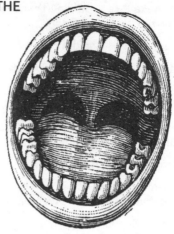

1997: Stanley Baxter

1996: Dave Allen

1995: Bruce Forsyth (for variety); Bob Monkhouse (for comedy)

1994: Spike Milligan; June Whitfield

1993: Ken Dodd

1992: Eric Sykes

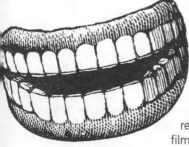

1991: Beryl Reid; George Burns received an International lifetime achievement award

1990: Ronnie Barker; Sir Norman Wisdom received a lifetime achievement award for stage; Roy Hudd received a lifetime achievement award for radio, and Peter Rogers received a lifetime achievement award for film comedy

THE ONLY COUNTRIES TO HAVE WON THE WIMBLEDON MEN'S SINGLES TITLE

UK – 35 wins (the most recent: Fred Perry in 1936)

USA – 33 wins (the most recent: Pete Sampras in 2000)

Australia – 21 wins (the most recent: Lleyton Hewitt in 2002)

France – 7 wins (the most recent: Yvon Petra in 1946)

Sweden – 7 wins (the most recent: Stefan Edberg in 1990)

New Zealand – 4 wins (the most recent: Tony Wilding in 1913)

Germany – 4 wins (the most recent: Michael Stich in 1991)

Spain – 1 win (Manuel Santana in 1966)

Czechoslovakia – 1 win (Jan Kodes in 1973)

Holland – 1 win (Richard Krajicek in 1996)

Croatia – 1 win (Goran Ivanisevic in 2001)

Switzerland – 1 win (Roger Federer in 2003)

Note: Jaroslav Drobny won the men's title in 1954 representing Egypt. He was in fact Czech, and later became British.

PEOPLE WHO HAVE SWITCHED ON THE OXFORD STREET LIGHTS

2002: Blue

2001: S Club 7

2000: Charlotte Church

1999: Ronan Keating

1998: Zoe Ball

1997: Peter Andre

1996: The Spice Girls

1995: The cast of *Coronation Street*

1994: Lenny Henry

1993: Sir Richard Branson

1992: Linford Christie

1991: Children from Westminster Children's Hospital

1990: Sir Cliff Richard

1989: Gorden Kaye

1988: Terry Wogan

1987: Derek Jameson

1986: Leslie Grantham and Anita Dobson

1985: Bob Geldof

1984: Esther Rantzen

1983: Pat Phoenix

1982: Daley Thompson

PEOPLE WHO HAVE SWITCHED ON THE BLACKPOOL ILLUMINATIONS

2002: Ronan Keating

2001: Steps

2000: Westlife

1999: Gary Barlow

1998: Chris de Burgh

1997: Michael Ball

1996: Eternal

1995: The Bee Gees

1994: Dame Shirley Bassey

1993: Status Quo

1992: Lisa Stansfield

1991: Derek Jameson and Judith Chalmers

1990: Julie Goodyear and Roy Barraclough

1989: Frank Bruno

1988: Andrew Lloyd Webber and Sarah Brightman

1987: Frank Bough

1986: Les Dawson

1985: Joanna Lumley

1984: Johannes Rau

1983: Doris Speed and the cast of *Coronation Street*

1982: Rear Admiral Sandy Woodward

WONDERFULLY NAMED DICKENS CHARACTERS

Doctor Neeshawts (*The Mudfog Papers*), Oswald Pardiggle (*Bleak House*), Paul Sweedlepipe (*Martin Chuzzlewit*), Doctor Soemup (*The Mudfog Papers*), Mortimer Knag (*Nicholas Nickleby*), Augustus Moddle (*Martin Chuzzlewit*), Quebec Bagnet (*Bleak House*), Simon Tappertit (*Barnaby Rudge*), Mercy Pecksniff (*Martin Chuzzlewit*), Morleena Kenwigs (*Nicholas Nickleby*), Chevy Slyme (*Martin Chuzzlewit*), Dick Swiveller (*The Old Curiosity Shop*), Conkey Chickweed (*Oliver Twist*), Sophy Wackles (*The Old Curiosity Shop*), Minnie Meagles (*Little Dorrit*), Canon Crisparkle (*The Mystery of Edwin Drood*), Peepy Jellyby (*Bleak House*), Nicodemus Boffin (*Our Mutual Friend*), Count Smorltork (*The Pickwick Papers*)

PEOPLE WHO HAD BAD ADOLESCENT ACNE

Dustin Hoffman, Victoria Beckham, Jennifer Capriati, Chris Morris, Jim Henson, Jack Nicholson, Janis Joplin, Mike Myers, F. Murray Abraham

PEOPLE WHO ARE FLUENT IN FOREIGN LANGUAGES

Mira Sorvino (Mandarin Chinese)

Imogen Stubbs (French)

Eddie Izzard (French)

Kate Beckinsale (French and Russian)

Geena Davis (Swedish)

Davina McCall (French)

Rachel Weisz (German)

Helena Bonham Carter (French)

Rupert Everett (French and Italian)

Kate Adie (Swedish)

Alan Bennett (Russian)

Prunella Scales (French)

Gabriel Byrne (Spanish)

Edward Norton (Japanese)

Natalie Portman (Hebrew)

PEOPLE WHO READ THEIR OWN OBITUARIES

Dave Swarbrick

Mark Twain

Wild Bill Hickok

Bob Hope

The Queen Mother

Harold Macmillan

Max Jaffa

Alfred Nobel

Ian Dury (heard it)

Bertrand Russell

P.T. Barnum

Daniel Boone

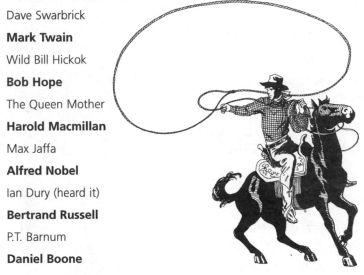

ALL THE PEOPLE WHO HAVE OPENED THE HARRODS SALES SINCE 1988

January 1988: Charlton Heston

July 1988: Dame Edna Everage

January 1989: Tony Curtis

July 1989: Sir Roger Moore and Brooke Shields

January 1990: Jason Donovan

July 1990: John Forsythe

January 1991: Sir Cliff Richard

July 1991: Graham Gooch and Viv Richards

January 1992: Diana Ross

July 1992: Nigel Mansell

January 1993: Tom Jones

July 1993: Burt Reynolds

January 1994: Richard Gere

July 1994: Betty Boothroyd and Rory Bremner

January 1995: Pierce Brosnan

July 1995: Chris O'Donnell and Damon Hill

January 1996: Gerard Depardieu

July 1996: Holly Hunter

January 1997: Goldie Hawn

July 1997: Daryl Hannah

January 1998: Cher cancelled after the death of her ex-husband Sonny Bono; it was therefore known as the Chairman's Sale

July 1998: Boyzone

January 1999: Cher

July 1999: Sophia Loren

January 2000: Raquel Welch

July 2000: Westlife

January 2001: Charlotte Church

July 2001: Salma Hayek

January 2002: Victoria Beckham

July 2002: Liberty X and Enrique Iglesias

January 2003: Holly Valance

July 2003: Natalie Imbruglia

PEOPLE WHO SURVIVED PLANE CRASHES

Clint Eastwood, Sir Bobby Charlton, Yasser Arafat, Dame Elizabeth Taylor, Peter Snow, David Coulthard, Frankie Dettori, Patrick Swayze, Sting, Luciano Pavarotti, Rowan Atkinson, Brian Blessed

PEOPLE WHO HAD HIPS REPLACED

Murray Walker, Maeve Binchy, Dave Prowse, Dame Elizabeth Taylor, Oscar Peterson, Peter Vaughan, Anita Pallenberg, Charlton Heston, Sir Jimmy Young, John Cleese, Gerd Muller, Bob Wilson, Tony Britton, Liza Minnelli (twice), The Duke of Kent

THE FIRST TEN CASTAWAYS ON *DESERT ISLAND DISCS*

First broadcast 29 January 1942

Vic Oliver (comedian)

James Agate (critic)

Commander Campbell (mariner and explorer)

C.B. Cochran (showman)

Pat Kirkwood (actress)

Jack Hylton (bandleader)

Captain Dingle (explorer)

Joan Jay (glamour girl)

The Reverend Canon W.H. Elliott (precentor of the Chapels Royal)

Arthur Askey (comedian)

WHAT A 10-STONE PERSON WOULD WEIGH ON OTHER PLANETS

Pluto – 7lb

The Moon – 1st 10lb

Mercury – 3st 11lb

Mars – 3st 11lb

Uranus – 9st 1lb

Venus – 9st 11lb

Saturn – 10st 11lb

Neptune – 11st 12lb

Jupiter – 25st 5lb

MPs WHO WERE THE BABY OF THE HOUSE OF COMMONS

Tony Benn (Labour; 25 in 1950)

David Steel (Liberal; 26 in 1965)

Stephen Dorrell (Conservative; 27 in 1979)

John Profumo (Conservative; 25 in 1940)

Charles Kennedy (SDP; 23 in 1983)

Paul Channon (Conservative; 23 in 1959)

Malcolm Rifkind (Conservative; 27 in 1974)

Matthew Taylor (Liberal; 24 in 1987)

WELL-KNOWN SONGS BASED ON CLASSICAL MUSIC

'Lady Lynda' (The Beach Boys) – based on Bach's *Jesu Joy of Man's Desiring*

'I Believe In Father Christmas' (Greg Lake) – based on Prokofiev's *Lieutenant Kije Suite*

'It's Now Or Never' (Elvis Presley) – based on De Capua's *O Sole Mio*

'Stranger In Paradise' (Tony Bennett) – based on Borodin's *Polotsvian Dances*

'Sabre Dance' (Love Sculpture) – based on Aram Khachaturian's ballet *Gayaneh*

'More Than Love' (Ken Dodd) – based on Beethoven's *Pathetique Sonata*

'Could It Be Magic' (Barry Manilow) – based on Chopin's *Prelude In C Major*

'Joybringer' (Manfred Mann's Earth Band) – based on Holst's *The Planets*

'A Lover's Concerto' (The Toys) – based on Bach's *Minuet In G*

'All By Myself' (Eric Carmen) – based on Rachmaninov's *Piano Concerto No. 2*

'Who's Afraid of The Big Bad Wolf' (1933) – based on Johann Strauss's 'Champagne Song' from *Die Fledermaus*

'Lullaby of Broadway' (1935) – based on Brahms's *Hungarian Dances* and Offenbach's 'Barcarolle' from *Tales of Hoffman*

'Where Did You Get That Hat' (1888) – based on Wagner's *Lohengrin* and *Die Meistersinger*

WELL-KNOWN SONGS BASED ON OTHER SONGS

'Love Me Tender' (1956) – based on George Poulton's 'Aura Lee' (1861)

'El Condor Pasa' (1933) – based on a Peruvian folksong

'Waltzing Matilda' (1903) – based on Robert Tannahill's 'Craigielea'

'Those Were The Days' (1968) – based on a traditional East European tune

'Don't Sit Under The Apple Tree' (1942) – based on 'Long Long Ago' (1833)

'It's All In The Game' (1951) – based on 'Melody' by Dawes (1912)

'She'll Be Comin' Round The Mountain (When She Comes)' (1899) – based on the hymn 'When The Chariot Comes'

'Hello Dolly' (1964) – based on 'Sunflower' by Mack David (1948)

'Midnight In Moscow' (1962) – based on the Russian song 'Padmas Koveeye Vietchera'

'My Sweet Lord' (1971) – based on Ronald Mack's 'He's So Fine' (1962)

FAMOUS RELATIVES OF OLYMPIC COMPETITORS

Grace Kelly (her father, John Kelly, Rowing 1920)

Roddy Llewellyn (his father, Sir Harry Llewellyn, Showjumping 1952)

Jean Simmons (her father, Charles Simmons, Gymnastics 1952)

Jonathon Porritt (his father, Arthur Porritt, 100 metres 1924)

Bobby Davro (his father, Bill Nankeville, 1500 metres 1948)

Charlotte Rampling (her father, Godfrey Rampling, 4x400 metres 1936)

Prince Rainier (his son, Prince Albert, Bobsleigh 1988)

Sir Rex Harrison (his son, Noel, Alpine Skiing 1952)

Tara Palmer-Tomkinson (her father, Charles Palmer-Tomkinson, Skiing 1964)

Andre Agassi (his father, Mike Agassi, Boxing 1948 and 1952 for Iran)

Hugh Laurie (his father, Ran Laurie, Rowing – Gold Medal winner – 1948)

Lindsay Davenport (her father, Volleyball 1968)

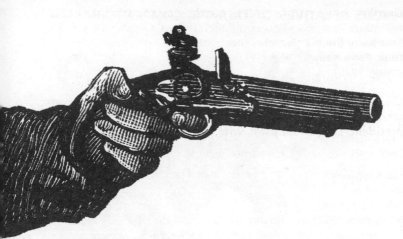

THE SPOOKY LINCOLN–KENNEDY COINCIDENCES

Lincoln was elected President in 1860 (having been elected to Congress in 1846); Kennedy was elected President in 1960 (having been elected to Congress in 1946)

Both presidents were directly concerned in civil rights for black people

Lincoln had a secretary named Kennedy; Kennedy had a secretary named Lincoln

Both presidents were shot in the head (from behind) and both presidents were with their wives when they were assassinated

Both wives had lost children while living at the White House

Both assassinations took place on a Friday and both presidents were warned that they might be assassinated but both refused to change their schedules

Lincoln was shot in a theatre by a man who hid in a warehouse; Kennedy was shot from a warehouse by a man who hid in a theatre

Kennedy was riding in a Lincoln when he was shot

Lincoln's assassin (John Wilkes Booth) was a Southerner in his twenties; Kennedy's assassin (Lee Harvey Oswald) was a Southerner in his twenties (both assassins were known by their three names)

Booth and Oswald were both shot before they could be tried

Lincoln was succeeded by his vice-president, Andrew Johnson, who was born in 1808; Kennedy was succeeded by his vice-president, Lyndon Johnson, who was born in 1908

Lincoln and Kennedy each had seven letters in their names; John Wilkes Booth and Lee Harvey Oswald each had 15 letters in their names; Andrew Johnson and Lyndon Johnson each had 13 letters in their names

NB A month before Lincoln was assassinated, he was in Monroe, Maryland; a year before Kennedy was assassinated, he was in Marilyn Monroe

PEOPLE WHO ENTERED COMPETITIONS TO IMITATE OR IMPERSONATE THEMSELVES AND LOST

David Bellamy (he was driving to an engagement one day, listening to a local radio station in his car. The station was running a 'Phone in and give us your David Bellamy impersonation' competition. He stopped at a telephone box, phoned in to take part – and came third)

Dolly Parton

Graham Greene (entered a competition to parody his style in the *Spectator* – came third)

Charlie Chaplin

Jason Donovan (sent in a tape to *Stars In Their Eyes* but was turned down)

Elvis Presley (entered an Elvis lookalike contest in a US burger joint but came third)

THE LAST LINES OF CLASSIC MOVIES

'The horror, the horror.' (*Apocalypse Now*)

'Madness. Madness.' (*The Bridge On The River Kwai*)

'That's right, that's right – attaboy, Clarence.' (*It's A Wonderful Life*)

'I used to hate the water – I can't imagine why.' (*Jaws*)

'The old man was right, only the farmers won; we lost, we'll always lose.' (*The Magnificent Seven*)

'Eliza? Where the devil are my slippers?' (*My Fair Lady*)

'Why, she wouldn't even harm a fly.' (*Psycho*)

'Well, Tillie, when the hell are we going to get some dinner?' (*Guess Who's Coming To Dinner*)

'We saw her many times again, born free and living free, but to us she was always the same, our friend Elsa.' (*Born Free*)

'Hello, everybody, this is Mrs Norman Maine.' (*A Star Is Born*)

'I haven't got a sensible name, Calloway.' (*The Third Man*)

'Thank you, thank you, I'm glad it's off my mind at last.' (*The 39 Steps*)

'Good, for a minute I thought we were in trouble.' (*Butch Cassidy And The Sundance Kid*)

'All right, Mr De Mille, I'm ready for my close-up.' (*Sunset Boulevard*)

'I now pronounce you men and wives.' (*Seven Brides For Seven Brothers*)

'Louis, I think this is the beginning of a beautiful friendship.' (*Casablanca*)

'Oh, Aunt Em, there's no place like home.' (*The Wizard of Oz*)

'The way we're swimming, old girl.' (*The African Queen*)

'Mediocrities everywhere, I absolve you, I absolve you, I absolve you, I absolve you. I absolve you all.' (*Amadeus*)

'Cool Hand Luke, hell, he's a natural born world-shaker.' (*Cool Hand Luke*)

'I guess we all died a little in that damn war.' (*The Outlaw Josey Wales*)

WOMEN WHO HAD GRANDFATHERS WHO WON 1954 NOBEL PRIZES

Olivia Newton-John (Max Born, won for Physics)

Mariel Hemingway (Ernest Hemingway, won for Literature)

PROOF THAT HELL IS EXOTHERMIC

This was a question in a University of Washington chemistry exam: 'Is Hell exothermic (gives off heat) or endothermic (absorbs heat)? Support your answer with proof.' Most students wrote about Boyle's Law: gas cools off when it expands and heats up when it is compressed. However, one student wrote this:

'First, we need to know how the mass of Hell is changing in time. So, we need to know the rate that souls are moving into Hell and the rate they are leaving. I think that we can safely assume that once a soul gets to Hell, it will not leave. Therefore, no souls are leaving. As for how many souls are entering Hell, let's look at the different religions that exist in the world today. Some of these religions state that if you are not a member of their religion, you will go to Hell. Since there are more than one of these religions and since people do not belong to more than one religion, we can project that all people and all souls go to Hell. With birth and death rates as they are, we can expect the number of souls in Hell to increase exponentially. Now, we look at the rate of change of the volume in Hell because Boyle's Law states that in order for the temperature and pressure in Hell to stay the same, the volume of Hell has to expand as souls are added. This gives two possibilities: (1) If Hell is expanding at a slower rate than the rate at which souls enter Hell, then the temperature and pressure in Hell will increase until all Hell breaks loose. (2) Of course, if Hell is expanding at a rate faster than the increase of souls in Hell, then the temperature and pressure will drop until Hell freezes over. So which is it? If we accept the postulate given to me by Ms. Therese Banyan during my Freshman year, 'That it will be a cold night in Hell before I sleep with you,' and take into account the fact that I still have not succeeded in having sexual relations with her, then (2) cannot be true and thus I am sure that Hell is exothermic.'

This student received the only A.

THE FIRST 10 COMMERCIALS BROADCAST ON BRITISH TV

ITV, Thursday, 22 September 1955:

Gibbs SR toothpaste

Cadbury's drinking chocolate

Kraft cheese

Dunlop tyres

***Woman* magazine**

Surf washing powder

National Benzole petrol

Lux soap

Ford cars

Guinness

OSCAR ONLYS

The **Only** role to garner two Oscars is Vito Corleone: Marlon Brando won the Best Actor Oscar in this role for *The Godfather* (1972), while Robert De Niro won the Best Supporting Actor Oscar in the same role for *The Godfather Part II* (1974). This film is also the **Only** sequel to win an Oscar as Best Film

The **Only** actor to win an Oscar for less than ten minutes' work: Anthony Quinn, who was on screen for only nine minutes in *Lust For Life* (1956)

The **Only** actress to win an Oscar for less than ten minutes' work: Dame Judi Dench, who was on screen for only eight minutes in *Shakespeare In Love* (1998)

The **Only** Oscar to win an Oscar: Oscar Hammerstein II (Best Song: 1941 and 1945)

The **Only** actress to win an Oscar for playing an Oscar nominee: Maggie Smith in *California Suite* (1978)

The **Only** silent film to win Best Picture: *Wings* (1927)

The **Only** actor to win a Best Actor Oscar when nominated alongside four previous Oscar winners: Adrien Brody for *The Pianist* (2003)

The **Only** actor to win a Best Actor Oscar in a foreign language film: Roberto Benigni for *Life Is Beautiful* (1998); note also that Robert De Niro's performance in *The Godfather Part II* was mostly in Italian

The **Only** actress to win a Best Actress Oscar in a foreign language: Sophia Loren for *Two Women* (1961)

The **Only** actress to win a Best Supporting Actress Oscar for playing the title role in a film: Vanessa Redgrave for *Julia* (1977)

The **Only** films in which all the members of the cast have been nominated for Oscars: *Who's Afraid of Virginia Woolf?* (four cast members 1966), *Sleuth* (two cast members 1972) and *Give 'em Hell Harry* (one cast member 1975)

The **Only** family in which three generations have won Oscars – the Hustons: Walter for *The Treasure of The Sierra Madre* (1948), John for *The Treasure of The Sierra Madre* and Anjelica for *Prizzi's Honor* (1985). Walter and John Huston are also the only father and son to win acting Oscars for the same film. Note also that Carmine Coppola, his son Francis and Francis's nephew Nicolas Cage all won Oscars

The **Only** mother and daughter to be nominated for Oscars in the same year: Diane Ladd and her daughter Laura Dern for *Rambling Rose* (1991)

The **Only** films to win 11 Oscars: *Ben-Hur* (1959) and *Titanic* (1997)

The **Only** films to get 11 Oscar nominations but not a single Oscar: *The Turning Point* (1977) and *The Color Purple* (1985)

The **Only** sisters to win Best Actress Oscars: Joan Fontaine for *Suspicion* (1941) and Olivia de Havilland for *To Each His Own* (1946). And they didn't speak to each other!

The **Only** twins to win Oscars: Julius J. Epstein and Philip G. Epstein (with Howard Koch) for *Casablanca* (1943)

The **Only** Oscar sold for more than half a million dollars: Vivien Leigh's for *Gone With The Wind*, which fetched $510,000 at auction in 1994

The **Only** posthumous acting Oscar was won by Peter Finch for *Network* (1976)

The **Only** actor to get two posthumous Oscar nominations: James Dean, for *East of Eden* (1955) and *Giant* (1956)

The **Only** animation film nominated for Best Film: *Beauty And The Beast* (1991)

The **Only** actress to win four Oscars: Katharine Hepburn, for *Morning Glory* (1932–33), *Guess Who's Coming To Dinner?* (1967), *The Lion In Winter* (1968) and *On Golden Pond* (1981). Jack Nicholson (two Best Actor and one Best Supporting Actor) and Walter Brennan (all as Best Supporting Actor) hold the record for the most Oscars for actors with three

The **Only** Best Supporting Actor winner to perform one-armed push-ups when he received his award: Jack Palance when he won for *City Slickers* (1991)

The **Only** father to win a Best Actor Oscar after his daughter had already won two Best Actress Oscars: Henry Fonda (*On Golden Pond*, 1981) after Jane Fonda had won for *Klute* (1971) and *Coming Home* (1978)

The **Only** daughter of a Best Actor winner to win an Oscar for Best Supporting Actress: Angelina Jolie for *Girl Interrupted* (1999); she is the daughter of Jon Voight, who won for *Coming Home* (1978)

The **Only** actors to get seven acting nominations without winning a single Oscar: Peter O'Toole and Richard Burton

The **Only** actress to get six acting nominations without winning a single Oscar: Deborah Kerr

The **Only** two actresses to compete against each other in both the Best Actress and the Best Supporting Actress categories in the same year: Holly Hunter and Emma Thompson in 1993

The **Only** actors to refuse Oscars: George C. Scott, *Patton* (1970) and Marlon Brando, *The Godfather* (1972)

The **Only** actor nominated as both Best Actor and Best Supporting Actor in the same year: Al Pacino (1992)

The **Only** octogenarian to win a Best Actress Oscar: Jessica Tandy for *Driving Miss Daisy* (1989)

The **Only** octogenarian to win a Best Supporting Actor Oscar: George Burns for *The Sunshine Boys* (1975)

The **Only** person to open the Oscar envelope to find his own name on the card: Irving Berlin (Best Song, 'White Christmas', 1942)

The **Only** man to be nominated for producer, director, writer and actor on the same film – twice – was Warren Beatty for *Heaven Can Wait* (1978) and *Reds* (1981)

The **Only** film in which the Best Director Oscar was shared by two men: *West Side Story* (Robert Wise and Jerome Robbins in 1961)

The **Only** women nominated as Best Director: Lina Wertmuller, *Seven Beauties* (1976), and Jane Campion, *The Piano* (1994)

The **Only** foreign language films nominated for Best Picture: *Grand Illusion* (1938, France), *Z* (1969, Algeria), *The Emigrants* (1972, Sweden), *Cries And Whispers* (1973, Sweden), *Il Postino* (*The Postman*; 1995, Italy), *Life Is Beautiful* (1998, Italy), *Crouching Tiger, Hidden Dragon* (2000, Taiwan)

The **Only** actors to win consecutive Oscars: Spencer Tracy (1937 and 1938), Jason Robards (1976 and 1977) and Tom Hanks (1993 and 1994)

The **Only** actresses to win consecutive Oscars: Luise Rainer (1936 and 1937) and Katharine Hepburn (1967 and 1968)

The **Only** actresses to get acting nominations five years running: Bette Davis (1938–42) and Greer Garson (1941–45)

The **Only** actors to get acting nominations four years running: Marlon Brando (1951–54) and Al Pacino (1972–75)

The **Only** films to win Best Actor and Best Actress Oscars: *It Happened One Night* (1934), *One Flew Over The Cuckoo's Nest* (1975), *Network* (1976), *Coming Home* (1978), *On Golden Pond* (1981), *The Silence of The Lambs* (1991) and *As Good As It Gets* (1997)

The **Only** films to win Oscars for Best Picture, Best Director, Best Actor, Best Actress and Best Screenplay: *It Happened One Night* (1934), *One Flew Over The Cuckoo's Nest* (1975) and *The Silence of The Lambs* (1991)

The **Only** films to win three acting Oscars: *A Streetcar Named Desire* (1951) and *Network* (1976)

The **Only** two actors to tie for Best Actor: Wallace Beery, *The Champ*, and Fredric March, *Dr. Jekyll and Mr. Hyde* (1931–32)

The **Only** two actresses to tie for Best Actress: Katharine Hepburn, *The Lion In Winter* and Barbra Streisand, *Funny Girl* (1968)

The **Only** actor to be nominated in both the leading and supporting categories for the same role: Barry Fitzgerald, *Going My Way* (1944)

The **Only** people to direct themselves to acting Oscars: Laurence Olivier, *Hamlet* (1948), and Roberto Benigni, *Life Is Beautiful* (1998)

The **Only** black actors to win Oscars: Hattie McDaniel (*Gone With The Wind*, 1939), Sidney Poitier (*Lilies of The Field*, 1963), Louis Gossett Jr. (*An Officer And A Gentleman*, 1982), Denzel Washington (*Glory*, 1989), Whoopi Goldberg (*Ghost*, 1990), Cuba Gooding Jr. (*Jerry Maguire*, 1996), Halle Berry (*Monster's Ball*, 2001), Denzel Washington (*Training Day*, 2001)

The **Only** actor to appear in three films that were nominated for Best Picture in the same year: Thomas Mitchell (*Stagecoach*, *Mr Smith Goes To Washington* and *Gone With The Wind* in 1939; he got the Best Supporting Actor Oscar for *Stagecoach*)

Note: Actors whose **Only** Oscars have been awarded for directing: Robert Redford (1980: *Ordinary People*), Warren Beatty (1981: *Reds*), Richard Attenborough (1982: *Gandhi*), Kevin Costner (1991: *Dances With Wolves*), Mel Gibson (1995: *Braveheart*)

SLOGANS SEEN OUTSIDE CHURCHES

Carpenter from Nazareth seeks joiners

Seven prayer-less days make one spiritually weak

Come in for a faith-lift

Come to Church in September and avoid the Christmas rush

Danger! Live Church!

Come to Ch**ch. What is missing? (UR – get it?)

Fight truth decay – brush up your Bible every day

Glory, Glory, Man Utd

Is life a Blur? Come to the Oasis

THE TOP PEOPLE IN THE COUNTRY (AFTER THE ROYAL FAMILY)

The Archbishop of Canterbury

The Lord High Chancellor (office under review)

The Archbishop of York

The Prime Minister

The Lord High Treasurer (although no such office exists at the moment)

Lord President of The Council

The Speaker of The House of Commons

The Lord Privy Seal

HEAD BOYS AT SCHOOL

Ian Hislop (Ardingly)

Hugh Dennis (University College School)

Sir Peter Hall (The Perse School)

Jonah Lomu (Wesley College)

Frank Bruno (Oak Hall)

Simon MacCorkindale (Haileybury)

Peter Jay (Winchester)

John Fowles (Bedford)

Lord William Rees-Mogg (Charterhouse)

Lord Douglas Hurd (Eton)

Lord David Owen (Mudd House Preparatory School)

Boris Johnson (Eton)

Nicholas Serota (Haberdashers' Aske's)

Steven Norris (Liverpool Institute)

Richard Curtis (Harrow – 'a freakish head of school')

Sir Ian McKellen (Bolton Grammar)

Alan Duncan MP (Beechwood Park Prep and Merchant Taylors')

Terry Jones (Royal Grammar School, Guildford)

Stuart Hall (Glossop Grammar)

Omar Sharif (Victoria College)

Peter Tatchell (Mount Waverley High School)

Simon Hughes MP (Christ College, Brecon)

Sir Tom Courtenay (Kingston High School)

HEAD GIRLS AT SCHOOL

Sarah, Duchess of York (Hurst Lodge)

Dame Norma Major (Peckham Comprehensive)

Baroness Margaret Thatcher (Kesteven and Grantham Girls' School)

Mo Mowlam (Coundon Court Comprehensive)

Dame Thora Hird (Morecambe Preparatory School)

Joan Bakewell (Stockport High School for Girls)

Gillian Shephard (North Walsham High School for Girls)

Kate Winslet (Redroofs Theatre School)

Baroness Lynda Chalker (Roedean)

Emma Nicholson (St Mary's, Wantage)

Baroness Sarah Hogg (St Mary's Convent, Ascot)

Francine Stock (St Catherine's, Guildford)

Kate Dimbleby (St Paul's)

Kate Hoey (Belfast Royal Academy)

Jill Dando (Broadoak Sixth-form Centre)

Minette Walters (Godolphin)

J.K. Rowling (Wyedean Comprehensive in Chepstow)

Esther McVey (Belvedere Girls' School, Liverpool)

SOME GENUINE AILMENTS

Lumpy Jaw (bacterial infection of the jaw with weeping sores)

Barbados Leg (elephantitis)

Painter's Colic (lead poisoning)

Iliac Passion (enduring pain in the lower three-fifths of the small intestine)

Parrot Disease (illness caused by inhaling dust contaminated by the droppings of infected birds)

Crab Yaws (tropical disease resembling syphilis with lesions on the foot)

Mad Staggers (often fatal gastric paralysis in horses)

Farmer's Lung (allergic reaction to fungi growing on hay, grain or straw)

Derbyshire Neck (enlargement of the thyroid gland visible as swelling on the neck)

Soldier's Heart (stress-related palpitations)

THE BBC'S ONLY FEMALE SPORTS PERSONALITIES OF THE YEAR

Anita Lonsborough (1962)

Dorothy Hyman (1963)

Mary Rand (1964)

Ann Jones (1969)

Princess Anne (1971)

Mary Peters (1972)

Virginia Wade (1977)

Jayne Torvill (with Christopher Dean) (1984)

Fatima Whitbread (1987)

Liz McColgan (1991)

Paula Radcliffe (2002)

FAMOUS PEOPLE WITH FAMOUS GODPARENTS

Winona Ryder (Timothy Leary)

Whitney Houston (Aretha Franklin)

Bertrand Russell (John Stuart Mill)

Jennifer Aniston (Telly Savalas)

Peter Scott (Sir J.M. Barrie)

Jonathan Aitken (Queen Juliana)

Mia Farrow (George Cukor and Louella Parsons)

Robert Cummings (Orville Wright)

Martin Amis (Philip Larkin)

Drew Barrymore (Steven Spielberg)

Earl Spencer (The Queen)

Andrew Parker Bowles (The Queen Mother)

Bridget Fonda (Larry Hagman)

Jeremy Thorpe (Megan Lloyd George)

Angelina Jolie (Jacqueline Bisset)

Sophie Dahl (Babs Powell)

THE WORLD'S GREATEST URBAN MYTH

Good Luck, Mr Gorsky: **On 20 July 1969, Neil Armstrong, commander of Apollo 11, was the first person to set foot on the moon. His first words – 'That's one small step for man, one giant leap for mankind' – were heard by millions. He then said: 'Good luck, Mr Gorsky.' People at NASA thought he was talking about a Soviet cosmonaut, but it turned out there was no Gorsky in the Russian space programme. Over the years Armstrong was frequently asked what he had meant by 'Good luck, Mr Gorsky', but he always refused to answer for fear of offending the man. When Mr Gorsky died, Neil Armstrong finally felt able to tell the story. When he was a kid playing in his back yard, he once had to fetch his ball from the neighbours' yard. As he dashed in, he overheard his neighbour Mrs Gorsky shouting at Mr Gorsky: 'Sex! You want sex? You'll get sex when the kid next door walks on the moon!'**

Alas, not only is the story untrue, but Neil Armstrong never even uttered the words 'Good luck, Mr Gorsky'. This story is an urban myth that has gathered currency on the internet. It's a prime example of the old saw that a lie can be halfway round the world before the truth has even got its boots on.

WONDERFULLY NAMED CHARACTERS FROM THE WORLD OF BERTIE WOOSTER

Barmy Fotheringay-Phipps, Stilton Cheesewright, Pongo Twistleton-Twistleton, Gussie Fink-Nottle, Biscuit Biskerton, Stiffy Stiffham, Catsmeat Potter-Pirbright, Dogface Rainsby, Oofy Prosser, Freddie Fitch-Fitch

STATISTICALLY THE MOST LANDED UPON MONOPOLY SQUARES

In order:

Trafalgar Square

Go

Marylebone Station

Free Parking

Marlborough Street

Vine Street

King's Cross Station

Bow Street

Water Works

Fenchurch Street Station

PEOPLE WHO GUESTED IN THE *BATMAN* TV SERIES

Shelley Winters (Ma Parker)

Ethel Merman (Lola Lasagne)

Tallulah Bankhead (Mrs Max Black)

Anne Baxter (Olga, Queen of the Cossacks)

Bruce Lee (Kato)

Glynis Johns (Lady Penelope Peasoup)

Jock Mahoney (Leo, one of Catwoman's accomplices)

James Brolin (Ralph Staphylococcus)

Michael Rennie (The Sandman)

George Sanders (Mr Freeze)

Zsa Zsa Gabor (Minerva)

**Roddy McDowall
(The Bookworm)**

Art Carney (The Archer)

Joan Collins (The Siren)

Vincent Price (Egghead)

Liberace (Chandell)

Cliff Robertson (Shame)

**Eartha Kitt
(Catwoman)**

Julie Newmar
(Catwoman)

**Lee Meriwether
(Catwoman)**

Edward G. Robinson
(cameo role)

George Raft (cameo role)

Phyllis Diller (cameo role)

Jerry Lewis (cameo role)

Gypsy Rose Lee (cameo role)

Rob Reiner (cameo role)

Sammy Davis Jr. (cameo role)

**Note: Robert F. Kennedy, Frank Sinatra, Jose Ferrer, Yul
Brynner, Dame Elizabeth Taylor, Gregory Peck, Mae West,
Gloria Swanson and Cary Grant all wanted to appear but no
parts could be found for them**

HOW TO SAY 'BEER' IN DIFFERENT LANGUAGES

cerveza (Spanish)

cerveja (Portuguese)

sor (Hungarian)

bière (French)

Bier (German)

bjór (Icelandic)

pombe (Swahili)

'pivo' (Russian)

öl (Swedish)

øl (Danish and Norwegian)

olut (Finnish)

bira (Turkish)

bir (Indonesian)

bere (Romanian)

birra (Italian)

'beera' (Greek)

fermentum/cervisia (Latin)

FAMOUS PEOPLE BORN ON THE VERY SAME DAY AS OTHER FAMOUS PEOPLE DIED

Donnie Wahlberg and Mies van der Rohe – 17.8.69

Davy Crockett and Frederick the Great – 17.8.1786

Billie Jean King and Lorenz Hart – 22.11.43

Laura Dern and Billy Rose – 10.2.66

Donald Trump and John Logie Baird – 14.6.46

Bryan Ferry and Bela Bartok – 26.9.45

Kevin Costner and George Morrow – 18.1.55

Kian Egan and Sir Alfred Hitchcock – 29.4.80

Rutger Hauer and Edvard Munch – 23.1.44

Phil Collins and C.B. Cochran – 31.1.51

Jason Donovan and Helen Keller – 1.6.68

Graham Chapman and Lord Baden-Powell – 8.1.41

Julio Iglesias and Elinor Glyn – 23.9.43

Yoko Ono and Gentleman Jim Corbett – 18.2.33

Anthea Redfern and Ernest Bevin – 14.4.51

Donna Summer and Sir Malcolm Campbell – 31.12.48

Adam Ant and Henri Matisse – 3.11.54

Michael Stipe and Albert Camus – 4.1.60

Frank Zappa and F. Scott Fitzgerald – 21.12.40

Che Guevara and Emmeline Pankhurst – 14.6.28

Sir James Savile and Harry Houdini – 31.10.26

Johnny Rotten and A.A. Milne – 31.1.56

Christina Aguilera and Ben Travers – 18.12.80

Victoria Principal and William Joyce (Lord Haw Haw) – 3.1.46

Julia Ormond and T.S. Eliot – 4.1.65

Tom Baker and King George V – 20.1.36

Billy Ocean and George Orwell – 21.1.50

Germaine Greer and W.B. Yeats – 29.1.39

Jerome Flynn and William Henry Beveridge – 16.3.63

Clyde Barrow and J.M. Synge – 24.3.09

Srinivas Venkataraghavan and John Maynard Keynes – 21.4.46

Mickey Rourke and Hilaire Belloc – 16.7.53

Patrick Ewing and Marilyn Monroe – 5.8.62

Anna Massey and Edith Wharton – 11.8.37

Lord Gus Macdonald and Leon Trotsky – 20.8.40

Adam Sandler and Hendrik Verwoerd – 6.9.66

Jacqueline Bisset and William Heath Robinson – 13.9.44

James Gandolfini and Dag Hammarskjöld – 18.9.61

Gwyneth Paltrow and Rory Storm – 27.9.72

Janeane Garofalo and Harpo Marx – 28.9.64

Richard Carpenter and Hermann Goering – 15.10.46

Winona Ryder and Duane Allman – 29.10.71

Larry Mullen Jr. and Augustus John – 31.10.61

k.d. lang and James Thurber – 2.11.61

Art Carney and Wilfred Owen – 4.11.18

Leonardo DiCaprio and Cyril Connolly – 11.11.74

Robert F. Kennedy and Queen Alexandra – 20.11.25

Kelly Brook and Merle Oberon – 23.11.79

David Mamet and Ernst Lubitsch – 30.11.47

Dennis Wise and Walt Disney – 15.12.66

Jay Kay and Trygve Lie – 30.12.68

COMIC BOOK SUPERHEROES AND THEIR CONCEALED IDENTITIES

Spiderman (Peter Parker)

Superman (Clark Kent)

Batman (Bruce Wayne)

Robin (Dick Grayson)

The Green Hornet (Britt Reid)

Supergirl (Linda Lee Danvers)

Batgirl (Babs Gordon)

The Incredible Hulk (Bruce Banner)

Captain Marvel (Billy Batson)

Wonder Woman (Diana Prince)

WOMEN WHO HAD SONGS WRITTEN FOR THEM

Marilyn Monroe – 'Candle In The Wind' (Elton John/Bernie Taupin)

Dame Elizabeth Taylor – 'Emotionally Yours' (Bob Dylan)

Christie Brinkley – 'Uptown Girl' (Billy Joel)

Joni Mitchell – 'Our House' (Graham Nash)

Billie-Jean King – 'Philadelphia Freedom' (Elton John/Bernie Taupin)

Joan Baez – 'It Ain't Me Babe' (Bob Dylan)

Kylie Minogue – 'Suicide Blonde' (Michael Hutchence)

Marianne Faithfull – 'Wild Horses' (Mick Jagger)

Geri Halliwell – 'Eternity' (Robbie Williams)

Nicole Appleton – 'Songbird' (Liam Gallagher)

Patti Boyd – 'Layla' (Eric Clapton)

Jenny Boyd – 'Jennifer Juniper' (Donovan)

Rita Coolidge – 'Delta Lady' (Leon Russell)

Judy Collins – Suite: 'Judy Blue Eyes' (Stephen Stills)

GREAT COUNTRY & WESTERN TITLES

'You're The Reason Our Kids Are Ugly' (Loretta Lynn)

'I Cheated Me Right Out of You' (Moe Bandy)

'You're Out Doing What I'm Here Doing Without' (Gene Watson)

'The Lord Knows I'm Drinkin'' (Cal Smith)

'She Got The Goldmine (I Got the Shaft)' (Jerry Reed)

'Now I Lay Me Down To Cheat' (David Allan Coe)

'You Just Hurt My Last Feeling' (Sammi Smith)

'She's Actin' Single (I'm Drinkin' Doubles)' (Gary Stewart)

'I'm Gonna Hire A Wino To Decorate Our Home' (David Frizzell)

'Divorce Me C.O.D.' (Merle Travis)

'Heaven's Just A Sin Away' (The Kendells)

'I Forgot More Than You'll Ever Know' (The Davis Sisters)

'I'm The Only Hell (Mama Ever Raised)' (Johnny Paycheck)

SOME MORE GENUINE SONG TITLES

'I'd Rather Be A Lobster Than A Wiseguy' (Edward Madden and Theodore F. Morse, 1907)

'(Potatoes Are Cheaper – Tomatoes Are Cheaper) Now's The Time To Fall In Love' (Al Lewis and Al Sherman, 1931)

'Hey Young Fella Close Your Old Umbrella' (Dorothy Fields and Jimmy McHugh, 1933)

'Caldonia (What Makes Your Big Head So Hard)' (Fleecie Moore, 1946)

'Aunt Jemima And Your Uncle Cream of Wheat' (Johnny Mercer and Rube Bloom, 1936)

'Come After Breakfast, Bring 'Long Your Lunch And Leave 'Fore Supper Time' (J. Tim Bryman, Chris Smith and James Henry Burris, 1909)

'I Love To Dunk A Hunk of Sponge Cake' (Clarence Gaskill, 1928)

'Who Ate Napoleons With Josephine When Bonaparte Was Away' (Alfred Bryan and E. Ray Gotz, 1920)

'All The Quakers Are Shoulder Shakers Down In Quaker Town' (Bert Kalmar, Edgar Leslie and Pete Wendling, 1919)

FAMOUS PEOPLE
WHO ARE VEGANS

Dannii Minogue, William Shatner, Alicia Silverstone, Woody Harrelson, Joaquin Phoenix, Moby, Bryan Adams, Carl Lewis, Uri Geller, k.d. lang, Sinéad O'Connor, Heather Small

SOME DEADLY AUSTRALIAN CREATURES

The Blue-Ringed Octopus – one bite or squirt causes immediate paralysis and death in minutes

The 'Sea Wasp' or Box Jellyfish – human survival rate almost zero; time from its transparent sting to death = 4 minutes

The Taipan Snake is 180 times more venomous than the King Cobra – one bite can kill 12,000 guinea pigs, and a human within three seconds

The Tiger Snake – death takes 12 hours. Antidote available but must be used within 30 minutes of bite; single snake has enough venom to kill 118 sheep

The Funnel-Web Spider – tree-dweller, one of the most dangerous spiders in the world; kills humans within 15 minutes

Conus Textile Shells – underwater sea-creature with 21 darts, each of which has enough poison to kill 300 people; death in minutes

Irukandji Jellyfish – deadly transparent sea creature with poisonous tentacles; sting causes heart attacks in humans, leaving swimmers to drown

The Saltwater Crocodile – kills 2,000 people a year because it is fast in and out of water; it can outrun a galloping horse and kills in seconds

The Great White Shark – the most dangerous of the many sharks in Aussie waters; kills in seconds with just one snap of its awesome teeth

Red-backed Spider – the female is the deadly variety and it kills in a few minutes but deaths have ceased since an antidote was found

PAIRS OF FAMOUS PEOPLE WHO DIED ON PRECISELY THE SAME DAY

Freddie Mercury (rock star) and Klaus Kinski (actor) – 24.11.91

Maria Callas (opera singer) and Marc Bolan (rock star) – 16.9.77

Fred Perry (tennis player) and Donald Pleasence (actor) – 2.2.95

Ben Travers (playwright) and Alexei Kosygin (former Soviet premier) – 18.12.80

G.K. Chesterton (writer) and Maxim Gorky (writer) – 14.6.36

Ronnie Kray (gangster) and Arthur English (comic actor) – 17.3.95

Woody Guthrie (folk singer) and Sir Malcolm Sargent (orchestral conductor) – 3.10.67

Rudolf Nureyev (ballet dancer) and Dizzy Gillespie (jazz musician) – 6.1.93

Sir P.G. Wodehouse (writer) and Sir Julian Huxley (scientist) – 14.2.75

Gilbert Harding (broadcaster) and Clark Gable (film star) – 16.11.60

Marvin Gaye (soul singer) and Rene Cutforth (broadcaster) – 1.4.84

Jim Laker (England cricketer) and Otto Preminger (film director) – 23.4.86

Orson Welles (film director and actor) and Yul Brynner (actor) – 10.10.85

Cecil Day-Lewis (poet) and Dame Margaret Rutherford (actress) – 22.5.72

Orville Wright (aviation pioneer) and Mahatma Gandhi (Indian leader) – 30.1.48

David Niven (actor and author) and Raymond Massey (actor) – 29.7.83

Sir Anthony Eden (former British prime minister) and Peter Finch (actor) – 14.1.77

Lord Bernard Miles (actor and producer) and Dame Peggy Ashcroft (actress) – 14.6.91

Sammy Davis Jr. (entertainer) and Jim Henson (the man behind the Muppets) – 16.5.90

River Phoenix (actor) and Federico Fellini (film director) – 31.10.93

Earl Spencer (Princess Diana's father) and Paul Henreid (actor) – 29.3.92

John F. Kennedy (US President) and Aldous Huxley (writer) – 22.11.63

General Leopoldo Galtieri (former Argentinian dictator) and Maurice Gibb (musician) – 12.1.2003

MEN WHO WERE THE SEVENTH SONS OF SEVENTH SONS

Glen Campbell

Perry Como

THE WORKING TITLES OF CLASSIC TELEVISION PROGRAMMES

***The Waltons*: Spencer's Mountain**

Happy Days: New Family In Town

***The Flintstones*: The Flagstones**

Coronation Street: Florizel Street

***Beverly Hills 90210*: The Class of Beverly Hills**

Diff'rent Strokes: 45 Minutes From Harlem

***Falcon Crest*: The Vintage Years**

The Man From UNCLE: Mr Solo

***The Partridge Family*: Family Business**

Seinfeld: The Seinfeld Chronicles

***Charlie's Angels*: The Alley Cats**

TRIBUTE BANDS

Led Zeppelin: Whole Lotta Led

The Beatles: The Bootleg Beatles

The Rolling Stones: The Counterfeit Stones

Status Quo: State of Quo

Radiohead: No Surprises

U2: The Joshua Trio

Oasis: Noasis

The Stranglers: No More Heroes

The Jam: All Mod Cons

The Eagles: The Illegal Eagles

The Corrs: The Coors

The Beautiful South: The Beautiful Southmartins

Queen: Royal Family

Steely Dan: Nearly Dan

Black Sabbath: Sabbra Cadabra

The Stranglers: The Men In Black

Erasure: Erasured

The Doors: The Australian Doors

Abba: Bjorn Again

EXTRAORDINARY BEQUESTS

In 1987, Bob Fosse, the choreographer and film director (he won an Oscar for *Cabaret*), left $378.79 to each of 66 people to 'go out and have dinner on me'; these included Liza Minnelli, Janet Leigh, Elia Kazan, Dustin Hoffman, Melanie Griffith, Neil Simon, Ben Gazzara, Jessica Lange and Roy Scheider

In 1974, Philip Grundy, a dentist, left his dental nurse £181,000 on condition that she didn't wear any make-up or jewellery or go out with men for five years

In 1955, Juan Potomachi, an Argentinian, left more than £25,000 to the local theatre on condition that they used his skull when performing *Hamlet*

In 1765, John Hart left his brother a gun and a bullet 'in the hope that he will put the same through his head when the money is spent'

Mr John Bostock left in his will £100 to the manager of the local Co-op for the provision, 'until the fund be exhausted', of a two-ounce bar of chocolate every week for each child under the age of five in the parish of Westgate-in-Weardale

An unnamed Irishman left £1500 in his will to the Department of Health and Social Security (as it then was) to repay the money he had received while on the dole

In 1950, George Bernard Shaw left a considerable portion of his estate for the purpose of replacing the standard English alphabet of 26 letters with a more efficient alphabet of at least 40 letters – it was never achieved

The British dramatist Richard Brinsley Sheridan told his son that he was cutting him out of his will with just a shilling. His son's reaction was, 'I'm sorry to hear that, sir. You don't happen to have the shilling about you now, do you?'

In 1856, Heinrich Heine, the German poet, left everything to his wife on the condition that she remarried 'so that there will be at least one man to regret my death'

In 1937, F. Scott Fitzgerald drew up a will in which he specified 'a funeral and burial in keeping with my station in life'. Three years later, just before his death, a much poorer Fitzgerald amended this provision to read 'cheapest funeral … without undue ostentation or unnecessary expense' – his funeral cost precisely $613.25

The longest will in the world was one drawn up for Frederica Cook, an American woman – when it was proved at London's Somerset House in 1925, it consisted of four bound volumes totalling 95,940 words. Amazingly, she didn't have all that much to leave

The shortest valid British will – which was contested but eventually passed after the 1906 case Thorne v. Dickens – consisted of three words: 'All for mother'. What caused the confusion was that the testator didn't mean his mother but his wife

William Shakespeare bequeathed to his wife, Anne, 'my second best bed'. This has been interpreted as a snub. In fact, his 'second best bed' was probably the one most used by the two of them and it was therefore a sentimental gesture. His best bed went to the male heirs of his elder daughter

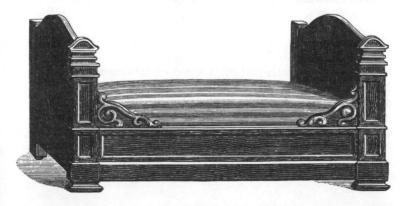

An unnamed Scotsman bequeathed each of his two daughters her weight in £1 notes. The elder, slimmer daughter received £51,200, while her younger, fatter sister got £57,433

In 1975, Edward Horley, a former Mayor of Altrincham, instructed his solicitors to buy a lemon, cut it in two and send one half to the income tax inspectorate and the other half to the tax collector with the message, 'Now squeeze this'

In 1997, Robert Brett, a Californian who wasn't allowed to smoke at home, left his entire fortune to his wife provided that she smoked four cigars a day for the rest of her life

A wealthy American banker left a codicil in his will cutting out two members of his family: 'To my wife and her lover, I leave the knowledge I wasn't the fool she thought I was. To my son, I leave the pleasure of earning a living. For twenty-five years he thought the pleasure was mine'

Charles Millar, a strait-laced Canadian lawyer who died in 1928 at the age of 73, had a bizarre sense of humour. He wondered how much people would do in the pursuit of money. To a preacher and a judge, who were both against gambling, he left shares in a racetrack that would make both men automatic members of a horse racing club. Both accepted. To a group of ministers who were anti-alcohol, Millar left $50,000 worth of shares in a brewery – they all accepted bar one. To three acquaintances who loathed each other, Millar bequeathed a holiday home in Jamaica which they were obliged to share – which they did. Most controversially, Millar bequeathed more than $500,000 to the Toronto woman who 'has given birth to the greatest number of children at the expiration of ten years from my death'. Millar's relatives tried – but failed – to overturn the will and, ten years later, four women who had each had nine children in the ten years shared the money

ANAGRAMS

'TO BE OR NOT TO BE: THAT IS THE QUESTION, WHETHER TIS NOBLER IN THE MIND TO SUFFER THE SLINGS AND ARROWS OF OUTRAGEOUS FORTUNE' is an anagram of: 'IN ONE OF THE BARD'S BEST-THOUGHT-OF TRAGEDIES, OUR INSISTENT HERO, HAMLET, QUERIES ON TWO FRONTS ABOUT HOW LIFE TURNS ROTTEN'

NEIL ARMSTRONG: 'THAT'S ONE SMALL STEP FOR A MAN, ONE GIANT LEAP FOR MANKIND' is an anagram of: 'THIN MAN RAN; MAKES A LARGE STRIDE, LEFT PLANET, PINS FLAG ON MOON! ON TO MARS!'

Eric Clapton (NARCOLEPTIC), Andi Peters (PEDESTRIAN) and Britney Spears (PRESBYTERIANS) all have names that can be anagramatized into single words

WORKABLE CARAMEL LIPS – Camilla Parker Bowles

ECCENTRIC MOUTH, MAN – Martine McCutcheon

LARGE FAT NOISE – Gloria Estefan

MANURE PLOT – Paul Merton

NOT ARENA KING – Ronan Keating

'ONLY JERK!' SCREAM – Jeremy Clarkson

HIM ALL SPOTTY – Timothy Spall

GROAN MADLY – Gary Oldman

HER ILLEGAL CHARM SALE – Sarah Michelle Gellar

MOANS LYRIC – Carly Simon

BLAME, COMPLAIN – Naomi Campbell

I'M AS CHEAP BENEATH – Stephanie Beacham

DOCILE OR PARANOID – Leonardo DiCaprio

NO NEAR SHOTS – Sharon Stone

DO 'ANNIE' TAKE – Diane Keaton

AMERICAN YELLS 'HI!' – Shirley Maclaine

NO ALIENS, DARLING – Gillian Anderson

I WARM BILLIONS – Robin Williams

REVIEW AGONY SURE – Sigourney Weaver

OLD WEST ACTION – Clint Eastwood

VALUES SLIM WIN – Venus Williams

ANORAK'S IN TOWN – Rowan Atkinson

NATIVE NODDY – Danny DeVito

CAP STAR TREK WIT – Patrick Stewart

PAY MR CLEAN-CUT – Paul McCartney

BEST PG – NEVER LIES – Steven Spielberg

GOD I DO COMPLAIN – Placido Domingo

GIRLIE LAW HELL – Geri Halliwell

DIET? TREMBLE! – Bette Midler

BLOB RECREATION – Robbie Coltrane

COOL OGRE IMMINENT – Colin Montgomerie

IN TONE – WHY SHOUT? – Whitney Houston

ERROR ON BIDET – Robert De Niro

EVIL LASS IN EROTICA – Alicia Silverstone

SUPER AMORAL FLIRT – Mariella Frostrup

RAN ALL JUICY – Julian Clary

NO, I DECLINE – Celine Dion

HERE IS SHINY CD – Chrissie Hynde

MARK A BITCH VOICE – Victoria Beckham (or BRAVO! I'M ACE THICK)

MORMON IDEAS – Marie Osmond

BURSTING PRESENCE – Bruce Springsteen

EACH TIMELY FALL – Michael Flatley

BEGS HUGE ROW – George W. Bush

SLICE SO MEAN – Monica Seles

GRASS AN AIDE – Andre Agassi

BORN INSANE? NO! – Anne Robinson

LOOKS IRK TERRIBLY – Robert Kilroy-Silk

ASCEND IN PARIS – Princess Diana

WOW! DOES INVENTIVE – Vivienne Westwood

SLOVENLY STEEL STAR – Sylvester Stallone

JUST A BROILER – Julia Roberts

HURRAH TO BORED ACTING! – Richard Attenborough

RIGHT FEE IN A FILM – Melanie Griffith

NO REAL CHARM BENEATH – Helena Bonham Carter

RUDE? I'M HYPED! – Eddie Murphy

FLOWERS AND WHAT THEY MEANT TO THE VICTORIANS

Syrian Mallow – 'Consumed by love'

Pansy – 'You occupy my thoughts'

Yellow Chrysanthemum – 'Slighted love'

Red Chrysanthemum – 'I love you'

Jonquil – 'Return my affection'

Yellow Tulip – 'Hopeless love'

Rose Maiden's Blush – 'If you love me, you will find it out'

American Cowslip – 'You are my divinity'

Creeping Willow – 'A love forsaken'

Orange Blossom – 'Your purity equals your loveliness'

GENUINE NAMES FOR FLOWERS AND PLANTS

Dog's-Tooth-Grass

Old Man's Beard

Jack-Go-To-Bed-At-Noon

Witches'-Butter

None So Pretty

Morning Glory

Love-In-Idleness

Devil's Snuffbox

Gill-Over-The-Ground

Elephant's-Ears

Adult actors who played children

Colin Welland *et al* (*Blue Remembered Hills*)

Richard Attenborough (*The Guinea Pig*)

Keith Barron (*Stand Up, Nigel Barton*)

Denholm Elliott *et al* (*School Play*)

Ginger Rogers (*The Major And The Minor*)

Joan Fontaine (*Letter From An Unknown Woman*)

Cary Grant (*Monkey Business*)

Bette Davis (*Payment On Demand*)

How rock groups got their names

Abba From the initials of the four members of the band: Agnetha, Björn, Benny and Anni-Frid. Anni-Frid, however, is now known as Frida. This means that the ABBA Fan Club is now known as the ABBF Fan Club.

Bad Company The band took their name from the title of a 1972 Jeff Bridges film.

The Beatles All The Beatles were fans of Buddy Holly and The Crickets and so John decided to call his band The Beetles. Then he changed it to 'Beatles' as they were a *beat* band.

Blue Oyster Cult From an anagram of Cully Stout Beer, which the band's manager and producer were drinking when they were trying to come up with a name for the band.

Crowded House Chose the name because of the cramped living conditions in their rented house.

Deacon Blue From a song by Steely Dan, 'Deacon Blues'.

Dexy's Midnight Runners 'Dexy' is a slang word for the pep pill Dexedrine.

Dire Straits A friend, noting their perilous financial position, suggested the name.

Dr Feelgood Took their name from the 1962 song 'Doctor Feel-Good', which the bluesman Piano Red recorded under the name Dr Feelgood & The Interns.

The Doobie Brothers 'Doobie' was Californian slang for a marijuana joint.

The Doors Taken from a line written by Aldous Huxley, 'All the other chemical Doors in the Wall are labelled Dope …'

Duran Duran From the name of the villain – played by Milo O'Shea – in the Jane Fonda film *Barbarella*.

Eurythmics Named after an early twentieth-century form of dance and mime ('Eurhythmics') based on Greek methods of teaching children music through movement.

Everything But The Girl Took their name from a second-hand shop where everything was for sale except for the people who worked there.

Fine Young Cannibals Took their name from a 1960 film *All The Fine Young Cannibals*, which starred Robert Wagner and Natalie Wood.

Foo Fighters Took their name from the nickname that Allied forces in World War Two gave to unidentified glowing spheres

Frankie Goes To Hollywood Took their name from a newspaper cutting about Frank Sinatra going into films.

Green Day Took their name from their own slang expression for 'good marijuana' ('it's a green day').

Happy Mondays Named after the Blue Order song, 'Blue Monday'.

Iron Maiden After a medieval torture device (consisting of a metal form with spikes on the inside).

Judas Priest Taken from the title of the Bob Dylan song 'The Ballad of Frankie Lee And Judas Priest'.

Korn The band members were trying to come up with names while they were drunk. One suggestion was met with the response, 'It would be as intelligent as calling it Korn.' So that's what they called it.

Led Zeppelin From the Keith Moon (then drummer with The Who) line – which he often used – 'That went down like a lead zeppelin.' The band later dropped the 'a' in lead.

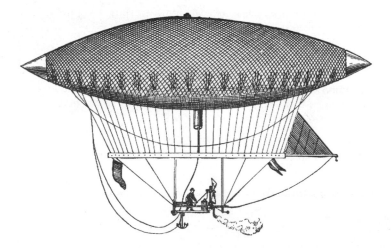

Level 42 Took their name from *The Hitchhiker's Guide To The Galaxy* by Douglas Adams, in which the number 42 is the answer to the 'meaning of life'.

The Lovin' Spoonful From the words of a Mississippi John Hurt song, 'Coffee Blues'; this is bluesmen's slang for what a man gives a woman during sex.

Lynyrd Skynyrd Named themselves after Leonard Skinner, a disliked gym teacher at their high school.

Mungo Jerry From T.S. Eliot's *Old Possum's Book of Practical Cats*.

Oasis The name came from a sports centre in Swindon.

The Pet Shop Boys Despite the persistent rumours – see also 10CC – they named themselves after a couple of friends who were running a pet shop in Ealing.

Pink Floyd They named themselves after legendary bluesmen, Pink Anderson and Floyd Council.

The Pogues Short for the Gaelic *pogue mahone*, which means 'kiss my arse'.

Prefab Sprout As a child, singer Paddy McAloon had misheard the words 'pepper sprout' in a Nancy Sinatra song as 'prefab sprout', and that's the name he always wanted to give his band.

The Pretenders After the Sam Cooke song, 'The Great Pretender'.

Pulp Originally known as Arabacus Pulp, a term apparently used in coffee manufacturing; they then dropped the first part of their name.

Radiohead From the Talking Heads song, 'Radiohead'.

The Righteous Brothers When the duo performed at black clubs, they were praised with the words, 'That's righteous, brother.'

The Rolling Stones Named themselves after a Muddy Waters song, 'Rollin' Stones'.

The Searchers Named themselves after the John Ford classic that starred John Wayne and Natalie Wood.

Simple Minds From the lyrics of the David Bowie song 'Jean Genie'.

The Small Faces They chose the name 'Faces' because, in Mod terms, they were all 'faces' (cool dudes). The word 'Small' came from the fact that all four members of the band were under 5 foot 6.

Soft Machine Took their name from a novel by William Burroughs (see also Steely Dan).

Spandau Ballet From graffiti seen on a Berlin loo wall by Robert Elms. Spandau was, of course, the prison in which leading Nazi war criminals were held.

Steely Dan From the William Burroughs novel *Naked Lunch* in which Steely Dan was a steam-powered dildo.

Super Furry Animals A friend gave them a T-shirt bearing the words 'Super Furry Animals' and they decided to adopt the name for their group.

The Teardrop Explodes Taken from a caption in a comic book.

Tears For Fears From the methods (in primal scream therapy) used by the psychiatrist Arthur Janov.

10cc Despite persistent rumours to the contrary, the truth is that this was just a name that came to Jonathan King, the group's mentor, in a dream.

Thin Lizzy Named after a robot in the *Beano* comic named Tin Lizzie. The band inserted the 'h' in Thin on the basis that it wouldn't be sounded in Ireland and might be worth a chuckle when it confused people.

The Thompson Twins Named after the bungling detectives in the *Tintin* comic strip.

Three Dog Night From the Australian slang for a freezing night (in the outback, a man would need to sleep with one dog to keep warm on a cold night, two dogs on a very cold night and three dogs on the coldest night).

The Velvet Underground Taken from the title of a pornographic book about sado-masochism.

Wet Wet Wet Took their name from words in a Scritti Politti song, 'Getting, Having And Holding'.

Z.Z. Top Billy Gibbons, the band's vocalist, was inspired by the Z beams on a pair of open hay-loft doors.

Extraordinary executions and non-executions

In the eighteenth and nineteenth centuries, people – including children – were hanged for incredibly trivial offences. In 1819, Thomas Wildish was hanged for letter-stealing; in 1750, Benjamin Beckonfield was hanged for the theft of a hat; in 1833, an unnamed nine-year-old boy was hanged for stealing a pennyworth of paint from a shop; in 1782, a 14-year-old girl was hanged for being found in the company of gypsies.

In 1948, William John Gray was sentenced to hang for the murder of his wife. However, he was reprieved after medical examiners ruled that hanging would cause him too much pain. This was based on the extent of injuries to his jaw. It was explained that if he were hanged, the noose wouldn't dislocate his neck and that he would either die of strangulation or he would be decapitated altogether, as his injured jawbone was too weak to hold the rope around his neck.

In 1679, Messrs Green, Berry and Hill were hanged at Tyburn for a murder they committed on … Greenberry Hill

On 16 August 1264 at precisely nine o'clock in the morning, Inetta de Balsham was hanged. The King's messenger arrived a few seconds later with a reprieve. The hangman ran up the stairs and cut the rope with a sword. The victim's face had already turned blue but she survived.

Similarly, in 1705, John Smith was hanged for burglary at Tyburn Tree. After he had been hanging for fifteen minutes, a reprieve arrived and he was cut down. He was revived and managed to recover. As a result of his experience, he became known as John 'Half-Hanged' Smith.

In 1736, Thomas Reynolds was hanged for robbery at Tyburn Hill. He was cut down and placed in a coffin. However, as the hangman's assistant was nailing down the coffin lid, the lid was pushed away and the assistant's arm was grabbed from within. Reynolds was then taken out of the coffin and to a nearby house, where he vomited three pints of blood and died.

In 1650, charged with the murder of her newborn baby (a crime that only ceased to be a capital offence in 1922), Ann Green was hanged at Oxford Gaol. After an hour, she was cut down but was seen to be twitching. One person jumped on her stomach and a soldier struck her on the head with his musket. Her body was then passed on to a professor of anatomy who was preparing to cut her open when he heard a noise from her throat. She was put into a warm bed and her breathing restarted. By the next day she was almost fully recovered and she was eventually pardoned.

On 23 February 1885, John Lee was due to be hanged at Exeter Gaol for the murder of his employer (on thin circumstantial evidence). However, after the hangman put the noose around his neck, the scaffold's drop wouldn't respond to the lever. Lee was returned to his cell while the hangman tested the drop with weights until it worked perfectly. A second attempt was made but, once again, the drop didn't work. When Lee stood on the scaffold for the third time, it again proved impossible. Lee was returned to his cell and later given a reprieve by the Home Secretary. He became famous as 'The Man They Couldn't Hang'.

Being a hangman was no insurance against being hanged. Four English hangmen were hanged: Cratwell in 1538 for robbing a booth at St Bartholomew's Fair; Stump-leg in 1558 for thieving; Pascha Rose in 1686 for housebreaking and theft, and John Price in 1718 for murdering an old woman.

Postscript: Albert Pierrepoint was Britain's last executioner. He hanged more than 400 people. After his retirement, he campaigned for abolition saying, 'I do not now believe that any of the hundreds of executions I carried out has in any way acted as a deterrent against future murder. Capital punishment, in my view, achieved nothing except revenge.'

PEOPLE AND THEIR TATTOOS

Davina McCall: alien on her bottom, rose on her wrist and a devil's horn on each hip

Kerry Katona: soaring bird on the base of her spine

Anna Kournikova: a sun on her bottom

Kelly Osbourne: small heart on her hip and a small etching on the back of her neck

Colin Farrell: ex-wife Amelia Warner's name on his finger and 'Carpe diem' on his forearm

Sarah Michelle Gellar: Chinese character for integrity on her lower back

David Beckham: sons' names across his back

Robbie Williams: lion on his shoulder with 'Born To Be Mild' underneath; on his other arm he has a Maori design. Also has the Alcoholics Anonymous Serenity Prayer tattooed on his arm, but has replaced the word 'God' with 'Elvis'

Eminem: 'Slit me' on his wrists; the name of his wife Kim on his stomach with a tombstone and the inscription 'Rot In Flames'; an Indian tribal tattoo on his forearm

Charlize Theron: fish – her mother has a matching tattoo

Jude Law: 'Sexy Sadie' on his arm

Angelina Jolie: a tattoo on her belly which reads 'Quod me nutrit me destruit' – 'What feeds me destroys me'

Roseanne: pink rose on left foot; ex-husband Tom Arnold's name on shoulder and bottom now replaced with flowers and fairies

Gerard Depardieu: star on arm

Ulrika Jonsson: devil on bottom

Mel C: Celtic band on arm, huge phoenix on back and Chinese dragon running the length of her calf

Mick Hucknall: federal symbol of Europe on arm

Cher: flower on bottom

Alexander McQueen: Japanese fish symbol on chest

Vanilla Ice: leaf on stomach

Drew Barrymore: butterfly and flower sprig on bottom

Ringo Starr: half moon on arm

Vinnie Jones: 'Leeds Utd' on leg

Sean Bean: '100% Blade' on arm

Madonna: 'MP' – standing for 'Madonna's Property' – and Marilyn Monroe's face on bottom

Julia Roberts: red heart with a Chinese character meaning 'strength of heart' on shoulder

Sir Sean Connery: 'Scotland Forever' and 'Mum and Dad' on arms

Björk: Icelandic rune on shoulder

Melanie Griffith: pear on bottom

Geri Halliwell: sundial design on top of back and jaguar further down

Marianne Faithfull: bird on hand

Chrissie Hynde: dolphin on arm

Dame Helen Mirren: pair of crosses on hand

FAMOUS NOVELS ORIGINALLY REJECTED BY PUBLISHERS

The Time Machine
(H.G. Wells)

The Mysterious Affair At Styles (Agatha Christie)

Harry Potter And The Philosopher's Stone (J.K. Rowling)

The Razor's Edge (W. Somerset Maugham)

The Good Earth (Pearl Buck)

The Picture of Dorian Gray (Oscar Wilde)

Moby Dick (Herman Melville)

The Naked And The Dead (Norman Mailer)

Northanger Abbey (Jane Austen)

Barchester Towers (Anthony Trollope)

The Ginger Man (J.P. Donleavy)

Catch-22 (Joseph Heller)

The Wind In The Willows (Kenneth Grahame)

A Time To Kill (John Grisham)

The Rainbow (D.H. Lawrence)

The Spy Who Came In From The Cold (John Le Carré)

Animal Farm (George Orwell)

Tess of The D'Urbervilles (Thomas Hardy)

Lord of The Flies (William Golding)

GREAT NOVELS AND THEIR ORIGINAL TITLES

Lady Chatterley's Lover (D.H. Lawrence): *Tenderness*

Roots (Alex Haley): *Before This Anger*

The Postman Always Rings Twice (James M. Cain): *Bar-B-Q*

The Mill On The Floss (George Eliot): *Sister Maggie*

Portnoy's Complaint (Philip Roth): *A Jewish Patient Begins His Analysis*

A Portrait of The Artist As A Young Man (James Joyce): *Stephen Hero*

East of Eden (John Steinbeck): *The Salinas Valley*

The Time Machine (H.G. Wells): *The Chronic Argonauts*

Valley of The Dolls (Jacqueline Susann): *They Don't Build Statues To Businessmen*

Catch-22 (Joseph Heller): *Catch-18*

Treasure Island (Robert Louis Stevenson): *The Sea-Cook*

Jaws (Peter Benchley): *The Summer of The Shark*

War And Peace (Leo Tolstoy): *All's Well That Ends Well*

Moby Dick (Herman Melville): *The Whale*

Of Mice And Men (John Steinbeck): *Something That Happened*

The Great Gatsby (F. Scott Fitzgerald): *The High-bouncing Lover*

Gone With The Wind (Margaret Mitchell): *Ba! Ba! Black Sheep*

Frankenstein (Mary Shelley): *Prometheus Unchained*

Book titles and their literary origins

From Here To Eternity* (James Jones): taken from Rudyard Kipling's *Gentlemen Rankers

Brave New World (Aldous Huxley): taken from William Shakespeare's *The Tempest*

For Whom The Bell Tolls* (Ernest Hemingway): taken from John Donne's *Devotions

The Moon's A Balloon (David Niven): taken from e.e. cummings's *& N &*

Now Voyager* (Olive Higgins Prouty): taken from Walt Whitman's *Leaves of Grass

Under The Greenwood Tree (Thomas Hardy): taken from William Shakespeare's *As You Like It*

Paths of Glory* (Humphrey Cobb): taken from Thomas Gray's *Elegy In A Country Churchyard

Of Mice And Men (John Steinbeck): taken from Robert Burns's *To A Mouse*

A Confederacy of Dunces* (John Kennedy Toole): taken from Jonathan Swift's *Thoughts On Various Subjects

Gone With The Wind (Margaret Mitchell): taken from Ernest Dowson's *Cynara*

The Grapes of Wrath* (John Steinbeck): taken from Julia Ward Howe's *The Battle Hymn of The American Republic

Tender Is The Night (F. Scott Fitzgerald): taken from John Keats's *Ode To A Nightingale*

The Dogs of War* (Frederick Forsyth): taken from William Shakespeare's *Julius Caesar

EXTRAORDINARY EVENTS THAT (ALMOST) DEFY EXPLANATION

DOUBLE PROOF A pair of identical American twin boys were separated at birth in 1940 and adopted by different people who didn't know each other. Each boy was named James, each boy married a woman named Linda, had a son named James Alan, and was then divorced. When they eventually met up at the age of 39, they found that their hobbies, experiences and tastes had been and were remarkably similar.

BABY LUCK Some coincidences are just too extraordinary. In 1975 in Detroit, a baby fell out of a building 14 storeys up. Fortunately, it landed on a man named Joseph Figlock and so survived. A year later, another baby fell from the same building and survived by falling on. … Joseph Figlock.

LIVE MUSHROOMS A nun at a convent in Clwyd tried but failed to grow mushrooms in the convent grounds. She died at the age of 79 in 1986, and a decent crop of mushrooms has grown on her grave every autumn since. Nowhere else in the convent do mushrooms grow.

SPONTANEOUS COMBUSTION In 1938, Phyllis Newcombe, 22, combusted spontaneously at a dance hall during a waltz. Many people witnessed this unexplained phenomenon, which has parallels with the combustion of a British pensioner, Euphemia Johnson, who died after suddenly bursting into fire during her afternoon tea.

A GOLDEN SHEEP In 1984, a Greek Orthodox priest was cooking a sheep's head when he discovered that the sheep had a jaw composed of 14-carat gold (worth some £4,000). The sheep had come from a herd owned by the priest's own brother-in-law and he couldn't come up with any plausible explanation – nor could the Greek ministry of agriculture when they looked into the case.

LET IT RAIN In 1986, American judge Samuel King was annoyed that some jurors were absent from his Californian court because of heavy rain, so he issued a decree: 'I hereby order that it cease raining by Tuesday.' California suffered a five-year drought. So in 1991 the judge decreed, 'Rain shall fall in California beginning February 27.' Later that day, California had its heaviest rainfall in a decade.

DEAD AGAIN In Bermuda, two brothers were killed precisely one year apart at the age of 17 by the same taxi driver carrying the same passenger on the same street. The two boys had each been riding the same moped.

A TIME TO DIE It is said that when a person dies their spouse often dies soon afterwards, but this is exceptional. Charles Davies died at 3.00 in the morning at his sister's house in Leicester. When his sister phoned his home in Leeds to tell his wife, she discovered that Charles's wife had also just died … at 3.00 in the morning.

SOME THINGS TO KNOW ABOUT US PRESIDENTS

Herbert Hoover (1929–33) and his wife both spoke fluent Chinese. Hoover was also the first president to have a telephone on his desk in the White House.

When Calvin Coolidge (1923–29) was being driven in a car, he would always insist that the driver didn't exceed 16mph.

Andrew Jackson (1829–37) once killed a man in a duel because he had insulted his wife.

Ulysses S. Grant (1869–77) was tone-deaf and once said: 'I only know two tunes. One of them is "Yankee Doodle" and the other isn't.'

George Washington (1789–97) had wooden false teeth.

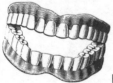

James Garfield (1881) could simultaneously write in Greek with one hand while writing in Latin with the other.

At up to 24 stones, William Taft (1909–13) was the heaviest president and once had the misfortune of getting stuck in the White House bathtub. At just over seven stones, James Madison (1809–17) was the lightest president.

Jimmy Carter (1977–81) developed the knack of reading at speed and was once tested and found to have 95 percent comprehension at a reading rate of 2,000 words a minute.

Ronald Reagan (1981–89) was the first – and so far only – president to have been divorced.

George Bush (1989–93), a chubby toddler, was nicknamed 'Fatty McGee McGaw' by his father.

James Buchanan (1857–61) was the first – and so far only – bachelor to become president. He also suffered from an unfortunate nervous twitch that caused his head to jerk frequently.

When he was young, Rutherford Hayes (1877–81) suffered from a strange phobia: the fear of going insane.

The first president to leave the US while in office was Theodore Roosevelt (1901–09): in 1906 when he visited the Panama Canal zone. He was also the first president to be a master of jujitsu.

Calvin Coolidge (1923–29) was famous for being a man of few words. At a White House dinner, a female guest told him that her father had bet her she wouldn't be able to get more than two words out of the president. 'You lose' were the only words he spoke to her.

LIVING PEOPLE WHO HAVE HAD PUBS NAMED AFTER THEM

Fred Trueman (Fiery Fred in Yorkshire)

Jack Walker (Uncle Jack's in Blackburn)

Sir Henry Cooper (Henry Cooper in London)

Sir Tom Finney (Tom Finney in Preston)

Prince Philip (Duke of Edinburgh in Bacton, Norfolk)

Dean Macey (The Silver Decathlete in Canvey Island)

Matthew Le Tissier (Matt Le Tissier in Southampton)

FAMOUS PEOPLE WHO WERE ADOPTED

Bill Clinton, Anna Ryder Richardson, Kate Adie, John Thomson, Ray Liotta, Nicky Campbell, George Cole, Eric Clapton, Gerald Ford, Daley Thompson, Dame Kiri Te Kanawa, Rob Newman, Debbie Harry, Mike McShane, Axl Rose, James Michener, Bo Diddley, Michael Denison, Michael Medwin, Helen Rollason, Wincey Willis

FAMOUS WOMEN WHO ADOPTED CHILDREN

Nicole Kidman, Dame Julie Andrews, Jamie Lee Curtis, Frances McDormand, Sharon Stone, Calista Flockhart, Drew Barrymore, Diane Keaton, Honor Blackman, Michelle Pfeiffer, Mia Farrow, Dawn French, Dame Shirley Bassey, Jilly Cooper, Dame Kiri Te Kanawa, Kirstie Alley, Penelope Keith

WOMEN WHO PUT THEIR BABIES UP FOR ADOPTION

Clare Short, Roseanne, Pauline Collins, Joni Mitchell, Sheila Mercier, Kate O'Mara, Linda Lovelace

ONLY CHILDREN

Shannon Elizabeth, Marilyn Manson, Craig David, Adrien Brody, Dale Winton, Teri Hatcher, Alan Bleasdale, David Essex, Barbara Windsor, Sir Elton John, Mick Hucknall, Bob Hoskins, Ulrika Jonsson, Uri Geller, Cherie Lunghi, Lord Melvyn Bragg, David Gower, Penelope Keith, Robert De Niro, Terry Venables, Clive James, Lester Piggott, Harold Pinter, Sir Peter Hall, Miriam Margolyes, Charlotte Church, Dame P.D. James, Vanessa-Mae, Jean-Paul Gaultier, Dame Ruth Rendell, Jacques Chirac, Frederick Forsyth, Sarah Michelle Gellar, Nick Faldo, Barbara Taylor Bradford, Chris Tarrant, Paul Merton, Dr David Starkey, Sir John Mortimer, Michael Parkinson, Ken Hom, David Copperfield, Ruby Wax, Aled Jones, Martina Hingis, Sam Mendes, Harry Enfield, Burt Bacharach, Sir Anthony Hopkins, Sir Peter Ustinov, Sam Torrance, Julie Burchill, Noel Edmonds, Lauren Bacall

ENGLISH COUNTIES AND THEIR VARIETIES OF APPLE

Kent: Kentish Fillbasket, Mabbott's Pearmain, Gascoyne's Scarlet, Golden Knob

Yorkshire: Green Balsam, Flower of The Town, French Crab, Acklam Russett

Hereford: King's Acre Pippin, Herefordshire Beefing, Lord Hindlip, Yellow Ingestrie

Lancashire: Golden Spire, Roseberry, Scotch Bridget, Proctor's Seedling

Surrey: Claygate Pearmain, Cockles Pippin, George Carpenter, Joybells, Scarlet Nonpareil

Devon: Michaelmas Stubbard, Crimson Costard, Devonshire Quarrenden, Star of Devon

Sussex: Crawley Beauty, Forge, Lady Sudeley, First And Last, Wadhurst Pippin

Hertfordshire: Lane's Prince Albert, Golden Reinette, Bushey Grove

Cornwall: Cornish Gilliflower, Glass Apple, Cornish Pine, Tommy Knight

PEOPLE WHO DIED ON THEIR BIRTHDAYS

Raphael (6 April 1483–1520 – and for good measure both days fell on Good Friday)

Shakespeare (23 April 1564–1616, though there is some doubt over his precise date of birth)

Frans Francken (6 May 1581–1642)

Joe Mercer (9 August 1914–1990)

Ingrid Bergman (29 August 1915–82)

Keith Boyce (11 October 1943–96)

THE LAST 50 PRESIDENTS OF THE CAMBRIDGE UNIVERSITY FOOTLIGHTS

2003: Stefan Golaszewski

2002: Ed Weeks

2001: James Morris

2000: Matt Green

1999: Kevin Baker

1998: Richard Ayoade

1997: Sarah Moule

1996: David Mitchell

1995: Charlie Hartill

1994: Robert Thorogood

1993: Mark Evans

1992: Dan Gaster

1991: Sue Perkins

1990: Henry Naylor

1989: Roland Kenyon

1988: Peter Bradshaw

1987: Tim Scott

1986: Nick Golson

1985: Kathryn Crew

1984: Nick Hancock

1983: Neil Mullarkey

1982: Tony Slattery

1981: Hugh Laurie

1980: Jan Ravens

1979: Robert Bathurst

1978: Martin Bergman

1977: Jimmy Mulville

1976: Chris Keightley

1975: Clive Anderson

1974: Jon Canter

1973: Robert Benton

1972: Steve Thorn

1971: Richard MacKenna

1970: Adrian Edwards

1969: Barry Brown

1968: Jonathon James-Moore

1967: Clive James

1966: Andrew Mayer

1965: Eric Idle

1964: Graeme Garden

1963: Tim Brooke-Taylor

1962: Robert Atkins

1961: Peter Bellwood

1960: Peter Cook

1959: Adrian Slade

1958: Peter Stroud

1957: Allan Mitchell

1956: Tim Berington

1955: Brian Marber

1954: Leslie Bricusse

People and the instruments they 'played' on the Bonzo Dog Band's 'The Intro and the Outro'

John Wayne – xylophone

Robert Morley – guitar

Billy Butlin – spoons

Adolf Hitler – vibes ('Nice!')

Princess Anne – sousaphone

Liberace – clarinet

Harold Wilson – violin

Eric Clapton – ukelele ('Hi, Eric')

Sir Kenneth Clark – bass saxophone ('A great honour, sir')

Peter Scott – duck call

Casanova – horn

General De Gaulle – accordion ('Really wild, General. Thank you, sir')

Val Doonican – himself

J. Arthur Rank – gong

KINGS AND THEIR UNFORTUNATE NICKNAMES

King Rudolf **The Sluggard** (King Rudolf III of Burgundy from 993 to 1032)

King Malcolm **The Maiden** (King Malcolm IV of Scotland from 1153 to 1165)

King Louis **The Fat** (King Louis VI of France from 1108 to 1137)

King Ferdinand **The Fickle** (King Ferdinand I of Portugal from 1367 to 1383)

King Charles **The Mad** (King Charles VI of France from 1380 to 1422)

King Ivan **The Terrible** (King Ivan IV of Russia from 1547 to 1584)

King Louis **The Stubborn** (King Louis X of France from 1314 to 1316)

King Charles **The Bad** (King Charles II of Navarre from 1349 to 1387)

King Henry **The Impotent** (King Henry IV of Castile from 1454 to 1474)

King Ethelred **The Unready** (King Ethelred II of England from 978 to 1016)

KINGS AND THEIR *FORTUNATE* NICKNAMES

King Louis **The Just** (King Louis XIII of France from 1610 to 1643)

King William **The Good** (King William II of Sicily from 1166 to 1189)

King Philip **The Handsome** (King Philip of Castile in 1506; he was married to Joan The Mad)

King Charles **The Victorious** (King Charles VII of France from 1422 to 1461)

King Henry **The Saint** (King Henry II of Germany from 1014 to 1024)

King Richard **The Lionheart** (King Richard I of England from 1189 to 1199)

King Philip **The Fair** (King Philip IV of France from 1285 to 1314)

King Ferdinand **The Great** (King Ferdinand I of Castile from 1035 to 1065)

King Charles **The Wise** (King Charles V of France from 1364 to 1380)

King Louis **The Well-Beloved** (King Louis XV of France from 1715 to 1774)

FAMOUS PEOPLE AND THE AGES AT WHICH THEY LOST THEIR VIRGINITY

Casanova (11)

Harold Robbins (11)

Shane Richie (12)

Jimi Hendrix (12)

Don Johnson (12)

Paul McGann (12)

Johnny Depp (13)

James Caan (13)

George Michael (13 – heterosexual sex)

Gillian Anderson (13 – 'I feel very ashamed looking back on it. It was only when I reached about 22 that I realized you could actually enjoy sex')

Mae West (13)

Bob Geldof (13)

Jon Bon Jovi (13)

Anton Chekhov (13)

Trevor Sorbie (14)

Dennis Waterman (14 – 'to an older woman')

Clint Eastwood (14 – with a 'friendly neighbour')

David Duchovny (14)

James Joyce (14)

Cher (14)

Nick Berry (14)

Phil Collins (14 – in an allotment)

Phillip Schofield (14)

Bruce Willis (14 – 'I was a 14-year-old bellboy at a Holiday Inn and it was the most incredible experience of my life. This really gorgeous chick started coming on to me, so we went down to the laundry room together. She guided me through it and things got kind of hot down there')

Kate Moss (14)

Natalie Wood (14)

King Charles II (15 – with his former wetnurse)

Sir Michael Caine (15 – 'I was 15 and we did it in a park')

Stephen Fry (15 – with a girl named Shelagh while listening to 'American Pie')

Sara Cox (15 – to a boy called Scott in a field full of sheep)

Jenny Eclair (15 – the boy had done it to win a £15 bet)

Charlie Sheen (15 – with a prostitute. 'The problem was she wanted $400 so we used my dad's credit card')

Dustin Hoffman (15 – with a girl who thought he was his older brother. 'She was a nymphomaniac called Barbara. She was 19 and I was 15½. My brother Ronnie threw a New Year's Eve party. It was over before it began but she thought she was making love to my brother and when she realized it was me, she screamed and ran out naked')

Björk (15)

Madonna (15 – in the back of a Cadillac with a guy called Russell)

Jerry Hall (15 – to a rodeo rider who kept his boots on)

Jo Brand (15)

Darren Day (16 – in Tesco's car park)

Brigitte Bardot (16 – with Roger Vadim)

John F. Kennedy (17)

Neil Morrissey (17 – 'I didn't have a clue what I was doing')

Frank Skinner (17 – with a prostitute in her 50s)

Lee Evans (17 – with the woman who became his wife)

Geri Halliwell (17 – to a boy called Toby, 'a sickly-looking ex-public schoolboy with a toffy accent')

Michelle Collins (17 – 'My virginity was something I'd hung on to but in the end I just thought, oh well, there it goes')

Joan Collins (17 – 'I was 17 and he was 33. It was just like my mother said – the pits')

Victoria Beckham (17)

Tina Hobley (17 – with her boyfriend after they'd been going out for exactly a year. 'But it was the first time for him, too, so it was very disappointing. It was all over before we got started')

Walt Disney (18 – on his birthday)

Barbra Streisand (18)

Brad Pitt (18)

Harry Enfield (18)

Zoe Ball (18)

Peter Stringfellow (18)

Jamie Lee Curtis (18)

Napoleon Bonaparte (18)

Brooke Shields (18 – with Dean Cain)

Danniella Westbrook (18)

Sir Cliff Richard (18 – with Carol Harris, the wife of Jet Harris of The Shadows)

Lord Jeffrey Archer (18 – in a wood)

Gail Porter (18 – 'Let's just say it didn't last very long and I wasn't the problem')

Leonardo DiCaprio (18)

Anthea Turner (18 –'to a 20-year-old student called Andy Sims. I felt incredibly happy afterwards. I thought: That's it, girl, now you've cracked it')

Marlon Brando (19 – with an older Colombian woman)

Leslie Thomas (19)

Mira Sorvino (20)

Victor Hugo (20)

Gillian Taylforth (20 – 'at the vital moment he called me Brenda')

Queen Victoria (21)

Jonathan Ross (21)

Dudley Moore (22)

Edvard Munch (22)

Ioan Gruffudd (22)

H.G. Wells (22)

John Peel (22)

Claire Sweeney (22)

Esther Rantzen (23)

D.H. Lawrence (23)

Elliott Gould (23 – with Barbra Streisand)

Mariah Carey (23)

John Cleese (24)

Isadora Duncan (25)

Bette Davis (26)

Sir Alfred Hitchcock (27)

Katy Hill (29 – on her wedding night)

William Gladstone (29)

George Bernard Shaw (29)

Lisa Kudrow (31 – 'I'm glad I waited till I was married. I decided my virginity was precious, an honour I was bestowing on a man')

Mark Twain (34)

Marie Stopes (40)

PEOPLE WITH ROSES NAMED AFTER THEM

Anna Ford, Penelope Keith, Sir Paul McCartney, Clive Lloyd, Geoffrey Boycott, Pam Ayres, Dame Vera Lynn, Prince Philip, Tina Turner, Jane Asher, Princess Michael of Kent, Sir Jimmy Savile, Sue Lawley, Dame Julie Andrews, Sir Bobby Charlton, Anne Diamond, Arthur Scargill, Jimmy Greaves, Michael Crawford, Sir Cliff Richard, Angela Rippon, Felicity Kendal, Maureen Lipman, Hannah Gordon, Joanna Lumley, Charlie Dimmock

REAL PEOPLE MENTIONED IN BEATLES SONGS

The Queen ('Penny Lane' and 'Mean Mr Mustard')

Edgar Allan Poe ('I Am The Walrus')

Harold Wilson and Edward Heath ('Taxman')

B.B. King, Doris Day and Sir Matt Busby ('Dig It')

Charles Hawtrey ('Two of Us')

Mao Tse-tung ('Revolution')

Sir Walter Raleigh ('I'm So Tired')

Peter Brown ('The Ballad of John And Yoko')

Bob Dylan ('Yer Blues')

THE INFINITE WISDOM OF MARK TWAIN

'There are several good protections against temptation, but the surest is cowardice.'

'Always do right. This will gratify some people, and astonish the rest.'

'When angry, count to four; when very angry, swear.'

'A flea can be taught everything a Congressman can.'

'It takes your enemy and your friend – working together – to hurt you to the heart: the one to slander you and the other to get the news to you.'

'I can live for two months on a good compliment.'

'I was born modest. Not all over but in spots.'

'I am opposed to millionaires – but it would be dangerous to offer me the position.'

'Fewer things are harder to put up with than the annoyance of a good example.'

'Man is the only animal that blushes – or needs to.'

'If you tell the truth you don't have to remember anything.'

'I must have a prodigious quantity of mind; it takes me as much as a week, sometimes, to make it up.'

'Man: a creature made at the end of the week's work when God was tired.'

'Such is the human race, often it seems a pity that Noah didn't miss the boat.'

'Education is what you must acquire without any interference from your schooling.'

'Familiarity breeds contempt ... and children.'

'The public is the only critic whose opinion is worth anything at all.'

'Confession may be good for my soul, but it sure plays hell with my reputation.'

'Good breeding exists in concealing how much we think of ourselves and how little we think of the other person.'

'Wit is the sudden marriage of ideas which, before their union, were not perceived to have any relation.'

'Life would be infinitely happier if we could only be born at the age of eighty and gradually approach eighteen.'

'Noise proves nothing. Often a hen who has merely laid an egg cackles as if she had laid an asteroid.'

'Courage is resistance to fear, mastery of fear, not absence of fear.'

'It is better to deserve honours and not have them than to have them and not deserve them.'

'We may not pay Satan reverence, for that would be indiscreet, but we can at least respect his talents.'

'What a good thing Adam had – when he said a good thing, he knew nobody had said it before.'

THE LABOUR PARTY LEADERS WHO NEVER BECAME PRIME MINISTER

Keir Hardie (1906–08), Arthur Henderson (1908–10, 1914–17), George Barnes (1910–11), William Adamson (1917–21), John Clynes (1921–22), George Lansbury (1932–35), Hugh Gaitskell (1955–63), Michael Foot (1980–83), Neil Kinnock (1983–92), John Smith (1992–94)

THE ADVENTURES OF BARRY HUMPHRIES

Before finding fame as Dame Edna Everage, Humphries was a Dadaist who performed a series of stunts in the name of art.

On his frequent flights between Australia and Britain, Humphries would pass the time by surreptitiously putting some Russian (or vegetable) salad in a sick bag and then, when other passengers were watching, he would pretend to throw up into the bag. He would then proceed to eat its contents. Humphries didn't restrict this 'gag' to aeroplanes but also performed it to a wider public. He would put some Russian salad on the pavement and then return to it later and eat it with a spoon. Once, in Fleet Street in the 1960s, a policeman approached him but was so sickened that he started retching. Humphries took the opportunity to disappear.

One of his favourite tricks was to get a female co-conspirator to dress up as a schoolgirl. The two of them would start kissing and when a policeman showed up to ask him what he was doing with a 'minor', he would flourish her birth certificate proving that she was, in fact, over 18.

One particularly unpleasant stunt was performed – like many of his others – on a train. His friend would board a train pretending to be blind with his leg in plaster and wearing a neck brace. Humphries would then get on board pretending to be a German and start abusing his friend, physically and verbally. Humphries was never challenged by other passengers. Meanwhile, after he got off, his friend would sit there saying, 'Forgive him, forgive him.'

For another stunt, Humphries would fill a public dustbin with rubbish and then, just before it reached the top, he would put in some really expensive food – smoked salmon, cooked chicken, Champagne – and cover this with a layer of rubbish. When people arrived, Humphries, dressed as a tramp, would astonish them by rummaging in the bin and pulling out fabulous delicacies.

In 1968, when the cinema was infested with a plague of ludicrous *avant-garde* films, Humphries invented a 'film director' named Martin

Agrippa, who had supposedly been working with the Blind Man's Cinema and who had made a film which had won the 'Bronze Scrotum' in Helsinki. Together with the (genuine) film director Bruce Beresford, he made a spoof film which was subsequently exhibited at several Festivals of Underground Cinema where it was taken entirely seriously.

With a group of friends, Humphries used to go to a shop every day at the same time and pay for a bar of Lux soap but never take the soap away. They would sometimes get strangers to do the same thing. Each time, the shopkeeper would say, 'You've forgotten your soap,' to which Humphries & Co. would respond, 'We don't want the soap, we just want to buy it!' Eventually, Humphries took the soap out of the shop but returned saying, 'I'm sorry, I forgot to leave the soap.' The shopkeeper eventually moved to another part of town.

One of Humphries's greatest stunts was performed while he was a university student. He took his seat on a Melbourne commuter train. At the first stop, one of his pals boarded the train and served him a grapefruit. At the next stop, another pal took away the grapefruit and gave him cornflakes. And so on – through the eggs and bacon and the coffee – until he had been served a full breakfast.

Humphries invented a 'film director' who had supposedly been working with the Blind Man's Cinema

FORMER WARM-UP MEN

Clive Anderson (*After Midnight*)

Mark Lamarr (*Harry Enfield*)

Michael Barrymore (*Larry Grayson's Generation Game*)

Brian Conley (*Wogan* – but was fired for being 'too funny')

Phill Jupitus (to touring bands – as Porky The Poet)

Rowland Rivron (for Ruby Wax)

Mike Myers (for Timmy Mallett)

Daniel Kitson (*The 11 O'Clock Show*)

Victor Borge (*Bing Crosby's Kraft Music Hall*)

Neil Innes (briefly for *Monty Python*)

Lee Hurst (*Have I Got News For You?*)

Gary Glitter (*Ready Steady Go*)

Peter Kay (*Parkinson*)

FAMOUS PEOPLE WITH FAMOUS ANCESTORS

Mike Myers – William Wordsworth

Patricia Cornwell – Harriet Beecher Stowe

Gena Lee Nolin – Sir Isaac Newton

Kyle MacLachlan – Johann Sebastian Bach

Cate Blanchett – Louis Blériot

Tom Hanks – Abraham Lincoln

Glenn Ford – President Martin Van Buren

Prince Philip – Queen Victoria

Helena Bonham Carter – Herbert Asquith

Judy Garland – President General Ulysses S. Grant

Dame Barbara Cartland – Robert The Bruce

Joyce Grenfell – Nancy Astor

David 'Kid' Jensen – Robert Louis Stevenson

William Holden – President Warren G. Harding

General Colin Powell – King Edward I

Basil Rathbone – King Henry IV

Richard Nixon – King Edward III

FAMOUS PEOPLE BORN ON THE VERY SAME DAY AS OTHER FAMOUS PEOPLE

Paul Azinger and Nigella Lawson (6.1.60)

George Foreman and Linda Lovelace (10.1.49)

Keith Chegwin and Paul Merton (17.1.57)

Richard Dunwoody and Jane Horrocks (18.1.64)

Eartha Kitt and Roger Vadim (26.1.28)

Tony Blackburn and Katharine Ross (29.1.43)

Charles Darwin and Abraham Lincoln (12.2.1809)

Jerry Springer and Stockard Channing and Peter Tork (13.2.44)

Sir Alan Bates and Barry Humphries (17.2.34)

Yoko Ono and Sir Bobby Robson (18.2.33)

Prince Andrew and Leslie Ash (19.2.60)

Douglas Bader and Eddie Waring (21.2.10)

Robert Mugabe and Sam Peckinpah (21.2.25)

Sheila Hancock and the Duchess of Kent (22.2.33)

Ainsley Harriott and John Turturro (28.2.57)

Mikhail Gorbachev and Tom Wolfe (2.3.31)

Michael Grade and Lynn Redgrave (8.3.43)

Prince Edward and Neneh Cherry (10.3.64)

Sir Michael Caine and Quincy Jones (14.3.33)

Damon Albarn and Michael Atherton (23.3.68)

Tommy Hilfiger and Peter Powell (24.3.51)

Lara Flynn Boyle and Sharon Corr (24.3.70)

John Major and Vangelis and Eric Idle (29.3.43)

Marlon Brando and Doris Day (3.4.24)

Francis Coppola and Sir David Frost (7.4.39)

Jimmy Osmond and Nick Berry (16.4.63)

Harold 'Dickie' Bird and Jayne Mansfield (19.4.33)

Sachin Tendulkar and Gabby Logan and Lee Westwood (24.4.73)

Andre Agassi and Uma Thurman (29.4.70)

Ben Elton and Neil Pearson (3.5.59)

Sir Albert Finney and Glenda Jackson (9.5.36)

Maureen Lipman and Donovan (10.5.46)

Bono and Merlene Ottey (10.5.60)

Ian Dury and Susan Hampshire (11.5.42)

Peter Gabriel and Stevie Wonder (13.5.50)

Steven Norris and Priscilla Presley (24.5.45)

Helena Bonham Carter and Zola Budd (26.5.66)

Jonathan Pryce and Ronnie Wood (1.6.47)

Stacy Keach and Charlie Watts (2.6.41)

Jackie Mason and Giorgio Armani (9.6.34)

Linda Evangelista and Elizabeth Hurley (10.6.65)

Jason Brown (aka J 5ive) and Kym Marsh (13.6.76)

Meryl Streep and Lindsay Wagner (22.6.49)

John Cusack and Mary Stuart Masterson (28.6.66)

Diana, Princess of Wales and Carl Lewis (1.7.61)

Pam Shriver and Neil Morrissey (4.7.62)

Sylvester Stallone and President George W. Bush (6.7.46)

Caroline Quentin and Richie Sambora (11.7.59)

Dame Diana Rigg and Natalie Wood (20.7.38)

Bonnie Langford and John Leguizamo (22.7.64)

Stanley Kubrick and Danny La Rue (26.7.28)

Kate Bush and Daley Thompson (30.7.58)

Jürgen Klinsmann and Lisa Kudrow (30.7.64)

Jason Robinson and Hilary Swank (30.7.74)

Mikey Graham and Ben Affleck (15.8.72)

Angela Bassett and Belinda Carlisle and Madonna (16.8.58)

Robert De Niro and John Humphrys (17.8.43)

Christian Slater and Edward Norton (18.8.69)

Sir Donald Bradman and Lyndon B. Johnson (27.8.08)

Lenny Henry and Michael Jackson (29.8.58)

Chrissie Hynde and Julie Kavner (7.9.51)

Goran Ivanisevic and Stella McCartney (13.9.71)

Tommy Lee Jones and Oliver Stone (15.9.46)

Mo Mowlam and Peter Shilton (18.9.49)

Jarvis Cocker and David Seaman (19.9.63)

Hansie Cronje and Catherine Zeta Jones (25.9.69)

Maria Whittaker and Thom Yorke (7.10.68)

Chris Tarrant and Charles Dance (10.10.46)

Amanda Burton and Fiona Fullerton (10.10.56)

David Threlfall and Les Dennis (12.10.53)

Ernie Els and Wyclef Jean (17.10.69)

Dannii Minogue and Snoop Dogg (20.10.71)

Michael Crichton and Dame Anita Roddick (23.10.42)

Dervla Kirwan and Caprice (24.10.71)

Hillary Rodham Clinton and Jaclyn Smith (26.10.47)

Matthew Hayden and Winona Ryder (29.10.71)

Rebecca Romijn-Stamos and Thandie Newton (6.11.72)

Eddie Irvine and Sean Hughes (10.11.65)

Daryl Hannah and Julianne Moore (3.12.60)

Keith Floyd and Richard Whiteley (28.12.43)

John Denver and Sir Ben Kingsley (31.12.43)

NON-PROFESSIONAL GOLFERS WHO SCORED HOLES-IN-ONE IN GOLF

Jimmy Tarbuck, Mike Reid, Richard Nixon, Graham Gooch, Bob Hope, Bing Crosby, Sir Henry Cooper, Michael Lynagh

PEOPLE WHO APPEARED IN BRITISH SOAPS AS THEMSELVES

Loyd Grossman (*Brookside*)

Freddie Trueman (*Emmerdale*)

Bernard Manning (*Coronation Street*)

Russell Grant (*Brookside*)

Princess Margaret (*The Archers*)

Chris Lowe (*Neighbours*)

Harold Macmillan (*The Archers*)

Martin Offiah (*Emmerdale*)

Bruce Grobbelaar (*Brookside*)

Carol Smillie (*Brookside*)

Graham Norton (*Brookside*)

Prince Charles (*Coronation Street*)

Marti Pellow (*Emmerdale*)

People who made guest appearances in situation comedies

Linda McCartney (*Bread*)

John Cleese (*Cheers*)

Vincent Hanna (*Blackadder The Third*)

Roy Hattersley (*Chef*)

Lulu (*Absolutely Fabulous*)

Kylie Minogue (*The Vicar of Dibley*)

George Hamilton (*Birds of A Feather*)

Larry King (*Spin City*)

Midge Ure (*Filthy, Rich & Catflap*)

Noel Edmonds (*The Detectives*)

Rolf Harris (*Goodnight Sweetheart*)

Sir Ludovic Kennedy (*Yes Minister*)

Carol Smillie (*2Point4 Children*)

Jenny Agutter (*Red Dwarf*)

Ainsley Harriott (*Red Dwarf*)

Timothy Spall (*Red Dwarf*)

Koo Stark (*Red Dwarf*)

Esther McVey (*Goodnight Sweetheart*)

Sean Bean (*The Vicar of Dibley*)

Jeremy Paxman (*The Vicar of Dibley*)

Twiggy (*Absolutely Fabulous*)

Laurence Llewelyn-Bowen (*The League of Gentlemen*)

Tamzin Outhwaite (*Men Behaving Badly*)

Leslie Ash (*Get Fit With Brittas*)

REAL PEOPLE WHO APPEARED IN *THE BEANO*

Chris Evans (with Dennis The Menace)

Geri Halliwell (with Minnie The Minx)

Linford Christie (with Billy Whizz)

Ronan Keating (with Plug from The Bash Street Kids)

Alan Shearer (with Ball Boy)

Michael Owen (with Ball Boy)

Ken Dodd (with Dennis The Menace's dog Gnasher)

Tony and Cherie Blair (with Ivy The Terrible)

David Jason as Del Boy Trotter (with Roger The Dodger)

Rowan Atkinson as Mr Bean (with Calamity James)

COLLECTORS OF ...

Old photographs (Brian May)

Dolls' houses and furniture (Dame Judi Dench)

1940s typewriters (Tom Hanks)

Ornamental ducks (Josie Lawrence)

Comics (Jonathan Ross)

Old radios (Steve Wright)

Bird and animal skulls (Vic Reeves)

Porcelain pigs (Janet Jackson)

Old tin-plate toys (Michael Barrymore)

***Planet of The Apes* memorabilia (Shane Richie)**

Shirley Temple memorabilia (Melissa Joan Hart)

Antique toys (Dustin Hoffman)

Antique books (John Simpson)

Old fruit machines (Sid Owen)

Literary autographs (Sir Tom Stoppard)

Art – particularly Victorian nudes (Ozzy Osbourne)

Beanie babies (Nick Carter)

Garden gnomes (Cerys Matthews)

Vintage Polaroid cameras (Brendan Fraser)

Dried insects – which she paints and frames (Claudia Schiffer)

Antique watches (Nicolas Cage)

Loo seats (Prince Charles)

American comic books (Lenny Henry)

Chairs (Brad Pitt)

Puppets (David Arquette)

Medical prosthetics such as eyes and limbs; vintage metal lunchboxes (Marilyn Manson)

Inflatable ducks (Kim Basinger)

Coat hangers (Penelope Cruz)

Snakes (Slash)

Thimbles (José Carreras)

PEOPLE WHO LAUNCHED THEIR OWN FRAGRANCES

Linda Evans – Forever Krystle

Dame Elizabeth Taylor – White Diamonds

Englebert Humperdinck – Release Me

Omar Sharif – Omar Sharif

Sophia Loren – Sophia

Björn Borg – Signature

Cynthia Lennon – Cynthia Lennon's Woman

Joan Collins – Scoundrel

Luciano Pavarotti – Luciano Pavarotti Parfum For Men

Catherine Deneuve – Deneuve

Naomi Campbell – Naomi

Jennifer Lopez – J-Lo

Christina Aguilera – Fetish

Isabella Rossellini – Manifesto

PEOPLE WHO LAUNCHED THEIR OWN PRODUCTS

Burt Reynolds – jewellery

Joan Collins – jeans

Paul Newman – salad dressing

Jerry Hall – swimwear

Pepsi and Shirlie – girls' clothes

Princess Stephanie – swimwear

Ken Kercheval – popcorn

Joan Rivers – jewellery

Denise Van Outen – T-shirts

Iman – Iman cosmetics

Bo Derek – shampoos, conditioners and fragrances for dogs (the brand name is Bless The Beast)

Kelly LeBrock – Kelly LeBrock's Homeopathic Remedy Kit For Kids

Jaclyn Smith – perfume and clothing

Clint Eastwood – Pale Rider Ale

Elle Macpherson – designer lingerie

Ted Nugent – beef jerky

Jay-Z – Roc-a-Wear clothing

Marie Osmond – cosmetics, porcelain dolls and clothing patterns

Christina Aguilera – cosmetics

Sadie Frost – Frost French clothing

Jennifer Lopez – clothing ($10 million deal with Tommy Hilfiger's younger brother)

Carlos Santana – shoes that 'radiate rhythm, passion and energy'

Loyd Grossman – pasta sauces

Chaka Khan – range of chocolates called Chakalates

Kylie Minogue – lingerie range called Love Kylie

Missy Elliott – lipstick: Misdemeanor Lipstick

Busta Rhymes – clothing range called Bushi

Jane Seymour – clothing range

PEOPLE WHO INSURED PARTS OF THEIR BODY

Michael Flatley – legs for £25 million

Bruce Springsteen – voice for £3.5 million

Dolly Parton – bust for £2 million

Ken Dodd – teeth for £4 million

Jamie Lee Curtis – legs for £1.5 million

Keith Richards – third finger of left hand for £1 million

Mark King – hands for £1 million

Jennifer Lopez – body for $1 billion (£660 million)

Tina Turner – lips for $1 million and breasts for $750,000 (£5 million overall)

Mariah Carey – body for £1 billion

Jenny Frost – body for £1 million

GUEST EDITORS OF FRENCH *VOGUE*

The Dalai Lama, Sir Alfred Hitchcock, Nelson Mandela, Federico Fellini, Joan Miró, Princess Caroline of Monaco, Salvador Dalí, Orson Welles, David Hockney, Martin Scorsese, Marc Chagall, Mikhail Baryshnikov, Roman Polanski

GUEST EDITORS

Lord Snowdon – *Country Life*

Cherie Blair – *Prima*

Mario Testino – *Visionaire*

Damien Hirst – *The Big Issue*

Joan Collins – *Marie Claire* (UK)

Jenny Eclair – *Loaded*

Isabelle Huppert – *Cahiers Du Cinema*

Gwyneth Paltrow – *Marie Claire* (US)

Jennifer Saunders & Joanna Lumley – *Marie Claire* (UK)

Sir Terence Conran   *Country Life*

Susan Sarandon – *Marie Claire* (US)

Roseanne – *New Yorker, National Enquirer*

Geri Halliwell – *New Woman*

Victoria Wood – *Radio Times*

Jerry Springer – *Chat*

Leonardo DiCaprio – *National Geographic* children's magazine

PEOPLE WITH FAMOUS AUNTS

Nigel Havers – Dame Elizabeth Butler-Sloss

Jemma Redgrave – Vanessa Redgrave

Macaulay Culkin – Bonnie Bedelia

Alessandra Mussolini – Sophia Loren

Bridget Fonda – Jane Fonda

Jodie Kidd – Vicki Hodge

George Clooney – Rosemary Clooney

PEOPLE WITH FAMOUS UNCLES

Alan Howard – Leslie Howard

Judge Jules – Rick Stein

Sir Bobby Charlton – Jackie Milburn

Ewan McGregor – Denis Lawson

Nicolas Cage – Francis Coppola

Harriet Walter – Christopher Lee

Jack Davenport – Jonathan Aitken

PARENTS OF TWINS

Ben Elton, Donald Sutherland, Phil Silvers, Gordon Ramsay, George W. Bush, Denzel Washington, Al Pacino, Ally McCoist, Jeremy Paxman, Cheryl Baker, Robert De Niro, Earl Spencer, Ivan Lendl, Jane Seymour, Nigel Benn, Fern Britton, Mollie Sugden, James Galway, Michael Buerk, Gary Oldman, Dean Gaffney, Pele, Pat Cash, Graham Gooch, Sir Alan Bates, David Essex, Baroness Margaret Thatcher, Mel Gibson, Mark Knopfler, Judy Finnigan, Stan Boardman, Cybill Shepherd, James Stewart, Ingrid Bergman, Bing Crosby, Mia Farrow, Günter Grass

FATHERS OF TRIPLETS

Rodney Bewes

Tony O'Reilly

Richard Thomas (John-Boy in *The Waltons*)

PEOPLE WITH A TWIN BROTHER/SISTER

Alanis Morissette (Wade)

Joseph Fiennes (Jake)

Vin Diesel (Paul)

Derek Thompson (Elaine)

Will Young (Rupert)

Matt Goss (Luke)

Alec Bedser (Eric)

Gayle Blakeney (Gillian)

Roger Black (Julia)

Reggie Kray (Ronnie)

Carol Thatcher (Mark)

Babs Beverley (Teddy)

Sir Henry Cooper (George)

Anthony Shaffer (Peter)

Isabella Rossellini (Ingrid)

Keith Chegwin (Jeff)

Alan Yentob (Robert)

John Sessions (Maggie)

Pier Angeli (Marisa)

John Boulting (Roy)

Tim Gullikson (Tom)

Elizabeth Carling (Laura)

Kiefer Sutherland (Rachel)

Jerry Hall (Terry – sister)

Lowri Turner (Catrin)

Benjamin Zephaniah (Velda)

MEN WHO HAD TWIN BROTHERS WHO DIED AT BIRTH OR IN CHILDHOOD

Elvis Presley, David Jason, Liberace, William Randolph Hearst, Ed Sullivan, Freddie Starr, Edgar Allan Poe, Leonardo da Vinci, Lewis Carroll, Oscar Wilde, Jay Kay

Andy Garcia was born with a partly formed twin on his shoulder

PEOPLE WHO CAME FROM LARGE FAMILIES

Sol Campbell (one of 10 children)

Tim Allen (one of 10 children)

Rosie Perez (one of 10 children)

Mel Gibson (one of 11 children)

David Emanuel (one of 11 children)

Lucas Radebe (one of 11 children)

Benny Goodman (one of 11 children)

Lewis Carroll (one of 11 children)

Brian Lara (one of 11 children)

Glen Campbell (one of 11 children)

Dolly Parton (one of 12 children)

Sir Gordon Richards (one of 12 children)

Little Richard (one of 12 children)

George Burns (one of 13 children)

Perry Como (one of 13 children)

Little Eva (one of 13 children)

Richard Burton (one of 13 children)

Nicolae Ceausescu (one of 13 children)

Me-One (one of 13 children)

Charles Bronson (one of 15 children)

Billy Blanks (one of 15 children)

Sonny Liston (one of 25 children)

People who have/had famous fathers-in-law

Gregor Fisher – Peter Vaughan

Woody Allen – André Previn

Jonny Lee Miller – Jon Voight

Barry Humphries – Sir Stephen Spender

Loyd Grossman – Sir David Puttnam

Anthony Quinn – Cecil B. De Mille

Axl Rose – Don Everly

Sir Charles Chaplin – Eugene O'Neill

Karen Dotrice – Wilfrid Hyde-White

Richard Wagner – Franz Liszt

Belinda Carlisle – James Mason

Sir David Frost – The Duke of Norfolk

John McEnroe – Ryan O'Neal

Vincent Hanna – Lord Gerry Fitt

W. Somerset Maugham – Dr Barnardo

Shannen Doherty – George Hamilton

Peter Lawford – Dan Rowan

Artie Shaw – Jerome Kern

Oskar Werner – Tyrone Power

Geraldo Rivera – Kurt Vonnegut Jr

W.H. Auden – Thomas Mann

Burt Lancaster – Ernie Kovacks

David O. Selznick – Louis B. Mayer

Daniel Day-Lewis – Arthur Miller

P.J. O'Rourke – Sidney Lumet

Tony Blair – Anthony Booth

Boris Johnson – Charles Wheeler

Andrew Marr – Lord Jack Ashley

Lauren Holly – Anthony Quinn

Jeremy Irons – Cyril Cusack

George Clooney – Martin Balsam

Arnold Schwarzenegger – Sargent Shriver

PEOPLE WHO HAVE/HAD FAMOUS MOTHERS-IN-LAW

**Liam Neeson
– Vanessa Redgrave**

Sidney Lumet
– Lena Horne

**Simon Williams
– Dame Celia Johnson**

Janet Dibley
– Janet Brown

**Gary Oldman
– Ingrid Bergman**

Martin Scorsese
– Ingrid Bergman

COUSINS

Christopher Lee and Ian Fleming

Ginger Rogers and Rita Hayworth

Jon Snow and Peter Snow

Richard Briers and Terry-Thomas

Whitney Houston and Dionne Warwick

Peter Townsend (Princess Margaret's ex-lover) and Hugh Gaitskell

Natasha Richardson and Jemma Redgrave

Patrick Macnee and David Niven

Rip Torn and Sissy Spacek

Carole Lombard and Howard Hawks

Lauren Bacall and Shimon Peres

John Inman and Josephine Tewson

Ronald Harwood and Sir Antony Sher

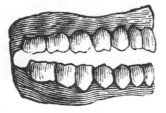

PEOPLE WHO OVERCAME STAMMERS

Bruce Willis, Carly Simon, Sir Winston Churchill, Harvey Keitel, King George VI, Sam Neill, Frankie Howerd, James Earl Jones, Martyn Lewis, Paul Young, W. Somerset Maugham, Marilyn Monroe, Charles Darwin, Arnold Bennett, Lewis Carroll, Nicholas Parsons

THE FIRST 10 SONGS PLAYED ON RADIO 1

'Flowers In The Rain' (The Move)

'Massachusetts' (The Bee Gees)

'Even The Bad Times Are Good' (The Tremeloes)

'Fakin' It' (Simon and Garfunkel)

'The Day I Met Marie' (Cliff Richard)

'You Can't Hurry Love' (The Supremes)

'The Last Waltz' (Engelbert Humperdinck)

'Baby Now That I've Found You' (The Foundations)

'Good Times' (Eric Burdon and the Animals)

'A Banda' (Herb Alpert and the Tijuana Brass)

THE FIRST 10 SONGS PLAYED ON *TOP OF THE POPS*

'I Only Want To Be With You' (Dusty Springfield)

'I Wanna Be Your Man' (The Rolling Stones)

'Glad All Over' (The Dave Clark Five)

'Stay' (The Hollies)

'Hippy Hippy Shake' (The Swinging Blue Jeans)

'Don't Talk To Him' (Cliff Richard and the Shadows)

'You Were Made For Me' (Freddie and the Dreamers)

'Twenty-four Hours From Tulsa' (Gene Pitney)

'She Loves You' (The Beatles)

'I Want To Hold Your Hand' (The Beatles)

WHAT FAMOUS PEOPLE DID IN WORLD WAR TWO

Sir Dirk Bogarde served as a captain in the Queen's Royal Regiment and saw action in France, Germany and the Far East. He also helped to liberate the Nazi concentration camp of Belsen.

Denholm Elliott served in the RAF until being shot down in a bombing mission over Denmark. He was captured and sent to a POW camp in Silesia for the last three years of the war. He gave a hugely praised performance as Eliza Doolittle in the camp production of *Pygmalion*.

Lord Denis Healey was a major in the Army and was the Beachmaster in the Anzio landings in Italy, for which he was mentioned in dispatches. He was also awarded a military MBE.

Tony Benn joined the RAF in 1943 at the age of 18. He got his wings just as Germany surrendered and so switched to the Fleet Air Arm to fight against Japan.

Kirk Douglas was a lieutenant in the US Navy and saw action in the Pacific before internal injuries suffered in combat led to an early discharge.

Paul Eddington joined ENSA but when he was called up registered as a conscientious objector. He was duly dismissed from ENSA but the war ended before his case (for being a conscientious objector) could be heard.

Sir Peter Ustinov served as a private in the Royal Sussex Regiment before being transferred to the position of David Niven's batman so that they could collaborate on the film _The Way Ahead_.

Hughie Green tried unsuccessfully to get into the RAF and so joined the Royal Canadian Air Force.

Richard Todd served with the Light Infantry, the Parachute Regiment and the 6th Airborne Division seeing action on (among others) D Day and in the Battle of the Bulge.

E W 'Jim' Swanton served as an acting major in the Royal Artillery before being captured in Singapore in 1942 and spending the rest of the war in a Japanese POW camp.

Enoch Powell rose through the ranks from private in the Royal Warwickshire Regiment to become a brigadier

Sammy Davis Jr. served in the US Army but was bullied by white southerners – five of whom once painted him white. However, he was taught to read by a black sergeant.

Sir Patrick Moore served in the RAF as a navigator with Bomber Command, reaching the rank of flight lieutenant.

Sheila Mercier served in the WAAF Signals, rising from section officer to adjutant.

Patrick Macnee served in the Royal Navy as a lieutenant, winning the Atlantic Medal.

Sir Ludovic Kennedy served in the Royal Navy (Volunteer Reserve) as a lieutenant and was also private secretary and ADC to the Governor of Newfoundland.

Sir Edmund Hillary served as a navigator in the Royal New Zealand Air Force in the Pacific.

Burt Lancaster served as a private in the American Fifth Army, having enlisted immediately after Pearl Harbor.

Ian Fleming served as assistant to the director of Naval Intelligence. After D Day, he was put in charge of Assault Unit No. 30, which was known as Fleming's Private Navy.

Kenneth Wolstenholme served as a bomber pilot in the RAF. He flew 100 missions over Germany and won the Distinguished Flying Cross (DFC) and Bar.

Walter Matthau served in the US Army in France (where he lost his virginity).

Tony Curtis served in the US Navy in the Pacific where he witnessed the Japanese surrender.

Jon Pertwee served as an officer in the Royal Navy (Volunteer Reserve). He served on HMS *Hood* and was lucky to be on shore leave when his ship was sunk by the *Bismarck* with only three survivors.

Ronald Searle was captured by the Japanese and was sent to the infamous Changi POW camp. He was also forced to work on the Burma–Siam railway.

Sir Kingsley Amis served as an officer in the Royal Corps of Signals and landed in Normandy three weeks after D Day.

Sir Michael Hordern was a Royal Navy officer and spent much of the war aboard the aircraft carrier *Illustrious* where he was also in charge of 'ship's entertainments'.

Donald Pleasence declared himself to be a conscientious objector at the start of the war and was sent to the Lake District to work as a forester. However, he had a change of heart and joined the RAF. He was shot down in France and spent the last year of the war in a German POW camp.

Sir Alec Guinness served in the Royal Navy in Combined Operations and captained a ship.

Marilyn Monroe worked in a Defense Plant while her then husband (James Dougherty) went into the Merchant Marines.

Audrey Hepburn starved in occupied Holland, living on two loaves of bread for one month.

Rod Steiger lied about his age to join the US Navy as a torpedoman on a destroyer in the South Pacific and saw action at Iwo Jima.

James Stewart saw active service as a pilot in the US Air Force with the rank of colonel.

Michael Foot was appointed acting editor of the London *Evening Standard*.

Dick Francis served as a pilot officer in the RAF, flying Lancaster and Wellington bombers.

Clive Dunn was captured and spent some of the war in a German POW camp.

Christopher Lee served in the RAF as a flight lieutenant and with Intelligence and Special Forces in the Western Desert, Malta, Sicily, Italy and Central Europe. He was mentioned in dispatches in 1944.

Jean Borotra was sports minister in the Vichy (pro-Nazi) French Government.

Bill Edrich was an RAF pilot who won the DFC for taking part in a daylight attack on Cologne in 1941. In one 48-hour period, he claims to have flown two bombing missions over occupied Europe, scored a century for Norfolk and made love to a local lass.

Tony Bennett served with the US Army in Europe as an infantryman.

Sir Jimmy Savile was sent down the mines as a Bevin Boy.

Murray Walker drove a tank.

PEOPLE WHO ATTENDED THE SAME SCHOOLS

Sir Ben Kingsley, Robert Powell, Michael Atherton and John Crawley (Manchester Grammar)

Sir Richard Branson and George Melly (Stowe)

Stephen Fry, Johnny Vaughan, Jonathan Agnew, Stephen Dorrell and John Suchet (Uppingham)

Sir Colin Cowdrey and Frederick Forsyth (Tonbridge)

Lord Brian Rix and A.J.P. Taylor (Bootham)

Bob Willis and Terry Jones (Royal Grammar, Guildford)

Kevin Whately, Rob Andrew, Rory Underwood and Craig Raine (Barnard Castle)

Peter Sissons and Steven Norris (Liverpool Institute High School For Boys)

Stewart Copeland, John Sergeant, John Standing, Tony Blackburn, Duncan Goodhew and Gareth Edwards (Millfield)

Mollie Sugden and Lord Denis Healey (Drake and Tonsons' Kindergarten)

Mick Fleetwood and Jeremy Irons (Sherborne)

Emile Heskey and Gary Lineker (City of Leicester School)

Jonathan King, David Dimbleby, Peter Gabriel and Nicky Henson (Charterhouse)

Bonnie Langford, Sarah Brightman and Nigel Havers (Arts Educational, London)

Sir P.G. Wodehouse, Raymond Chandler, Bob Monkhouse and Peter Lilley (Dulwich)

Jamie Theakston, Christopher Hampton, Sir Tim Rice and Tom Sharpe (Lancing)

Kelly Brook and Naomi Campbell (Italia Conti)

Chris Patten and Julian Clary (St Benedict's)

David Gilmour and Sir Peter Hall (The Perse School, Cambridge)

Ian Hislop and Terry-Thomas (Ardingly)

Imogen Stubbs, Shirley Conran, Harriet Harman, Celia Brayfield and Flora Fraser (St Paul's Girls)

Phil Tufnell, Bernard Jenkin, Barry Norman and Geoffrey Palmer (Highgate)

Beryl Reid and Judith Chalmers (Withington)

Nicky Campbell and Magnus Magnusson (Edinburgh Academy)

Peter Purves, Chris Lowe and Jimmy Armfield (Arnold)

Sir Malcolm Rifkind, Scott Hastings, Gordon Kennedy and Gavin Hastings (George Watson's)

Jeremy Paxman and Denholm Elliott (Malvern Boys)

Neil Diamond and Barbra Streisand (Erasmus Hall High, New York)

John Major and Raymond Briggs (Rutlish School, Merton)

Roger Lloyd Pack, Gyles Brandreth, Irina Brook and Amanda Craig (Bedales)

Rupert Everett, Michael Ancram, Lawrence Dallaglio, Edward Stourton and Piers Paul Read (Ampleforth)

Katherine Hamnett, Mary Archer, Nicola Horlick and Amanda Wakeley (Cheltenham Ladies)

Sir Stirling Moss, Alan Ayckbourn, Sir Michael Bonallack, Gerald Harper and Simon MacCorkindale (Haileybury)

Chris de Burgh, Captain Mark Phillips, Ian Balding and Toby Balding (Marlborough)

Kyran Bracken, Bill Cash, Sir Arthur Conan Doyle and Charles Laughton (Stonyhurst)

Jeremy Clarkson, Nick Raynsford and Graeme Garden (Repton)

Kenneth Clarke and Leslie Crowther (Nottingham High School)

Dame Judi Dench and Margaret Drabble (The Mount, York)

Chubby Checker and Eddie Fisher (South Philadelphia High)

Des Lynam and Paul Scofield (Varndean Grammar)

Sir Alastair Burnet and Martin Bell (The Leys)

John Cleese, John Inverdale, Clive Swift, Simon Russell Beale and Chris Serle (Clifton)

Kenneth Cranham and Ken Livingstone (Tulse Hill Comprehensive)

Michael Winner and A.A. Gill (St Christopher, Letchworth)

John Gummer and Dinsdale Landen (King's, Rochester)

Peter Cook, Brough Scott and Ted Dexter (Radley)

Jools Holland and William G. Stewart (Shooters' Hill)

Robert Redford and Stacy Keach (Van Nuys High, California)

Andi Peters, Michael Aspel and Geoffrey Robinson (Emanuel)

Sir Ian McKellen and Nigel Short (Bolton Boys)

Jenny Agutter, Fiona Fullerton, Joanna David and Hayley Mills (Elmhurst)

Dame Maggie Smith and Miriam Margolyes (Oxford High)

Barry Cryer and Gerald Kaufman (Leeds Grammar)

Les Dennis and Sir Paul McCartney (Stockton Wood Primary)

Helena Bonham Carter, Angela Lansbury and Fay Weldon (South Hampstead High)

Rory Bremner, Christopher Lee, David Suchet, Peter Snow and Robin Oakley (Wellington College)

Michael Buerk and Johnnie Walker (Solihull)

Graham Greene and Michael Meacher (Berkhamsted)

Indira Gandhi, Claire Bloom and Dame Iris Murdoch (Badminton)

David Hockney and Adrian Moorhouse (Bradford Grammar)

Michael Fish and Michael Praed (Eastbourne)

Emma Thompson, Charlotte Coleman and Sue Carpenter (Camden School For Girls)

Tim Pigott-Smith, Lord Richard Attenborough, Sir David Attenborough and Mark Cox (Wyggeston Grammar)

Ann-Margret and Bruce Dern (New Trier High, Illinois)

Michael Palin and Sir Rex Harrison (Birkdale)

Hugh Grant, Simon Hughes, Alan Rickman, Keith Vaz and Mel Smith (Latymer Upper)

Mark Nicholas, Lord David Owen and Richard Adams (Bradfield)

Matthew Pinsent, Bamber Gascoigne and Patrick Macnee (Eton)

Keith Floyd and Lord Jeffrey Archer (Wellington, Somerset)

Esther Rantzen and Eleanor Bron (North London Collegiate)

Alan Bennett and John Craven (Leeds Modern)

Harold Pinter and Sir Michael Caine (Hackney Downs)

Salman Rushdie, Christopher Brasher, Alan Howarth, Andrew Rawnsley, Nicholas Winterton and Robert Hardy (Rugby)

Douglas Adams, Keith Allen, Jack Straw, Noel Edmonds and Griff Rhys-Jones (Brentwood)

Sir Peter Ustinov, Imogen Stubbs, Tony Benn, Shane MacGowan, Gavin Rossdale, Matthew Freud, Nigel Planer, Corin Redgrave and Lord Andrew Lloyd Webber (Westminster)

Baroness Lynda Chalker and Sarah Miles (Roedean)

Sir Tom Stoppard and Ade Edmondson (Pocklington)

Barry Davies and Brian Moore (Cranbrook)

John Patten and Paul Merton (Wimbledon College)

Samantha Bond, Nigella Lawson and Davina McCall (Godolphin and Latymer)

Tony Blair and Rowan Atkinson (Durham Choristers Preparatory School)

John Wayne, Cameron Diaz and Snoop Dogg (Long Beach Polytechnic High School)

CONVENT SCHOOLGIRLS

Dame Helen Mirren, Joanna Lumley, Barbara Windsor, Donna D'Errico, Caroline Aherne, Zoe Ball, Sue Barker, Samantha Fox, Patsy Kensit, Genevieve Bujold, Janet Dibley, Marianne Faithfull, Cherie Booth Blair, Kathy Burke, Ann Widdecombe, Sarah Kennedy, Mia Farrow, Dillie Keane, Stephanie Beacham, Kristin Scott Thomas, Lisa Butcher, Andrea Corr, Caroline Corr, Sharon Corr

PEOPLE WHO WERE BULLIED AT SCHOOL

Gwyneth Paltrow (because she was 'gawky')

Harrison Ford (because he 'liked to hang out with girls')

Anthea Turner (because of her 'posh' accent)

Gillian Anderson (because of her 'independent' and 'bossy' attitude)

Prince Charles (because he was heir to the throne – was especially bullied during rugby games)

Marcella Detroit (because she was Jewish)

Mel Gibson (because of his American accent at his Australian school)

Sandra Bullock (because she was 'ugly')

Tom Cruise (because he 'was always the new kid in town')

Norman Pace (because he was so small)

Michelle Pfeiffer (because of her 'big lips')

Damon Albarn (because the other boys thought he was a 'gayboy')

Betty Boo (because she was a bookworm)

Sophie Dahl (by a boy who fancied her but whom she rejected)

Whitney Houston (because her 'hair was too straight' and her 'skin was too white')

Dannii Minogue (because she appeared on an Australian TV variety show at the age of ten)

Woody Allen (because of his name, Allen Konigsberg – 'I'd tell them my name was Frank, but they'd still beat me up')

Kate Winslet ('I was mentally bullied' – because of her weight)

Martin Clunes (taunted about his looks)

Patrick Swayze (because he liked to dance)

Ralph Fiennes ('for being a poof')

Joe Jackson (for being 'a bit of a misfit there, a sensitive kid who was into reading and classical music')

Jude Law (at a comprehensive in south-east London where suspects in the Stephen Lawrence murder were pupils; he moved to a private school where he was also bullied)

Dervla Kirwan (because she was shy)

Christina Aguilera (because she appeared on TV. In 2000, she got her own back on one of the bullies by driving in her sports car to the McDonald's where the girl worked. 'I heard you were working here and wanted to say hello,' she said)

Eminem (because his mum used to move all the time)

Victoria Beckham (because of her wealthy background; girls at school would push her around and swear at her in the playground and call her names because she had spots)

Ricky Martin (became the victim of a school bully called Manuel at the age of ten: 'He used to push me around and goad me into having a scrap, but I never fought back,' says Ricky)

Gabrielle (because of a lazy eyelid on her right eye, which made her look different from the other children at school)

Robert Carlyle (because he had no shoes and long hair)

Winona Ryder (because of her androgynous look)

Bryan McFadden (because of his 'puppy fat')

PEOPLE WHO WERE BULLIES (SELF-CONFESSED) AT SCHOOL

Stella McCartney, Jack Straw, David Schwimmer, Fiona Phillips, John Hegley, Charlie Drake

PEOPLE WHO WERE EDUCATED AT HOME

Dame Agatha Christie, Gerald Durrell, Molly Keane, C. S. Lewis, Sir Yehudi Menuhin, Alexander Graham Bell, Caitlin Moran, The Queen, George Bernard Shaw, Mary Wesley, Britney Spears, Joaquin Phoenix, The Everly Brothers

PEOPLE AND THEIR NICKNAMES FROM SCHOOLDAYS

Prince Andrew – The Sniggerer

Prince Edward – Jaws

Prince Philip – Flop

Prince William – Wombat

George Michael – Yog

Kate Moss – Mosschops

Cindy Crawford – Crawdaddy

Felicity Kendal – Fatty Foo

Beryl Bainbridge – Basher

Bob Geldof – Liver Lips

Kate Winslet – Blubber

Steven Spielberg – The Retard

Tony Robinson – Mighty Mouse

Sir Michael Caine – The Professor

Steve Wright – Concorde

Ronnie Wood – Cleopatra

Liam Gallagher – Weetabix

Noel Gallagher – Brezhnev

Sara Cox – Tefal (because of her high forehead) and Crazy Legs (because she was born with a clickyhip and has bent knees)

Michael Owen – Mincer

Cameron Diaz – Skeletor (because she was so skinny)

Alice Beer – Half-pint

Elle Macpherson – Smelly Elly

Rebecca Romijn-Stamos – Jolly Blonde Giant

Victoria Beckham – Acne Face

Ricky Martin – Kiki (this is also slang in Asia for 'pussy')

Geri Halliwell – Pancake (because of her flat chest)

Thom Yorke – Salamander (on account of his 'weird, wonky, reptile eyes')

Leonardo DiCaprio – The Noodle

Fiona Apple – Dog

Rowan Atkinson – Moon Man, Doopie and Zoonie

Puff Daddy – Born Sean Combs, he was given the nickname Puff because, as a child, he would huff and puff when angry

Sophia Loren – The Stick or Toothpick (because she was so thin)

Will Smith – The Prince (given to him by a teacher because of his regal attitude)

Denise Richards – Fish Lips

Kate Hudson – Hammerhead Shark (her brother's nickname because of the space between her eyes)

Charlie Dimmock – Charlie Bubbles (her headmaster's nickname for her because of her curls)

Jeff Goldblum – Bubwires ('because I had braces on my teeth when nobody else did and I think they were saying "barbed wires"')

Justin Timberlake – Brillo Pad (because of his curly locks)

Sophie Anderton – Thunder-thighs

Robert De Niro – Bobby Milk (because he was so white)

Nicole Kidman – Stalky

Kylie Minogue – Shorty

Davina McCall – Div

Gisele Bundchen – Oli (short for Olive Oyl because she was so tall and skinny)

Shane Filan – Shorty

Britney Spears – Boo-Boo

Elijah Wood – Little Monkey

PEOPLE WHO WERE EXPELLED FROM SCHOOL

Martin Amis (from Battersea Grammar for bunking off school at the age of 14 for a few months to play a part in the film *A High Wind In Jamaica*)

Roger Daltrey (from Acton Grammar School for smoking and refusing to wear school uniform)

Boy George (from Eltham Green School for – according to his headmaster – 'not coming to school and not working')

Jackie Collins (from Francis Holland School for smoking)

Jade Jagger (from St Mary's Calne for sneaking out on a date with her then boyfriend Josh Astor)

Stephen Fry (from Uppingham for theft)

Guy Ritchie (from Stanbridge Earls School near Andover for being in a girl's room or for snorting sulphate on Sports Day – depending on whether you listen to his dad or to him)

Macy Gray (from boarding school after, she says, reporting a dean who made improper physical contact)

Dan Aykroyd (from St Pius X Preparatory Seminary for committing acts of 'minor' delinquency)

Nicolas Cage (from elementary school for putting dead grasshoppers in the egg salad on picnic day)

Salma Hayek (from a Louisiana boarding school for setting alarm clocks back three hours)

Marilyn Manson (from a private conservative Christian school)

Kevin Spacey (from a military academy for hitting a classmate with a tyre)

Jeremy Clarkson (from Repton for many minor offences which his headmaster compared to being poked in the chest every day for five years)

Gabriel Byrne (from a seminary after being caught smoking in a graveyard)

Jeremy Beadle (from Orpington Secondary Modern for – among other things – hanging a pair of trousers on a flagpole)

Joshua Jackson (from two schools – one for poor attendance and the other for 'being mouthy')

Matthew Modine (from at least two high schools)

Jim Broadbent (from Leighton Park, just before his A-levels, for drinking)

PEOPLE WHO GOT FIRSTS AT UNIVERSITY

Imogen Stubbs (English, Cambridge)

Martin Bell (English, Cambridge)

David Baddiel (English, Cambridge)

Sir Roy Strong (History, Queen Mary College, London)

Arthur C. Clarke (Physics and Maths – in two years – King's College, London)

Lord Douglas Hurd (History, Cambridge)

Vanessa Feltz (English, Cambridge)

Michael Portillo (History, Cambridge)

Lord Maurice Saatchi (Economics, LSE)

Gordon Brown (History, Edinburgh)

Lord Denis Healey (Greats, Oxford)

Chris Smith (English, Cambridge)

Martin Amis (English, Oxford)

Laura Bailey (English, Southampton)

Louis Theroux (History, Oxford)

PEOPLE WHO GOT THIRDS AT UNIVERSITY

Lord John Birt

Baroness Barbara Castle

Tariq Ali

Lord Home

W.H. Auden

Jack Higgins

Margaret Hodge

Johnny Vegas

Carol Vorderman

Richard Whiteley

Anthony Powell

Imran Khan

PEOPLE WHO DROPPED OUT OF COLLEGE

Michael Douglas, Richard Dreyfuss, Carly Simon, David Gower, Bill Cosby, Jon Snow, Warren Beatty, Mick Jagger, Jane Fonda, Candice Bergen, Matt Damon, Christie Brinkley, Kate Beckinsale, Richard Stilgoe

AMERICANS AND THEIR CLASSMATES' RATINGS

Billy Crystal – voted Wittiest Student In His Class

Tom Cruise – voted Least Likely To Succeed

Sylvester Stallone – voted Most Likely To End Up In The Electric Chair

Sandra Bullock – voted Most Likely To Brighten Your Day

Robin Williams – voted Least Likely To Succeed

Meg Ryan – voted Cutest Girl In Class

Gillian Anderson – voted Girl Most Likely To Go Bald (because of her hairstyles) and Most Likely To Be Arrested

Halle Berry – voted Prom Queen but was forced to share the title with a 'white, blonde, blue-eyed, all-American girl'

Matthew Fox – voted Most Likely To Appear On *Hee-Haw*

Eddie Murphy – voted Most Popular

Chris Tucker – voted Most Humorous

John Leguizamo – voted Most Talkative

PEOPLE WHO ENDOWED SCHOLARSHIPS AT THEIR OLD SCHOOLS

Hugh Grant (Latymer Upper)

Jeremy Irons (Sherborne)

PEOPLE WHO WENT TO FINISHING SCHOOL

Mary Wesley   Anne Robinson   **Zsa Zsa Gabor**

FILM GAFFES

In *Charlie's Angels* (2000), when Drew Barrymore lifts up Lucy Liu to spin her around and kick the baddie, Drew calls out 'Lucy!' to get her attention – even though Lucy Liu's character's name is 'Alex'. See also *The Doors* (1991), when Meg Ryan calls Val Kilmer 'Val' instead of 'Jim', his character's name, and *The War of The Roses* (1989), in which Michael Douglas addresses Danny DeVito's character as 'DeVito'.

In *Rear Window* (1954), James Stewart has a cast on his leg for the whole film, which is fine except that in one scene the cast switches legs.

In *The Bible* (1966), the actor playing Adam has a belly button …

In *Spider-Man* (2002), Peter shoots his web at a lamp and pulls it across the room, smashing it, but seconds later it's back on the dresser in one piece.

In *Robin Hood: Prince of Thieves* (1991), the sheriff uses the expression '10.30'. Clocks didn't exist in the twelfth century.

In *Commando* (1985), the Porsche is wrecked on the left side – until Arnie drives it away and it's fine.

In *Harry Potter And The Philosopher's Stone* (2001), at the start-of-term feast Harry sits down on one side of the table next to Ron. When the food is served, Harry is on the other side of the table, next to Hermione.

In *Austin Powers In Goldmember* (2002), we learn that Austin Powers left school in 1959. This means that the family holiday in Belgium, when he was a baby, would have been between 1941 and 1944 when Belgium was occupied by the Nazis.

In *The Bridge On The River Kwai* (1957), Alec Guinness – who won an Oscar for his role – has his name spelt with just one 'n' in the final credits. Christopher Walken also had his name misspelled: in the credits of *Annie Hall* (1977).

In *The Perfect Storm* (2000), when the men are watching movies, there's a copy of *Blade Runner (Director's Cut)* on the table. The director's cut was released in 1992, but this movie is set in 1991.

In *Gladiator* (2000), in a battle scene, a chariot is turned over and a gas cylinder can be seen in the back.

In *The Maltese Falcon* (1941), as Sam Spade (Humphrey Bogart) slaps Joel Cairo (Peter Lorre), the latter's bow-tie changes from polka dots to stripes.

In *Speed* (1994), Harry (Jeff Daniels) is shot by Jack (Keanu Reeves) in the *left* leg but we later see him limping on the *right* leg.

In *The Wedding Singer* (1998), Julia's wedding was supposed to take place on Sunday, 5 August 1985. But in 1985, August 5th fell on a Monday.

In *The Last Temptation of Christ* (1988), you can see the label in Christ's robe.

In *It's A Wonderful Life* (1946), the old man's cigar disappears when he sends young George to deliver a prescription.

In *Spartacus* (1960), you can clearly see a vaccination scar on the arm of Spartacus (Kirk Douglas).

In *The Silence of The Lambs* (1991), Clarice Starling (played by Jodie Foster) has blue eyes, but the actress playing her as a child has brown eyes.

In *My Best Friend's Wedding* (1997), when Jules is trying on her dress she's wearing a white bra with a visible strap. Later, this becomes a black bra.

In *Pearl Harbor* (2001), Kate Beckinsale is seen wearing a bikini – even though the bikini wasn't invented until 1946 (five years later).

In *The Commitments* (1991), Imelda (Angeline Ball) decides not to go off with her family on a caravan holiday to the Isle of Man. Unfortunately for her family (who do go), the Isle of Man bans caravans.

In *48 Hours* (1982), Eddie Murphy is handcuffed when he leaves jail. The handcuffs then disappear but later reappear.

O Brother Where Art Thou? (2000) shows George 'Babyface' Nelson on his way to the electric chair. But George Nelson was never arrested in Mississippi, and anyway he wasn't executed but was killed by police near Chicago.

In *Born On The Fourth of July* (1989) you can hear 'American Pie', but this was released three years after the film was set.

In *The Matrix: Reloaded* (2003), there is a scene during a powercut where car headlights also go out.

OPERA

Key dates in the history of opera: 1597 – the first opera (Peri's *Dafne*); 1637 – the first public opera house opened in Venice; 1778 – La Scala was built; 1865 – Wagner wrote *Tristan Und Isolde*.

The longest operas – including intervals – performed at the Royal Opera House are all written by Wagner and are *Götterdämmerung* (6 hours), *Die Meistersinger Von Nurnberg* (5 hours, 40 minutes), *Siegfried* (5 hours, 25 minutes).

The shortest opera ever published is *The Deliverance of Theseus* (Darius Milhaud – 7 minutes, 27 seconds).

The most frequently performed operas at the Royal Opera House (since World War Two) are *La Bohème* (Puccini), *Carmen* (Bizet), *Aïda* (Verdi), *Tosca* (Puccini), *Rigoletto* (Verdi).

Famous opera haters include Jean Jacques Rousseau, George Bernard Shaw and Voltaire.

Things said about opera: 'Opera is when a guy gets stabbed in the back and, instead of bleeding, he sings' (Ed Gardner); 'Going to the opera, like getting drunk, is a sin that carries its own punishment with it and that a very severe one' (Hannah More); 'Opera is like a husband with a foreign title: expensive to support, hard to understand, and therefore a supreme social challenge' (Cleveland Amory); 'People are wrong when they say the opera isn't what it used to be. It is what it used to be. That's what's wrong with it' (Noël Coward).

Most curtain calls received by an opera singer: 165 (Luciano Pavarotti in 1988 in Berlin).

'Opera is when a guy gets stabbed in the back and, instead of bleeding, he sings' (Ed Gardner).

Extraordinary middle names

Joan HENRIETTA Collins

Rowan SEBASTIAN Atkinson

Mel COLUMCILLE Gibson

Gene ALDEN Hackman

Woody TRACY Harrelson

Rob HEPLER Lowe

Joseph ALBERIC Fiennes

Geri ESTOLLE Halliwell

Quincy DELIGHT Jones

Kate GARRY Hudson

Jack SIEGFRIED Ryder

Leonardo WILHELM DiCaprio

Russell IRA Crowe

Mark FREUDER Knopfler

Bob PRIMROSE Wilson

John MARWOOD Cleese

Robson GOLIGHTLY Green

Jo VELDA O'Meara

Lawrence BRUNO NERO Dallaglio

Jeremy DICKSON Paxman

Uma KARUNA Thurman

Damon ERNEST DEVERAUX Hill

Hugh JOHN MUNGO Grant

Sir Terence ORBY Conran

Ben GEZA Affleck

Emile IVANHOE Heskey

Famous women born with the first name Mary

Lauren Hutton, Dame Barbara Cartland, Dusty Springfield, Kathleen Turner, Christine Hamilton, Debbie Reynolds, Lily Tomlin, Dorothy Lamour, Sissy Spacek, Bo Derek, Meryl Streep, Debra Winger, Farrah Fawcett, Tipper Gore, Mae West.

FAMOUS PEOPLE WHO USE THEIR MIDDLE NAMES AS FIRST NAMES

Barbara Jane Horrocks

David Jude Law

Laura Reese Witherspoon

Keith Rupert Murdoch

Marvin Neil Simon

Ruz Fidel Castro

Desmond John Humphrys

Mary Debra Winger

Olive Marie Osmond

Walter Bruce Willis

Charles Robert Redford

Roberta Joan (i.e. Joni) Mitchell

William Bradley Pitt

George Ivan (i.e. Van) Morrison

Gordon Angus Deayton

James Gordon Brown

Michael Terry Wogan

Henry Warren Beatty

Michael Sylvester Stallone

Dorothy Faye Dunaway

Christina Brooke Shields

John Richard Whiteley

Thomas Sean Connery

Rosalie Anderson (i.e. Andie) MacDowell

PEOPLE NAMED AFTER SOMEONE/SOMETHING FAMOUS

Halle Berry (after the Halle Brothers department store)

Christopher Walken (named Ronald – a first name he dropped – after the actor Ronald Colman)

Heath Ledger (after Heathcliff in *Wuthering Heights*)

John Leguizamo (after the actor John Saxon)

Natasha Richardson (after the heroine in Tolstoy's *War And Peace*)

Charisma Carpenter (after an Avon perfume)

Dido (after the African warrior queen)

Marilyn Monroe – born Norma Jean Baker (after the actress Norma Talmadge)

Dale Winton (after the actor Dale Robertson)

Dustin Hoffman (after the cowboy star of the silent movies Dustin Farnum)

Mariel Hemingway (after a bay in Cuba)

Gloria Hunniford (after the actress Gloria Swanson)

Glenn Hoddle (after the bandleader Glenn Miller)

Sugar Ray Leonard (after the musician Ray Charles)

Whitney Houston (after the American TV soap star Whitney Blake)

Shirley Maclaine and Shirley Jones (after Shirley Temple)

Chelsea Clinton (after the song 'Chelsea Morning')

Dame Thora Hird (after the song 'Thora, Speak To Me Thora')

Martina Hingis (after the tennis star Martina Navratilova)

Dennis Bergkamp (after the footballer Denis Law)

Bette Midler (after the actress Bette Davis)

Oprah Winfrey (after Orpah, from the Bible's Book of Ruth; it was misspelt on her birth certificate)

Gillian Taylforth (after the dancer Gillian Lynne)

PEOPLE WHOSE NAMES ARE USED IN COCKNEY RHYMING SLANG

George Best – guest

Jeremy Beadle – needle

Tommy Steele – eel

Melvyn Bragg – shag

Richard Todd – cod

Cilla Black – back

David Bowie – blowy (in the sense of windy)

Sir Michael Caine – pain

Sir Edward Heath – teeth

Gregory Peck – cheque

Jane Russell – mussel

Doris Day – way

Mickey Rooney – loony

CELEBRITIES WHOSE NAMES ARE USED IN NEW RHYMING SLANG

Giorgio Armani – sarnie

Niki Lauda – powder

Christian Slater – later

Roberta Flack – sack

Calvin Klein – fine

Thelonius Monk – skunk

Kate Moss – toss

Britney Spears – beers

Fat Boy Slim – gym

Ronan Keating – meeting

Gloria Gaynor(s) – trainers

Carmen Miranda – veranda

Axl Rose – nose

Ringo Starr – bar

Belinda Carlisle(s) – piles

Sylvester Stallone – phone

UNUSUAL NAMES FAMOUS PEOPLE HAVE GIVEN THEIR CHILDREN

Lennon – Liam Gallagher and Patsy Kensit

Keelin – Jerry Garcia

Pixie, Fifi Trixiebelle and Peaches – Bob Geldof and Paula Yates

Heavenly Hiraani Tiger Lily – Michael Hutchence and Paula Yates

Homer – Matt Groening

Kidatia – Quincy Jones

Rufus Tiger and Tiger Lily – Roger Taylor (of Queen)

Bria – Eddie Murphy

Happy – Macy Gray

Jaden Gil – Steffi Graf and Andre Agassi

Denim – Toni Braxton

Jermajesty (boy) – Jermaine Jackson

Moon Unit, Dweezil, Diva and Emuukha Rodan – Frank Zappa

Dandelion (now Angela) – Keith Richards

Rain – Richard Pryor

Elijah Blue and Chastity Sun – Cher

Dakota Mayi – Don Johnson and Melanie Griffith

Navarone – Priscilla Presley

Dog – Sky Saxon

Rumer Glenn, Scout Larue and Tallulah Belle – Bruce Willis and Demi Moore

Brooklyn (girl) – Donna Summer

Brooklyn and Romeo (boys) – Victoria and David Beckham

Missy – Damon Albarn

Satchel – Spike Lee

Satchel – Woody Allen

Piper Maru – Gillian Anderson

Willow – Gabrielle Anwar

Starlite Melody – Marisa Berenson

Memphis Eve and Elijah Bob Patricius Guggi Q – Bono

Zowie (now Joey) – David Bowie

Sailor Lee – Christie Brinkley

Phoenix Chi – Mel B

Free – Barbara Hershey and David Carradine

Kansas – David Carradine

Tyson – Neneh Cherry

Braison Chance and Destiny Hope – Billy Ray Cyrus

Morgana – Morgan Freeman

Skylar – Sheena Easton

Arrana and Blue Angel – The Edge

Colton Jack – Chris Evert

Atiana Cecilia – Oscar de la Hoya

Chiara-Charlotte – Catherine Deneuve and Marcello Mastroianni

Lily-Rose Melody – Johnny Depp and Vanessa Paradis

Mallory Loving – Rick Derringer

Gracie Fan – Danny DeVito and Rhea Perlman

Caleb – Jack Nicholson

Brawley King – Nick Nolte

Gulliver – Gary Oldman

Morgane – Roman Polanski

Maesa – Bill Pullman

Elettra-Ingrid – Isabella Rossellini

Justice – Steven Seagal

Sage Moonblood – Sylvester Stallone

Amadeo – John Turturro

Ocean and Sonnet – Forest Whitaker

Mercedes – Val Kilmer and Joanne Whalley

Chance Armstrong – Larry King

Samaria – LL Cool J

Rainie – Andie MacDowell

Arpad Flynn – Elle Macpherson

Speck Wildhorse – John Cougar Mellencamp

And also: George Foreman named four of his sons George

PEOPLE WHO CHANGED THEIR NAMES

Sir Elton John (Reginald Dwight)

Meg Ryan (Margaret Hyra)

Alice Cooper (Vincent Furnier)

P.J. Proby (James Smith)

Elkie Brooks (Elaine Bookbinder)

Ricky Martin (Enrique Morales)

Joan Rivers (Joan Molinsky)

Kiki Dee (Pauline Matthews)

Woody Allen (Allen Konigsberg)

Martin Sheen (Ramon Estevez)

Macy Gray (Natalie McIntyre)

Hammer (Stanley Burrell)

Engelbert Humperdinck (Gerry Dorsey)

Bono (Paul Hewson)

Bo Derek (Mary Cathleen Collins)

Calvin Klein (Richard Klein)

Harry Hill (Matthew Hall)

David Copperfield (David Kotkin)

Bill Wyman (William Perks)

Omar Sharif (Michael Shalhoub)

James Garner (James Baumgarner)

David Bowie (David Jones)

Vic Reeves (Jim Moir)

Cilla Black (Priscilla White)

Jodie Foster (Alicia Foster)

Pat Benatar (Patricia Andrejewski)

Sid Owen (David Sutton)

Barry Manilow (Barry Pincus)

Michael Keaton (Michael Douglas)

Theresa Russell (Theresa Paup)

Me-One (Erik Martin)

Carmen Electra (Tara Leigh Patrick – advised by Prince to change: Carmen after the opera and Electra after the goddess)

Eminem (Marshall Mathers III)

Queen Latifah (Dana Owens)

Tom Cruise (Thomas Cruise Mapother IV)

Ice Cube (O'Shea Jackson)

Donna Karan (Donna Faske)

Larry King (Lawrence Zeiger)

Nathan Lane (Joseph Lane)

Ralph Lauren (Ralph Lifshitz)

Spike Lee (Shelton Lee)

Courtney Love (Courtney Menely)

Toni Morrison (Chloe Wofford)

Ozzy Osbourne (John Michael Osbourne)

Bernadette Peters (Bernadette Lazzara)

Tim Allen (Tim Allen Dick)

Snoop Dogg (Cordozar Broadus)

Shania Twain (Eileen Twain)

Wynonna (Christina Ciminella)

Puff Daddy (Sean Combs)

Marilyn Manson (Brian Warner – he named himself after Marilyn Monroe and Charles Manson)

Jay-Z (Shawn Carter)

Joaquin Phoenix (Joaquin Bottom – his surname was changed by his parents, which suggests that his older brother, the late actor River Phoenix, was once called River Bottom)

Sonique (Sonia Clarke)

Shaggy (Orville Burrell)

Norman Cook (Quentin Cook)

Stockard Channing (Susan Williams Antonia Stockard)

Ms Dynamite (Niomi Daley)

Eric Clapton (Eric Clapp)

Tina Turner (Annie Mae Bullock)

Doris Day (Doris Kapelhoff)

Axl Rose (William Bailey)

Michael Barrymore (Michael Parker)

Whoopi Goldberg (Caryn Johnson)

Billy Idol (William Broad)

Meatloaf (Marvin Aday)

Michael Crawford (Michael Dumble-Smith)

Dave Allen (David Tynan-O'Mahoney)

Chevy Chase (Cornelius Chase)

Lulu (Marie Lawrie)

Elaine Paige (Elaine Bickerstaff)

Grandmaster Flash (Joseph Saddler)

Elle Macpherson (Eleanor Gow)

Tom Jones (Thomas Woodward)

Demi Moore (Demetria Guynes)

Georgie Fame (Clive Powell)

Siouxsie Sioux (Susan Ballion)

Sir Cliff Richard (Harry Webb)

Winona Ryder (Winona Horowitz)

Jane Seymour (Joyce Frankenberg)

Christian Slater (Christian Hawkins)

Sir Michael Caine (Maurice Micklewhite)

Manfred Mann (Michael Lubowitz)

Sigourney Weaver (Susan Weaver – took the name from her favourite book, *The Great Gatsby*)

Elvis Costello (Declan McManus)

Dame Julie Andrews (Julia Wells)

Anne Bancroft (Anna Italiano)

Bobby Davro (Robert Nankeville)

Mel Brooks (Melvin Kaminsky)

Charles Aznavour (Shahnour Aznourian)

Iggy Pop (James Osterburg)

Stevie Wonder (Steveland Judkins)

Diane Keaton (Diane Hall)

Gary Numan (Gary Webb)

Les Dennis (Leslie Heseltine)

Jennifer Jason Leigh (Jennifer Morrow)

Paul Jones (Paul Pond)

The Edge (David Evans)

Nicolas Cage (Nicholas Coppola)

Jack Palance (Walter Palanuik)

Tammy Wynette (Virginia Pugh)

Mica Paris (Michelle Wallen)

Sting (Gordon Sumner)

Janis Ian (Janis Fink)

Chris de Burgh (Christopher Davidson)

Captain Sensible (Ray Burns)

Lou Reed (Louis Firbank)

Tony Curtis (Bernard Schwartz)

Adam Ant (Stewart Goddard)

Charles Bronson (Charles Buchinski)

Donna Summer (Donna Gaines)

David Essex (David Cook)

ALIASES

Mr Bellacon and Paul Cruise – Tom Cruise

Mr Dripnoodle – Johnny Depp

Tipsy McStagger and Phil S. Stein – Robbie Williams

Mr Hugh Jarse – George Michael

Miss Trixie Firecracker and Lili Paris – Geri Halliwell

Miss Flo Cha – Mel C

Mr Tyne and Mr Wear – Ant and Dec

Claris Norman – Madonna

Pussy Jones – Dannii Minogue

Peter Gunn – Eminem

Bobby Dee – Kevin Spacey

A.N. Other – Prince Edward (in an Austrian hotel)

Sir Humphrey Handbag – Sir Elton John

Miss R. Dynastar – Vanessa-Mae

Miss Cupcake – Mariah Carey

Doctor Frank'n'furter – Abs 5ive

Sabrina Duncan – Shirley Manson

Miss Honey – Nicole Kidman

Bambi Shots – Anastacia

Mary Black – Courtney Love

PEOPLE WITH FOUR INITIALS

V.H.B.M. Bottomley (Virginia Bottomley)

J.P.M.S. Clary (Julian Clary)

N.K.A.S. Vaz (Keith Vaz)

K.P.T.F. Duffy (Keith Duffy)

C.P.A.G. Windsor (The Prince of Wales)

M.J.C.C. Rutherford (Mike Rutherford)

SARDINES

The word SARDINE refers to any of several species of small food fish of temperate waters that are also known as pilchards – especially when adult. Sardines are shoaling fish that live near the surface feeding on plankton. This ends the encyclopaedia definition.

SARDINES are sensitive fish. They move away from their shoaling grounds and don't return for decades after naval battles.

SARDINES can improve your memory – according to a study of children in 1987. People with memory disorders have low levels of acetyl choline which certain foods – such as sardines – can mitigate.

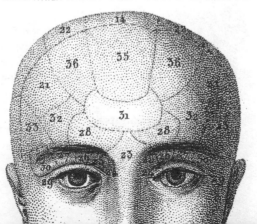

SARDINES were sold for years in cans with keys which would inevitably break as you tried to turn them, leaving razor-sharp edges. This led to cut fingers, a lot of swearing, oil going everywhere and no sardines for tea. In the past few years, they have been sold flat in cans with a ring-pull (like a soft drink) or standing up in a can which is opened with a tin opener (like a can of baked beans). In the dark days of the old-style sardine can key, nearly half of the shoppers surveyed complained about sardine-can keys breaking off or cutting them.

The Norwegian city of Stavanger uses as its symbol and crest the key to a tin of SARDINES.

In *Beyond The Fringe*, Alan Bennett described life as being 'rather like a tin of SARDINES – we're all of us looking for the key'.

Traditionally SARDINES were encouraged to rise to the surface of the sea by the fishermen drumming their feet on the bottom of the boat. The foaming shoals would then be scooped up in quantity.

In Britain, tinned SARDINES are one of our cheapest foodstuffs. If we want to describe someone as broke, we talk about them living on a diet of sardines.

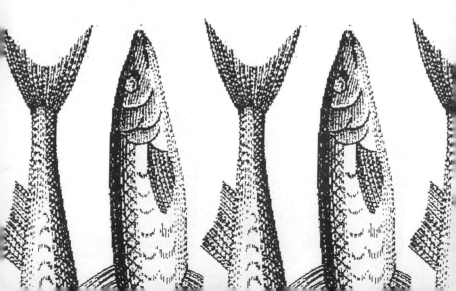

The French take SARDINES seriously. They sell prime quality tinned sardines – skinned and boned, in extra virgin olive oil – and even sell vintage sardines: date-stamped with the year they were captured because good sardines improve in the can so long as the can is regularly turned. The French value sardines so highly that there was even a Pierre Cardin sardine can, and a museum totally dedicated to sardines, in Sete, features stuffed sardines, pictures of sardines and live sardines in tanks. The museum's creator said, 'The fish are part of our culture.'

According to a 1991 survey commissioned by John West, seven out of ten men who eat a lot of canned fish – including SARDINES – head for the top and half rate themselves more successful than others. However, only 5 percent said they bounced back quickly after criticism, compared to 25 percent of non-fish eaters.

Some 14 million tins of SARDINES – the equivalent of 5,400 tons – are sold annually in Britain.

Like all oily fish, SARDINES (especially fresh ones) are marvellous for lowering cholesterol and are therefore an important guard against heart disease.

SARDINES can help cancer sufferers. Trials at Edinburgh Royal Infirmary showed that a fatty acid in sardine oils prevents patients losing weight by blocking a substance produced by tumours that destroys body tissue. This is important because about half of cancer patients lose weight – some so severely that it kills them.

In Alexandria, Minneapolis, no man is allowed to make love with the smell of SARDINES on his breath.

In Marseille, France, a 4,500 piece jigsaw depicting a two-acre SARDINE was laid out by thirty people in one week in 1992.

In 1995, millions of dead SARDINES were washed ashore along the Australian New South Wales coast when a mystery illness led to them suffocating after mucus blocked their gills.

In 1994, in Lima, Peru, 1,500 young people made a three-mile-long SARDINE sandwich in an attempt to get into the Peruvian *Guinness Book of Records.*

In Ipswich, Queensland, in Australia, SARDINES rained down from the sky in 1989. The fish were sucked up from the sea by a strong updraft of air and fell to the ground like hail. The local cats were said to be delighted.

There's the true story of the young boy who was told by his teacher to write about the harmful effects of oil on fish for his homework. He wrote, 'My mummy opened a tin of SARDINES. The sardines were covered in oil and they were all dead'.

The European Patents Office says that the most commonly requested item among its 31 million patent documents is SARDINE-flavoured ice cream. A spokesman says, 'No one believes that it actually exists until they've called it up and seen it themselves.'

PEOPLE WHO APPEARED IN ADVERTISEMENTS WHEN THEY WERE CHILDREN

Jonathan Ross (Rice Krispies)

Patsy Kensit (Birds Eye frozen peas)

Simon Le Bon (Persil)

Michael Portillo (Ribena)

Jodie Foster (Coppertone)

Martyn Lewis (Cow & Gate baby food)

B.B. King (Pepticon health tonic)

Keith Chegwin (Marathon)

Emma Bunton (Milky Bar)

Leslie Ash (Fairy Liquid)

Kate Winslet (Sugar Puffs)

Drew Barrymore (Gainsburgers)

Mike Myers (Datsun)

Sarah Michelle Gellar (Burger King; she couldn't say 'burger' and so needed a speech coach)

Melissa Joan Hart (Splashy – a bath toy)

Kirsten Dunst (a doll with bodily functions on US TV)

Yasmine Bleeth (was a Johnson & Johnson baby)

Jeff Daniels (McDonald's)

Rick Schroder (had appeared in about 60 adverts by the age of seven)

Brooke Shields (was the Ivory Snow baby at the age of 11 months)

Christian Bale (Pac-Man cereal)

Jessica Biel (Pringles crisps)

Danniella Westbrook (Asda)

FORMER FLATMATES

Tommy Lee Jones and Al Gore

Sir Michael Caine and Terence Stamp

Lauren Holly and Robin Givens

M. Emmet Walsh and William Devane

Ewan McGregor and Jude Law

Joel & Ethan Coen, Frances McDormand and Holly Hunter

Marilyn Monroe and Shelley Winters

David Baddiel and Frank Skinner

Charles Bronson and Jack Klugman

Charles Manson and Dennis Wilson

Peter Howitt and Kevin McNally

Cary Grant and Randolph Scott

Dustin Hoffman, Gene Hackman and Robert Duvall

Lesley Joseph and Maureen Lipman

David Niven and Errol Flynn

James Stewart and Henry Fonda

Michael Douglas and Danny DeVito

Mel Gibson and Geoffrey Rush

Ted Hughes and Peter O'Toole

Matt Damon and Ben Affleck

Zoe Ball and John Thomson

PEOPLE AND THE SPORTS THEY PLAYED

Shannon Elizabeth could have become a professional tennis player

Matthew Perry was ranked number 2 at tennis in Ottawa at the age of 13

Yanni was a member of the Greek national swimming team

Kurt Russell left acting in 1971 to pursue a career in minor league baseball

Hilary Swank swam in the Junior Olympics; she was also a top gymnast

Queen Latifah was a power forward on two state championship basketball teams in high school

Sonique 'could have competed on an international level' in the pentathlon as a teenager

Josh Hartnett turned to acting only after his soccer career ended

George Clooney once tried out for the Cincinnati Reds baseball team

Heath Ledger nearly became a professional ice hockey player but chose acting over sport when given an ultimatum

Gisele Bundchen originally wanted to be a professional volleyball player

Allison Janney wanted to be a competitive figure skater but a freak accident ended her chances

Dr Benjamin Spock won a rowing gold medal at the 1924 Olympics

Tommy Lee Jones is a champion polo player

Chevy Chase used to work as a tennis professional at a club

Paul Newman once achieved second place in the gruelling Le Mans 24 Hour Race

Richard Harris won a Munster Cup medal playing in the second row for Garryowen in 1952 and might well have gone on to play Rugby Union for Ireland had he not contracted TB

Richard Gere won a gymnastics scholarship to the University of Massachusetts

Keanu Reeves was the goalkeeper in his high school ice-hockey team, where he earned the nickname 'The Wall' and where he was voted MVP (Most Valuable Player)

Arnold Schwarzenegger was not only a bodybuilding champion but also won the Austrian Junior Olympic Weightlifting Championship

Julio Iglesias used to play in goal for Real Madrid's second team

Robert De Niro learned to box for his Oscar-winning role as Jake La Motta in *Raging Bull* and was so good that La Motta himself said that he could have taken it up professionally

Bill Cosby was good enough at American football to be offered a trial with the Green Bay Packers

William Baldwin was a good enough player to have originally considered a professional baseball career with the New York Yankees

Kirk Douglas once supplemented his meagre earnings with professional appearances in the ring as a wrestler

Billy Crystal attended college on a full baseball scholarship but decided not to pursue a career in the sport

Peter O'Toole 'distinguished himself on the rugby field' when he served in the navy in 1950–52

David Suchet played rugby union on the wing for Richmond RFC

Jim Brown embarked on an acting career only after having been a star at American football

Davy Jones was an apprentice jockey before joining The Monkees; however, it was only after he retired from singing and made a racing comeback that he had his first win as a jockey

Warren Beatty was offered scholarships as an American football player by several universities but turned them all down to concentrate on acting

Tom Cruise was an all-round sporting star at school but it was his wrestling that led to his acting career: he was in the school wrestling team but after injuring his knee turned to acting instead

Ian McShane could have followed his father into a career with Manchester United but he turned down the opportunity in order to pursue acting

Jack Palance worked as a professional boxer – which was how he got the broken nose that helped him to earn parts playing the heavy

Mickey Rourke had 26 amateur fights in the 1970s and then quit when his acting career took off; in recent years, he has returned to the ring with some success

Liam Neeson boxed for a local team from the age of nine until the age of 17 (in one early match his nose was broken and he had it set on the spot by his manager)

Jonathan Dimbleby was the 1964 showjumping champion of the south of England

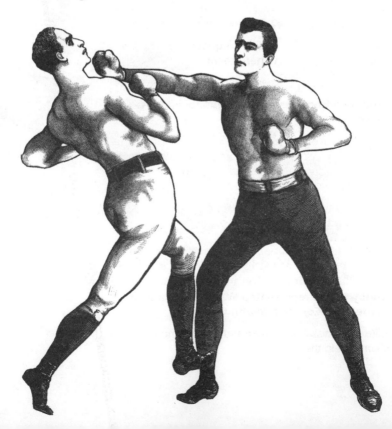

Roy Walker was a champion hammer thrower

Amanda De Cadenet trained four hours a day to become an Olympic gymnast (unsuccessfully)

Sheryl Crow was a competitive hurdler

Mel C ran for Cheshire county when she was a schoolgirl

Alanis Morissette takes part in triathlons

Sarah Michelle Gellar was a competitive figure skater for three years and was ranked third in New York State

Geena Davis tried in 1999 to qualify for the US Women's Olympic Archery team

Ellen DeGeneres considered becoming a professional golfer

Ross Davidson was an international water-polo player

Jonathan Cake won a Cambridge Blue for rugby after being drafted in at the last moment as a replacement, but gave up the game because there were only so many auditions he could go to with a bashed-in nose

Paul McGann was a junior triple-jump champion considered good enough to compete in a future Olympic Games

Rolf Harris was Junior Backstroke Champion of all Australia in 1946

Gabby Logan represented Wales at gymnastics in the 1990 Commonwealth Games

Kate Hoey was Northern Ireland's high jump champion in the 1960s

PEOPLE WHO PLAYED FOR – OR HAD TRIALS WITH – FOOTBALL CLUBS

Sir David Frost (Nottingham Forest)

David Essex (Leyton Orient)

The Duke of Westminster (Fulham)

Des O'Connor (Northampton Town)

Bradley Walsh (Brentford)

Eddie Large (Manchester City)

Stan Boardman (Liverpool)

Angus Deayton (Crystal Palace)

Rod Stewart (Brentford)

Gordon Ramsay (played twice for Rangers)

Stuart Hall (Crystal Palace)

Rick Savage (Sheffield United)

Gavin Rossdale (Chelsea)

Audley Harrison (Watford)

Lee Latchford-Evans (Wimbledon)

Nicky Byrne (Leeds United)

Ralf Little (Swindon and Millwall)

FORMER BEAUTY QUEENS

Joan Blondell (Miss Dallas 1926)

Dorothy Lamour (Miss New Orleans 1931)

Zsa Zsa Gabor (Miss Hungary 1936 – stripped of the title for being too young)

Veronica Lake (Miss Florida 1937 – stripped of the title for being too young: 'Being disqualified after you've won something is a pretty good way to lose.')

Lauren Bacall (Miss Greenwich Village 1942)

Cloris Leachman (Miss Chicago 1946)

Gina Lollobrigida (Miss Italy 1946)

Vera Miles (Miss Kansas 1948)

Debbie Reynolds (Miss Burbank 1948)

Anita Ekberg (Miss Sweden 1950)

Sophia Loren (Miss Elegance 1950)

Shirley Jones (Miss Pittsburgh 1952)

Imelda Marcos (Miss Manila 1953)

Kim Novak (Miss Deepfreeze 1953)

Raquel Welch (Miss Photogenic 1953)

Dyan Cannon (Miss West Seattle 1957)

Cybill Shepherd (Miss Teenage Memphis 1966)

Shakira Caine (Miss Guyana 1967)

Kim Basinger (Miss Junior Athens 1969)

Oprah Winfrey (Miss Black Tennessee 1971)

Lynda Carter (Miss World USA 1973)

Michelle Pfeiffer (Miss Orange County 1976)

Sharon Stone (Miss Crawford County 1976)

Marla Maples (Miss Resaca Beach Poster Girl 1983)

Halle Berry (Miss USA 1986 – first runner-up)

Helena Christensen (Miss Denmark 1986)

Jeri Ryan (Miss Illinois 1989)

Ali Landry (Miss USA 1996)

PEOPLE WHO PLAY/PLAYED IN BANDS

Russell Crowe is in a band named 30 Odd Foot of Grunts

Kevin Bacon formed the Bacon Brothers with his older brother Michael

Joe Pesci was lead vocalist with Joey Dee and the Starlighters

Johnny Depp was in a series of garage bands, one of which (The Kids) opened for Iggy Pop; later he became a member of the band P (with Steve Jones of the Sex Pistols and Flea of the Red Hot Chilli Peppers)

Gary Sinise formed The Bonsoir Boys in 1997

Director Mike Figgis was once in a band with Bryan Ferry

Stephen King and Matt Groening are in a band called Rock Bottom Remainders

David Lynch plays bass in a heavy metal group called Blue Bob

Ricky Gervais sang in a band named Seona Dancing

Ruud Gullit used to play bass guitar in a band named Revelation Time

Richard Gere was the lead singer with The Strangers

Loyd Grossman was the singer and guitarist with a group called Jet Bronx and the Forbidden which got to number 49 in 1977 with 'Ain't Doin' Nothin''

Kevin Costner was the vocalist with the group Roving Boy

Melvyn Bragg was lead singer of a group named Memphis 5; he was also in a skiffle group playing tea-chest bass

Nigel Havers was in a pop group with his brother (they used to sing Herman's Hermits-type songs)

Diane Keaton sang with The Roadrunners

Leslie Ash was a backing singer in the group Smiley & Co

Tony Blair was the lead singer in a university band, The Ugly Rumours

Michelle Collins started her career as a backing singer with Mari Wilson

Damon Hill played guitar in a punk band named Sex Hitler and the Hormones (with fellow aspiring racing drivers)

Chevy Chase played drums for a college group that included Donald Fagen and Walter Becker of Steely Dan

Roger Black played bass guitar for the amateur punk group The Psychedelic Vegetables

Jeremy Vine used to play drums in a rock band called Flared Generation

Patsy Kensit sang with Eighth Wonder

PEOPLE WHO GUESTED ON RECORDS

Rick Wakeman played synthesizer on 'Space Oddity' (David Bowie)

Brian Jones played oboe on 'Baby You're A Rich Man' (The Beatles)

Peter Gabriel played flute on 'Lady D'Arbanville' (Cat Stevens)

Billy Joel played piano on 'Leader of The Pack' (The Shangri-Las)

Elton John played piano on 'He Ain't Heavy, He's My Brother' (The Hollies)

Jack Bruce played bass on 'Sorrow' (The Merseys)

George Harrison played guitar on 'Badge' (Cream)

Eric Clapton played guitar on 'While My Guitar Gently Weeps' (The Beatles)

Paul Weller played guitar on 'Champagne Supernova' (Oasis)

David Gilmour played guitar on 'Wuthering Heights' (Kate Bush)

Ritchie Blackmore played guitar on 'Just Like Eddie' (Heinz)

Phil Collins played drums on 'Puss 'N Boots' (Adam Ant)

Mark King played bass on 'If I Was' (Midge Ure)

Stevie Wonder played harmonica on 'I Feel For You' (Chaka Khan)

SOME PEOPLE AND THE SONGS ON WHICH THEY PLAYED BACKING VOCALS

David Bowie – 'It's Only Rock And Roll' (The Rolling Stones)

Sir Tim Rice – 'Lily The Pink' (The Scaffold)

Sheryl Crow – 'Silver Girl' (Fleetwood Mac)

Eric Clapton – 'All You Need Is Love' (The Beatles)

Rupert Everett – 'American Pie' (Madonna)

Britt Ekland – 'Tonight's The Night' (Rod Stewart)

George Michael – 'Nikita' (Elton John)

Donovan – 'Yellow Submarine' (The Beatles)

Mick Jagger – 'You're So Vain' (Carly Simon)

Paul Young – 'Black Coffee In Bed' (Squeeze)

Phil Spector – 'My Sweet Lord' (George Harrison)

Bruce Springsteen – 'Street Hassle' (Lou Reed)

Luther Vandross – 'Young Americans' (David Bowie)

Sir Paul McCartney – 'Mellow Yellow' (Donovan)

Jimmy Somerville – 'Suspicious Minds' (Fine Young Cannibals)

John Lennon – 'Fame' (David Bowie)

Eric Clapton – 'I Wish It Would Rain Down' (Phil Collins)

Kate Bush – 'Games Without Frontiers' (Peter Gabriel)

Sting – 'Money For Nothing' (Dire Straits)

Michael Douglas – 'When The Going Gets Tough (The Tough Get Going)' (Billy Ocean)

Billy Idol – 'Dancin' Clown' (Joni Mitchell)

David Beckham – 'Out Of Your Mind' (Victoria Beckham – he sang on the first take which, apparently, wasn't subsequently used)

Roger Daltrey – 'Bad Attitude' (Meat Loaf)

George Michael – 'The Last Kiss' (David Cassidy)

Belinda Carlisle – 'Pearl's Café' (The Specials)

Richard Ashcroft, Patsy Kensit and Meg Mathews – 'All Around The World' (Oasis)

Sting – 'Shape' (Sugababes)

WHAT THEY DID BEFORE BECOMING FAMOUS

Michael Gambon – apprentice toolmaker

Geena Davis – live mannequin in a New York department store

Roy Walker – shipyard worker (and worked on the *QE2* in Belfast)

Phill Jupitus – press officer for The Housemartins

Charlie Dimmock – apple-picker, airport check-in clerk

Harvey Keitel – shoe salesman and court stenographer, having joined the US Marines at the age of 16 and served in the Lebanon

Paul O'Grady – social worker

Renée Zellweger – bartender assistant

Lucy Lawless – worked in a gold mine

Huey Lewis – slaughtered rabbits: he had to hit them over the head with a pipe, then skin them and gut them

Johnny Vaughan – grill chef, jewel courier, sales assistant, video shop manager

Beck – painted signs, moved refrigerators, took ID photos at the YMCA in New York, worked in a video store

Neve Campbell – ballerina

Hugh Grant – advertising account executive

Tom Clancy – insurance agent

George Clooney – sold insurance door to door, cut tobacco in Kentucky

Ellen DeGeneres – vacuum cleaner saleswoman

Dennis Franz – postman ('the worst postman in the history of the Post Office')

Whoopi Goldberg – bricklayer, bank teller, make-up artist for a funeral parlour

John Goodman – bouncer

Dustin Hoffman – toy seller at Macy's, attendant in a psychiatric institution

Russell Crowe – bingo caller

Vin Diesel – bouncer

Matthew Modine – electrician, macrobiotic chef

Kevin Richardson – played a Ninja Turtle at the Disney–MGM Studios theme park

J.K. Rowling – worked at the Amnesty International office in London and then at the Chamber of Commerce in Manchester

Meg Ryan – journalist

Mariella Frostrup – press officer for UB40

Davina McCall – singing waitress in Paris

Liam Neeson – forklift driver at the Guinness brewery in Belfast

Melinda Messenger – air stewardess

Björk – fish factory employee

Josh Hartnett – video store clerk

Chris Isaak – funeral parlour assistant

Sue Perkins – cleaned toilets for a hotel in Croydon for £1.50 an hour

Nathan Lane – police bail interviewer

Peter Gabriel – milliner

Elvis Costello – computer programmer at the Elizabeth Arden factory

Bob Geldof – meat packer

Tom Jones – glove cutter

Sir Ben Kingsley – penicillin tester

Madonna – worked in Burger King; also as a lifeguard and a lift operator

Robert Redford – pavement artist

Tina Turner – maid

Joe Cocker – plumber

Sir Elton John – messenger boy

Willem Dafoe – magazine binder at *Penthouse*, carpenter and electrician

Gloria Estefan – Spanish and French interpreter for customs at an American airport

Bill Withers – manufactured aeroplane loo seats

Tom Hanks – bellhop

Kylie Minogue – video shop worker

Jon Bon Jovi – served in Burger King

James Caan – rodeo rider

Kathy Bates – cashier in the gift shop in New York's Museum of Modern Art

Simon Le Bon – lumberjack

Mick Jagger – hospital porter

Cher – receptionist in a department store

Ozzy Osbourne – slaughterhouse labourer

Annie Lennox – fish filleter

Bob Hoskins – nightclub bouncer

Rod Stewart – grave digger

Vic Reeves – pig farmer

Warren Beatty – cocktail bar pianist

Jeremy Irons – social worker

Michelle Pfeiffer – supermarket assistant

Sir Sean Connery – french polisher

Dame Diana Rigg – coffee bar assistant

Julie Walters – nurse

DROVE TAXIS

Pierce Brosnan, Michael Keaton, Alan Alda, Oliver Stone

Note also: Stephen Fry, Prince Philip, Lord Andrew Lloyd Webber, Michael Jackson, John Wayne, Liberace and Keith Allen bought London cabs for their own personal use

FORMER TEACHERS

Sarah Kennedy, Sting, Bryan Ferry, Patricia Hodge, Jim Bowen, Sebastian Faulks, Gabriel Byrne, Dame Anita Roddick, Billy Crystal (substitute teacher), Luciano Pavarotti (elementary school), Dawn French, Oliver Stone (in Vietnam)

WORKED AS LION-CAGE CLEANERS

Clive James, Sylvester Stallone

WORKED AS WAITERS AND SERVED FAMOUS PEOPLE

Richard Gere (once served Robert De Niro)

Dido (once dropped 16 glasses of white wine and a tray on Stephen Fry when waitressing at Cafe Flo in London)

SERVED IN THE ISRAELI ARMY

Dr Ruth Westheimer, Uri Geller, Debra Winger, Vidal Sassoon

AUDITIONED UNSUCCESSFULLY FOR THE MONKEES

Charles Manson, Stephen Stills

FORMER HAIRDRESSERS

Chuck Berry, Lewis Collins, Alison Moyet, Mike McGear, Yazz, Danny DeVito, Sid James, Michael Barrymore (at Vidal Sassoon), Twiggy, Jayne Middlemiss, Delia Smith, Whoopi Goldberg, Tionne Watkins (shampooist), Richard Ashcroft (for just two days), Willy Russell

WHAT THEY ORIGINALLY INTENDED TO BE

Whitney Houston – vet

Alec Baldwin – lawyer

Rowan Atkinson – electrical engineer

Britt Ekland – vet

Paul Theroux – doctor

Eddie Izzard – accountant

Michael Palin – explorer

Jeremy Irons – vet

Gary Numan – airline pilot

Marilyn Monroe – schoolteacher

Dame Agatha Christie – professional musician

Lynn Redgrave – cook

Dennis Quaid – musician

George Lucas – racing driver

Pope John Paul II – actor

Patricia Routledge – headmistress

William H. Macy – vet

Bruce Dickinson – vet

Bruce Oldfield – teacher

Mel Gibson – chef

Angelina Jolie – funeral director

Charisma Carpenter – teacher

Julio Iglesias – lawyer

Tobey Maguire – chef

David Duchovny – a bathtub (he was six at the time)

Dustin Hoffman – concert pianist

Lisa Kudrow – doctor

Jennifer Lopez – hairstylist

J.C. Chasez – carpenter

Kathleen Quinlan – gymnastics teacher

Forest Whitaker – classical tenor

Lance Bass – astronaut (and passed the NASA exams)

Charlie Dimmock – forensic scientist

Morgan Freeman – fighter pilot

Liz McLarnon – lawyer

Janet Jackson – lawyer

Hannah Waterman – vet

Emma Bunton – a pony (she was a young child at the time)

Ricky Gervais – a vet (when he was seven) and a marine biologist (when he was ten)

Ethan Hawke – newsreader

Claudia Schiffer – lawyer

Eminem – comic-book artist

Colin Farrell – footballer

STARTED OUT AS SECRETARIES

Cilla Black, Anneka Rice, Caroline Aherne, Su Pollard, Sarah, Duchess of York, Ulrika Jonsson, Belinda Carlisle, Shania Twain, Anne Robinson, Betty Boothroyd, Catherine Keener, Joan Allen

TRAINED AS BALLET DANCERS

Victoria Principal

Leslie Caron

Clare Francis

Morgan Freeman

Charlize Theron

Caroline Quentin

Rachel de Thame

Jane Seymour (danced with the London Festival Ballet at the age of 13)

Mira Sorvino (performed in a professional production of *The Nutcracker* at the age of 12)

Penelope Cruz

Jennifer Ellison (Under-10 World Ballet Champion, Senior Champion at 14)

Sarah Jessica Parker (was with the Cincinnati Ballet and the American Ballet Theater)

WORKED AS SINGING TELEGRAMS

Sinéad O'Connor, Carol Smillie, Julian Clary, Chris Evans (Tarzan-o-gram), Virginia Madsen, Michaela Strachan, Keith Duffy

TRAINED TO BE DOCTORS BUT DIDN'T FINISH

Neil Diamond, Giorgio Armani, Lew Ayres (who went on to play Dr Kildare), Robert Dole, Wim Wenders, Christopher Isherwood, Roger Black, Robin Givens, Ralf Little, Dustin Hoffman, Bill Murray, William Roache

EX-POLICEMEN

Christopher Dean, Lord Jeffrey Archer, Dave Dee (and as such attended the scene of the crash in which Eddie Cochran died), Ray Reardon, Geoff Capes, John Arlott, Josef Locke, John Savident

PEOPLE WHO LIVED IN THEIR CARS

Brad Pitt

Chris Tarrant

Lenny Kravitz (a Ford Pinto)

Hilary Swank (with her mother when she was a kid)

Bob Hoskins (in a jeep after an expensive divorce)

GENUINE CAR BUMPER STICKERS

CAUTION: I drive just like you!

Don't Drink and Drive – you might spill some

This car is insured by the Mafia – you hit me, they hit you

Be careful – 90 percent of people are caused by accidents

Sorry, I don't date outside my species

Rehab is for Quitters

Not all dumbs are blonde

I took an IQ test and the results were negative

I don't brake for pedestrians

If you lived in your car, you'd be home by now

Honk if you've been married to Elizabeth Taylor

If you think I'm a lousy driver, you should see me putt

Learn from your parents' mistakes – use birth control

Of course I'm drunk – what do you think I am, a stunt driver?

Eat Well, Stay Fit, Die Anyway

YOU! Out of the gene pool!

You can't drink all day long if you don't start first thing in the morning

If you don't like the way I drive, get off the pavement

How many roads must a man travel down before he admits he is lost?

My wife's other car is a broom

I'm not a complete idiot – some parts are missing

He who laughs last thinks slowest

Ex-Saudi Arabian shoplifter – no hand signals

Instant asshole, just add alcohol

Beer isn't just for breakfast

PERSONALIZED CAR NUMBER PLATES

COM 1C (Jimmy Tarbuck)

1 PRO (Ray Reardon)

HRH 1 (The Queen)

777 SM (Sir Stirling Moss)

1 CUE (Jimmy White)

K7 (Duke of Kent)

OFF 1A (Martin Offiah)

8 DEB (Paul and Debbie Daniels)

P17 TSY and PAT 5Y (Patsy Palmer)

RH 666 (Robert Hardy)

EH 1 (Engelbert Humperdinck)

BOX 1T (Barry McGuigan)

MOVE 1T (Sir Cliff Richard)

MCP 1 (Martin Pipe)

CSM 43 (Colin Montgomerie)

1 MB (Max Bygraves)

BJM LAF1 (Bernard Manning)

KD 11 (Ken Dodd)

D1 SCOX (Judge Jules)

D1 DDY (David Hamilton)

NW 1 (Sir Norman Wisdom)

M1 BAD (Roy Keane)

AL 9 (Alan Shearer)

COLE 5 (Andy Cole)

K8 YER (Kieron Dyer)

PN 2000 (Phil Neville)

L11 BOW (Lee Bowyer)

H6 WELL (Harry Kewell)

QUALIFIED PILOTS

John Travolta, Nicholas Lyndhurst, Greg Norman, The Prince of Wales, Niki Lauda, Kurt Russell, Gary Numan, Kris Kristofferson, Gore Vidal (got his licence at the age of 10), B.B. King, Treat Williams, Tom Cruise, Luke Goss, John Grisham

TOILETS

Sir John Harington (1561–1612) invented the toilet for Queen Elizabeth I after she'd banned him from her court for circulating smutty stories. So she allowed him to return. Sir John's toilet did the job – up to a point – but there were unpleasant side effects.

The reason so many houses bear the legend 'Queen Elizabeth I stayed here' is because she used to move on every time the stench became too much to bear.

The Victorian plumber, Thomas Crapper, perfected the system we all know and use: the siphon flush which, by drawing water uphill through a sealed cistern, is both effective and hygienic. Crapper was born in the village of Thorne: an anagram of throne. He also invented (and patented) the stair tread.

TALKING TOILETS

In British English and its sister Englishes, we have a huge number of synonyms for the toilet, such as bathroom, biffy, bog, can, chamber of commerce, cloakroom, comfort station, convenience, cottage (public toilet), crapper (after dear Thos.), donicker, dunny (originally Australian), gents', the geography (American euphemism, as in 'Can you show me the *geography* of the house?'), head (nautical), jakes, john, johnny, karzy, ladies', latrine, lavatory (which is, strictly speaking, a vessel for washing), little boys'/girls' room, loo, men's/women's room, personal hygiene station, powder-room, privy (an outdoor toilet), rest-room, sanctum sanctorum, shot-tower, smallest room, throne, washroom and WC (water closet).

TOILET FACTS

The most impossible item to flush is a ping-pong ball

In a survey, it was discovered that 91 percent of 30,000 British women surveyed won't sit down properly on public toilets but instead adopt a semi-sitting, squatting position

Psycho was the first Hollywood film that showed a toilet flushing – thereby generating many complaints

The first toilet air-freshener was a pomegranate stuffed with cloves

The idea of separate cubicles for toilets is a relatively modern invention; the Romans, for example, sat down together in large groups

In Victorian times, loo seats were always made of wood: the well-to-do sat on mahogany or walnut while the poor put up with untreated white pine

The Victorians gave their loos names such as Cascade, Optimus, Alerto, Pluvius, Deluge, Tornado, Aquarius, Niagara, Planetas and the Subito

The town council of Cheltenham Spa once voted to replace the words 'Men' and 'Women' on their public toilets with 'Ladies' and 'Gentlemen' in order 'to attract a better class of person'

In the Middle Ages, 'waste' from public latrines ran directly into the river or the sea

ROYALS ON THE THRONE

In 1988, Australian officials built a special toilet for the Queen at a cost of £35,000. Then they decided to build a second – at the same cost – in case Prince Philip needed to go at the same time. Neither toilet was used.

Prince Charles insists on having his own wooden toilet seat installed wherever he's going.

Just before the Queen opened the Westminster and Chelsea hospital of which she was to be patron, officials realized that the hospital's initials would be WC and quickly changed the name to Chelsea and Westminster.

When Queen Victoria visited Trinity College Cambridge, she looked down at the River Cam, which was basically an open sewer, and seeing the toilet paper asked Dr Whewell, the Master of Trinity, what were all those pieces of paper floating down the river. The Master replied, 'Those, ma'am, are notices that bathing is forbidden.'

The death of Queen Victoria's beloved Albert was as a direct result of poor sanitation – he died of typhoid in 1861 (in 1870, one in every 3,000 people in Britain died of typhoid).

King Edward VII bought a 'WC enclosure in the form of an attractive armchair upholstered in velvet' for his mistress, the actress Lily Langtry.

TOILETS AROUND THE WORLD

In a 1992 survey by Andrex Moist Toilet Tissue, British public toilets were voted among the worst in the world, just ahead of those in Thailand, Greece and France.

The Japanese have invented the Shower Toilet. Originally designed for invalids, it boasts a self-raising seat cover, a bidet, water jets, a heated seat, a hot-air dryer and a fan for the removal of smells, all operated with an infra-red control. The Japanese have also built toilets that resemble coffee shops, churches and space stations, one that speaks your weight, and one that is a bicycle.

In 1993, Juan Bernaus was sentenced to three years' jail in Argentina for switching the 'Ladies' and 'Gents' signs round on public toilets.

An American jeweller has built the world's most expensive toilet, made of gold, diamonds, rubies and emeralds, with a mink seat – it costs $175,000.

TOILET PAPER

Before the invention of toilet paper, people used shells or stones, bunches of herbs, or at best a bit of sponge attached to a stick which they rinsed with cold water.

The Victorians were so delicate they couldn't bring themselves to use the words 'toilet paper'; instead they said 'curl papers'.

In 1986, Nathan Hicks of St Louis, Missouri shot his brother Herbert dead because he used six toilet rolls in two days.

The French use less toilet paper (8½lb per person per year) than any other European people; the Swedes use the most (18½lb), while the British are sixth in the European loo roll table with 10lb. In total we use nearly 1.5 billion loo rolls, more than 200,000 tons a year.

American civil servants' pay checks are recycled to make toilet rolls.

Hermann Goering refused to use regulation toilet paper and used to bulk-buy soft white handkerchiefs instead.

American researchers spent $100,000 on making the discovery that three out of four people hang their toilet rolls so that the paper is pulled down to be torn off rather than up.

The world's oldest piece of toilet paper – thought to be 1,200 years old – was found buried under an Israeli garage.

An American toilet manufacturer in California has created loo rolls made from hay. It is not known whether this is the same Californian company that in 1992 started selling 'camouflage' toilet paper for hunters to use so that fellow hunters don't mistake them for whitetailed deer.

CELEBRITIES AND TOILETS

Judy Garland and Lenny Bruce both died on the loo; King George II died after falling off a loo.

In 1993, Barbra Streisand got stuck in a toilet at Liza Minnelli's apartment during a party; fellow guests Jack Nicholson and Michael Douglas couldn't break down the door and so the building's porter had to come up to release her.

Actor George Hamilton was once trapped in the toilet of a restaurant, but he was rescued after a few minutes.

Jack Nicholson has a dead rattlesnake embedded in the clear plastic seat of his toilet.

While Gerald Ronson was at Ford Prison, he had to clean toilets, a job also once performed by the singer Tasmin Archer (at a recording studio) before she became famous. By contrast, the late Little 'The Loco-Motion' Eva found herself cleaning toilets in police stations *after* her days of fame.

Sir Winston Churchill did not believe in using toilet seats. He had them for his guests but when his plumber asked him what sort of seat he would have on his own loo, he responded, 'I have no need of such things.'

In 1994, Chuck Berry was obliged to pay £550,000 to sixty women he had filmed using the toilets in his restaurants.

Marti Pellow, the lead singer of Wet Wet Wet, was born in a public toilet in Clydebank.

People who have been pestered for autographs in toilets

Joan Collins stopped giving autographs after someone slid a piece of paper under a loo door and asked her to sign it.

Minnie Driver was also asked to give an autograph after someone slid a piece of paper under a loo door but merely said, 'Could we do this outside?'

Andrea Corr was asked for an autograph while she was throwing up. 'I couldn't believe it. I told her it might be a good idea if I washed my hands first.'

Julia Roberts was asked for an autograph while she was on the loo. She said, 'I'm the tiniest bit busy.'

Pierce Brosnan was asked while using a urinal. He obliged but: 'I refused the guy's request to say "shaken not stirred".'

Toilet quotes

'You must know that it is by the state of the lavatory that a family is judged' (Pope John XXIII)

'The biggest waste of water in the country by far. You spend half a pint and flush two gallons' (Prince Philip in a 1965 speech)

'Everything a man brings to his marriage is consigned to the downstairs loo' (Kelly Hoppen, an interior designer)

PEOPLE AND THE NAMES THEY GAVE THEIR PETS

Renée Zellweger: a dog (collie/retriever) named Woofer

Britney Spears: two Yorkshire terriers named Mitzy and Baby, a Rottweiler named Cane and a poodle named Lady

Jessica Simpson: a pig named Brutus

Cameron Diaz: a cat named The Little Man

Paul O'Grady: a dog (golden retriever) named Bruno

Natalie Imbruglia: a dog (King Charles spaniel) named Charlie

Ozzy Osbourne: dogs named Baldrick (a bulldog), Sugar, Sonny, Raider, Duster and Phoebe

Samantha Mumba: a dog (shih-tzu) named Foxy

Sarah Michelle Gellar: a dog (Maltese terrier) named Thor

Natalie Appleton: a dog (chihuahua) named Chiquita

Nicole Appleton: a dog (chihuahua) named Godzilla

Drew Barrymore: a dog named Flossie (once saved Drew's life by waking her in a house fire)

Sara Cox: a dog (basset hound) named Snoop (after Snoop Dogg)

Daniel Radcliffe: dogs (border collies) named Binka and Nugget

Tara Palmer-Tomkinson: a dog (Burmese mountain dog) named Wolfgang

Derren Brown: a parrot named Figaro

Courtney Love: a dog named Bob Dylan

Melissa Joan Hart: a duck named Flipper and dogs named Holly Ochola and Permani Pele

Axl Rose: a dog named Sumner (Sting's surname at birth)

Julia Roberts: a dog named Gatsby

Anna Carteret: a cat named Michael Jackson

Matt LeBlanc: a dog (Dobermann) named Shadow

Isabella Rossellini: a dog (dachshund) named Ferdinando

William Shatner: a dog (Dobermann pinscher) named Kirk

Uma Thurman: a dog (chow chow) named Muffy

Steve Martin: a cat named Dr Carlton B. Forbes

David Baddiel: a cat named Chairman Meow

Victoria and David Beckham: dogs (Rottweilers) named Puffy and Snoopy

Jennifer Jason Leigh: dogs named Bessie and Otis

Kirsten Dunst: cats named Inky, Taz and Zorro

Hilary Swank: dogs named Lucky and Tanner, a rabbit named Luna, a parrot named Seuss and a cat named Deuce

Brendan Fraser: a dog (chihuahua) named Lucy

Ralph Lauren: a dog (bearded collie) named Rugby

Valentino: dogs (pugs) named Molly and Maggie

Domenico Dolce and Stefano Gabbana: dogs (yellow Labradors) named Lola and Dali

Giorgio Armani: cats – a Blue Russian named Uli and three Persians: Nerone, Micia and Charlie

A.J. McLean: dogs (Yorkshire terriers) named Vegas and Jack Daniels

Dame Elizabeth Taylor: parrots named Dick and Liz

Leonardo DiCaprio: a dog (poodle) named Rufus

Jim Carrey: a dog (Labrador) named Hazel (who gets a professional massage three times a week and lives in a $20,000 three-room dog house, complete with plush sofa)

George Michael: a dog (Labrador) named Hippy

Robbie Williams: a cat named Our Lady Kid

Madonna: a dog named Pepito

Geri Halliwell: a dog (shih-tzu) named Harry

Adam Sandler has a bulldog named Meatball

FEARS & PHOBIAS

Flying Dennis Bergkamp, Whitney Houston, Aaron Spelling, The Dalai Lama, Lenny Kravitz, Mike Oldfield, Lesley Joseph, Bret Easton Ellis, Bob Newhart, Muhammad Ali, Joanne Woodward, Sam Shepard, Billy Bob Thornton, Whoopi Goldberg, Cher, Glenda Jackson, Aretha Franklin, Emily Mortimer, Sharleen Spiteri, Dina Carroll, John Peel, Justin Timberlake, Joaquin Phoenix, Patsy Palmer

Germs &/or Dirt Michael Jackson, Howard Hughes, Marlene Dietrich, Prince

Clowns Billy Bob Thornton, Puff Daddy/P. Diddy, Johnny Depp

The Dark Nancy Dell'Olio, Melinda Messenger, Christina Aguilera, Joan Collins, Baroness Margaret Thatcher, Stephen King, Melanie Sykes, Tracey Emin

Heights Prince, Tara Fitzgerald, Vic Reeves, Martin Clunes, Ann Widdecombe, Will Young

Snakes Sarah, Duchess of York, Madeleine Albright, Isla Blair, Ross Kemp, Stephen King

Needles &/or Injections Martine McCutcheon, Angela Griffin

Earthquakes Kevin Bacon, George Clooney

Cats Julius Caesar, Napoleon, King Henry II

Spiders Leo McKern, Stephen King, Claudia Winkleman

OTHER PEOPLE AND THEIR FEARS & PHOBIAS

Lee Evans (the colour green – he once freaked out when he was made to wear a green suit)

Rachel Weisz (frogs – she's been known to go without a bath rather than evict amphibian intruders from her ground-floor bathroom)

The Dalai Lama (caterpillars)

Billy Bob Thornton (antiques)

Kate Beckinsale (metaphobia – fear of throwing up)

Christina Ricci (gerbils)

Matthew McConaughey (tunnels and revolving doors)

Queen Christina of Sweden (fleas)

Ernest Hemingway (telephones – because of his fear of the American income tax office)

Sigmund Freud (train travel)

Caroline Quentin (rats)

Queen Elizabeth I (roses)

Princess Margaret (dolls)

Madonna (thunder)

Judy Garland (horses)

Sir Alfred Hitchcock (policemen – he refused to learn to drive for fear of being stopped by a policeman)

Graham Greene (blood and bats)

Robert Mitchum (crowds)

Sid Caesar (haircuts)

Robert De Niro (dentists)

Natalie Wood (water – she was to die by drowning)

Nicholas Lyndhurst (tall buildings)

Leslie Grantham (moths)

FAMOUS PEOPLE WHO BOUGHT HOUSES THAT HAD BELONGED TO OTHER FAMOUS PEOPLE

Brian Jones bought A.A. Milne's house, Cotchford Farm in Hartfield, West Sussex

Pete Townshend bought Alfred, Lord Tennyson's house in Twickenham

Pete Townshend also bought Ronnie Wood's house, the Wick in Richmond, Surrey (which he'd bought from John Mills)

Lord Jeffrey Archer bought Rupert Brooke's house, the Old Rectory in Grantchester, Cambridgeshire

Nick Mason bought Camilla Parker-Bowles's house in Corsham, Wiltshire

Engelbert Humperdinck bought Jayne Mansfield's house in Beverly Hills, California

Burt Reynolds bought Al Capone's ranch in Florida

Jacqueline Bisset bought Clark Gable and Carole Lombard's house in Benedict Canyon, California

Martin Clunes bought Field Marshal Montgomery's home, the Old Rectory in Beaminster, Dorset

Noah Wyle bought Bo Derek's ranch (for £1.6 million) in Santa Barbara, California

Robert Kilroy-Silk bought Ozzy Osbourne's house in Little Chalfont, Buckinghamshire

Paul O'Grady (aka Lily Savage) bought Vic Reeves's house in Aldington, Kent, which had once been owned by Sir Noël Coward

Davinia Murphy bought Noel Gallagher's house – Supernova Heights – in North London

Jerry Seinfeld bought Billy Joel's 30-acre Long Island beachfront estate in 2000 – the only problem was there was a covenant on the property banning 'Jews or showbusiness types'. Seinfeld, like Joel, fits both categories so he did the same thing that Joel did and bought it through a corporation

John Cleese bought Bryan Ferry's Holland Park, London house in 1977 (for £80,000); he sold it in 2001 for £5 million

Madonna bought Diane Keaton's Beverly Hills home for £4.4 million

Earl Spencer bought David Gilmour's West London house for £4.5 million

Vic Reeves bought Tom Baker's house near Maidstone in Kent

PEOPLE AND THE INSTRUMENTS THEY CAN PLAY

Piano Dustin Hoffman, Sir Anthony Hopkins, Clint Eastwood, Richard Gere, Rupert Everett

Clarinet Woody Allen, Ricki Lake (also flute, piano and piccolo)

Banjo George Segal, Ewan McGregor (can also play the French horn)

Guitar Renée Zellweger, Serena Williams, Michael Ancram, Tony Blair, Gary Sinise (bass)

Saxophone Bill Clinton, James Gandolfini (also plays the trumpet), Darius Danesh

Cello Prince Charles, Emily Watson

Tuba John Malkovich

Accordion Gabriel Byrne

Mandolin Nicolas Cage – for his role in *Captain Corelli's Mandolin*

Violin Russell Crowe – for his role in *Master And Commander*

PEOPLE WHO EXPERIENCED BAD STAGE FRIGHT

Sir Derek Jacobi avoided the theatre for two years after drying as Hamlet in 1980.

Lord Laurence Olivier went through a bout of terrible stage fright when he was running the National Theatre and playing Othello. Olivier said, 'All I could see were the exit signs and all I wanted to do was run off the stage each night towards them.'

Freddie Starr became addicted to Valium because of his stage fright.

The first time the Irish singer Enya appeared on stage she took fright, fled and had to be coaxed back by a psychologist.

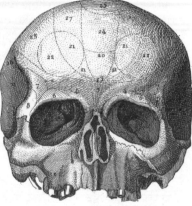

John Sessions fled the stage during a performance of *My Night With Reg* in 1995 because of stage fright, but he returned.

Barry Humphries suffers from stage fright 'every night' and has 'to overcome a tremendous reluctance to get on stage'.

Tim Roth started out as a stage actor on the fringe. Now he sticks to films because his stage fright leads him to having 'nightmares' about the theatre.

Marvin Gaye had such bad stage fright that he once tried to escape by climbing out of his dressing room.

Stephen Fry suffered such bad stage fright in *Cell Mates* (as well as other problems) that he left the country.

Dawn French was sick every night when she starred in *Then Again* in the West End. 'Every night I go on I'm knocking a couple of weeks off my life because of the stress.'

Barbra Streisand returned to the stage after stage fright put her off. On her return she said, 'It has taken me 2,700 hours and $360,000 worth of psychotherapy to be able to sing.' Streisand puts her stage fright partly down to a PLO death threat in 1967, which caused her to forget her lines on stage.

Elvis Presley's hip-wiggling started out as stage fright. According to Carl Perkins, 'Elvis was so nervous his legs would shake. One day he did it and the crowd went wild. He asked guitarist Scotty Moore, "What'd I do?" and Moore replied, "I don't know but do it again."'

In 1999, Paul McGann found the experience of performing at the Bush Theatre in Shepherd's Bush, London, so intimate that he vowed never to appear on stage again.

Uma Thurman has avoided stage work since 1996 after bursting into tears in an off-Broadway show.

Vanessa Redgrave was struck with panic while appearing in *The Prime of Miss Jean Brodie* and didn't perform on stage for another six years.

Tea Leoni had such bad stage fright while recording the pilot for *The Naked Truth* that she threw up five times.

In 2001, Robbie Williams announced he was going to take time off because he was suffering from stress and stage fright.

Judy Garland tried hypnosis but found that Irish whiskey worked better.

THINGS THAT NEW WORKERS ARE ASKED TO FETCH

A tub of elbow grease, invisible nails, a pair of rubber scissors, a dozen sky-hooks, a left-handed monkey-wrench, a glass hammer, a long weight, a horizontal ladder, a right-handed mug, a tin of striped paint

KISSING

The first kiss was supposedly delivered by God. According to Genesis, God breathed the 'spirit of life' into Adam. This has come to be interpreted symbolically as a kiss, which is why so many religious ceremonies include kissing.

A study by a Canadian anthropologist demonstrated that 97 percent of women shut their eyes during a kiss but only 37 percent of men did. The late actor Anthony Quinn had an explanation: 'Many a husband kisses with his eyes wide open. He wants to make sure his wife is not around to catch him.' Chico Marx (of the Marx Brothers) would have agreed. Chico was an habitual philanderer. When his wife caught him French kissing a girlfriend, he replied, 'I wasn't kissing her, I was whispering in her mouth.'

Kissing on the lips is something the Romans started. A husband returning from work would kiss his wife's lips to see if she'd been boozing during the day. The Romans had three different types of kiss: *basium*, the kiss on the lips; *osculum*, a friendly kiss on the cheek, and *suavium*, the full monty. In fact, the Romans were so keen on kissing that the Emperor Tiberius was obliged to ban the practice after an epidemic of lip sores. Until the Romans invaded, the British had no word for 'kissing'.

The French Kiss itself – tongues and all – was invented in the Brittany village of Pays de Mont as a substitute for sex because the population was growing too fast.

Kissing got a bad press because of Judas Iscariot, who used the kiss as a sign of betrayal. In exchange for 30 pieces of silver, Judas identified Jesus to his enemies in the Garden of Gethsemane by kissing him. This is probably the earliest known example of kiss and tell.

In writing – particularly in greetings cards and in love letters – we use XXXXs to represent kisses. The origins of this go back to the days when people who couldn't write signed their name with an X. To emphasize their sincerity, they would then kiss their mark – in the same way that they would have kissed a Bible when swearing an oath on it. This practice of kissing the X led to the X representing a kiss. The Romans also sealed the signing of contracts with a kiss.

Kissing under the mistletoe at Christmas is an English tradition that has been exported to other countries. It started with the Kissing Bough, which had mistletoe at its centre. When the Christmas Tree replaced the Kissing Bough, the mistletoe was salvaged and given its own unique position in the Yuletide ritual.

Human beings are not the only mammals that kiss. Polar bears and kangaroos kiss. Chimpanzees can and do French kiss. Sealions rub mouths, a male mouse licks the mouth of a female mouse and an elephant sometimes brushes its trunk against another elephant's lips.

Everyone knows that Lord Nelson said, 'Kiss me, Hardy.' However, some revisionists have claimed that what he really said was 'Kismet, Hardy', i.e. 'fate'. In fact, Hardy (an ancestor of Stan Laurel's partner, Oliver) understood him to say 'Kiss me' and that is what he duly did. Nelson said, 'Now I am satisfied,' and died about twenty minutes later, thanking God that he'd done his duty.

The Anti-Kissing League was formed in 1909 in America by people who considered kissing unhealthy.

How and where you kiss used to be a sign of where you stood in the social 'pecking' order. Equals kissed each other on the cheek. The lower you ranked to another person, the lower you had to kiss them. Thus a slave would kiss his master's feet, and a prisoner – not allowed even that close – would be obliged to kiss the ground near the foot, i.e. kiss the dirt.

Rodin's _The Kiss_ is one of the world's most important pieces of sculpture. The figure – completed in 1886 – of two naked lovers kissing has not been entirely free from controversy. In the US in the last century, it was deemed to be too strong for the public and was exhibited in a special room.

The most kissed statue in the world is not The Kiss but a marble statue of Guidarello Guidarelli, a sixteenth-century Italian soldier. At the end of nineteenth century, a rumour went around that any woman who kissed the statue would marry a fabulous man. Some five million kisses later, Guidarello's mouth is significantly redder than the rest of him.

One person who regretted kissing a work of art was Ruth van Herpen, who in 1977 was obliged to pay the restoration costs of a painting she had kissed and blighted with her red lipstick. In court, she declared that she 'only kissed it to cheer it up: it looked so cold'.

Alice Johnson, a 23-year-old American waitress, won a car in Santa Fe after kissing it for 32 hours and 20 minutes in a 1994 competition. She loosened four teeth in the process.

An American insurance company discovered that men were less likely to have a car accident on the way to work if they were kissed before they set off.

If you are late, you are said to have 'kissed the hare's foot'. Glandular fever is referred to as 'the kissing disease' (because that is how it is easily spread among adolescents). In the US a person who has been sacked is said to have been given the 'kiss-off'. A sailor who in olden times 'kissed the gunner's daughter' had been tied to the breech of a cannon and flogged. A person vomiting is said to be 'kissing the porcelain bowl'.

As all internet surfers know, the acronym KISS stands for 'Keep It Simple, Stupid'.

In Sicily, members of the Mafia have stopped kissing each other because the way they kissed was a dead giveaway to the police and mobsters were getting arrested.

SCREEN KISSES

The first film kiss was in, appropriately enough, the 1896 movie *The Kiss*. The protagonists were John C. Rice and May Irwin.

The film with the most kisses is the 1926 *Don Juan*, in which John Barrymore performed 191 kisses with different women. This was before the 1930 Hays Code, which banned 'excessive and lustful kissing'.

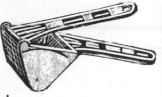

Greta Garbo didn't relish kissing scenes with Fredric March, her co-star in *Anna Karenina*, so she ate garlic before every such scene. Diana Rigg did the same before kissing George Lazenby in *On Her Majesty's Secret Service*. Julia Roberts hated kissing Nick Nolte while making *I Love Trouble*. At one point she sent a memo to the producer saying, 'If he puts his tongue in my mouth one more time I'm walking off the set.'

Nepal bans films featuring kisses by Nepalese actors. The same is true of Bangladesh and Macao.

The most famous kiss in a Hollywood film is probably that between Burt Lancaster and Deborah Kerr in *From Here To Eternity*.

The first genuine French kiss in a Hollywood movie was between Warren Beatty and Natalie Wood in the 1961 film *Splendor In The Grass*.

The first kiss in an Indian film didn't take place until the 1978 film *Love Sublime*, when Shashi Kapoor and Zeenat Aman embraced. An Indian minister described the kissing scenes as 'an insult' and called for a mass protest.

Bing Crosby – or so his co-stars claimed – had really bad breath, probably a result of his pipe-smoking. Clark Gable's bad breath wasn't improved by the whisky he regularly drank or the false teeth he wore, and Vivien Leigh hated having to kiss him in *Gone With The Wind*.

KISSING AROUND THE WORLD

Eskimos rub noses, as do a good many other peoples. Polynesians like a nose rub but also enjoy the *mitakuku*, which involves biting hairs from eyebrows. Trobriand islanders bite each other's eyelashes. In China, they touch each other's cheeks and then sniff. In the Pacific Islands, they inhale each other's breath. In Gambia, a man holds the back of a lover's hand against his nose. In Knightsbridge people put their cheeks a few inches apart from each other and say 'Mmmm'.

After World War Two, Americans were so keen to see the Japanese embrace the American way of life that during their occupation they ordered Japanese film makers to put kisses in their films. Some feat, in films that were invariably about Samurai warriors.

In Sorocaba, Brazil, they outlawed kissing in public places – specifically 'the cinematographic kiss, in which salivas mix to swell the sensuality'.

If you're in Scotland and are offered a 'Glasgow kiss', or in Liverpool a 'Kirby kiss', you'd better refuse unless you want a head butt.

Oliver Cromwell banned kissing on Sundays – even for married couples – on pain of a prison sentence.

In 1837, Thomas Saverland tried to kiss a woman who promptly bit off part of his nose. Saverland took her to court but lost, the judge commenting, 'When a man kisses a woman against her will, she is fully entitled to bite his nose, if she so pleases.'

In 1969, there was a mass kiss-in in the town of Inca on the island of Mallorca. Young lovers were being fined 500 pesetas for kissing in public, so a group of couples held a 'snogfest'. The police charged them and they were fined a total of 45,000 pesetas before being released.

KISSING AND HEALTH

The World Health Organization issued a warning against passionate kissing for World Aids Day 1991 – although current medical thinking is that you can't get AIDS from snogging.

Kissing is good for your teeth. According to dentists, kissing encourages saliva, which acts as a mouthwash that helps prevent tooth decay. However, a 1994 report by the German Dental Association claimed that French kissing could give you toothache on the basis that 'tongues can make holes in teeth'.

Kissing can prevent illness. When you absorb someone else's saliva, you also receive their enzymes, which gives you their immunities – a kind of antibiotic. Of course, kissing can pass on diseases too.

Kissing a frog doesn't necessarily get you a prince but it might get rid of your cold sore, thanks to a chemical secreted from frog skins.

A really tongue-twisting kissing session exercises 39 different facial muscles and can burn up 150 calories – more than a 15-minute swim. An ordinary peck uses up just three calories.

THINGS SAID ABOUT KISSING

'Yet each man kills the thing he loves … The coward does it with a kiss, the brave man with a sword!' (Oscar Wilde, *The Ballad of Reading Gaol*)

'What of soul was left, I wonder, when the kissing had to stop' (Robert Browning)

'You must remember this, a kiss is just a kiss' (Dooley Wilson in *Casablanca*)

'I think less is more when it comes to kissing in the movies' (Julia Roberts)

'Sweet Helen, make me immortal with a kiss' (Christopher Marlowe, *Dr Faustus*)

'People who throw kisses are hopelessly lazy' (Bob Hope)

**'I kiss'd thee ere I kill'd thee. No way but this –
Killing myself, to die upon a kiss' (Shakespeare, *Othello*)**

'Kissing don't last: cookery do!' (George Meredith)

'There is always one who kisses and one who only allows the kiss' (George Bernard Shaw)

THE GREATEST SCENE IN MOVIE HISTORY – OR JUST THE MOST IMITATED?

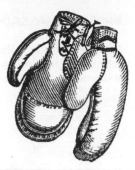

Excerpt from the back-of-the-cab dialogue between Marlon Brando and Rod Steiger in *On The Waterfront*

Charley Malloy (Rod Steiger) has been instructed by Johnny Friendly (Lee J. Cobb) to stop his brother Terry (Marlon Brando) from testifying against Friendly's crooked union activities. Charley tries everything – even threatening his brother with a gun – until, at this climactic point in the scene, he acknowledges his failure by saying wistfully …

CHARLEY: How much you weigh, slugger? When you weighed 168 pounds, you were beautiful. You could have been another Billy Conn. That skunk we got you for a manager, he brought you along too fast.

TERRY: It wasn't him, Charley, it was you. Remember that night in the Garden you came down to my dressing room and you said, 'Kid, this ain't your night. We're going for the price on Wilson.' You remember that? *This ain't your night.* My night! I coulda taken Wilson apart! So what happens? He gets the title shot outdoors in the ballpark and what do I get? A one way ticket to Palooka-ville. You was my brother, Charley, you shoulda looked out for me a little bit. You shoulda taken care of me just a little bit so I wouldn't have to take them dives for the short end money.

CHARLEY: I had some bets down for you. You saw some money.

TERRY: You don't understand! I coulda had class! I coulda been a contender. I coulda been somebody. Instead of a bum, which is what I am, let's face it. It was you, Charley.

Defeated, Charley lets Terry leave. Charley is executed by Johnny Friendly's henchmen. Terry takes on Friendly and, after an epic fight, wins.

UNICEF AMBASSADORS

Sir Roger Moore, Julio Iglesias, Emmanuelle Béart, Sir Edmund Hillary, Imran Khan, Liam Neeson, George Weah, Lord Richard Attenborough, Liv Ullmann, Sir Peter Ustinov, Jane Seymour, Robbie Williams, Zinedine Zidane, Susan Sarandon, Nana Mouskouri, Martin Bell, Michael Jackson, Samantha Mumba

FAMOUS PEOPLE AND THEIR ALLERGIES

Tom Cruise (cats)

Beyonce Knowles (perfume)

Dannii Minogue (wheat, dairy products and yeast)

Lisa Faulkner (cats)

Sandra Bullock (horses)

Tony Robinson (cats and feathers)

Roger Cook (cucumbers)

Steve Wright (feathers)

Gaby Roslin (wheat)

Honor Blackman (cats)

Beverley Callard (avocados)

Andi Peters (chocolate)

Sue Townsend (monosodium glutamate)

Clint Eastwood (horses)

Susan Hill (wasps)

Nick Hancock (cats and dogs)

Bill Clinton (flowers)

Richard E. Grant (alcohol)

Donald Sutherland (cigarette smoke)

Drew Barrymore (garlic and coffee)

Naomi Campbell (tuna)

Sharon Stone (caffeine)

Iggy Pop (milk)

Trisha Goddard (lactose)

CELEBRITIES AND WHO THEY CHOSE AS THEIR BEST MAN

GROOM	BEST MAN
Marco Pierre White	**Michael Winner**
Uri Geller (renewing vows)	**Michael Jackson**
Chris Evans	**Danny Baker**
Dennis Taylor	**Ian Woosnam**
David Bailey	**Mick Jagger**
Kenneth Clarke	**John Selwyn Gummer**
Jeremy Irons	**Christopher Biggins**
Bob Geldof	**Dave Stewart**
Kenneth Branagh	**Brian Blessed**
John McEnroe	**Björn Borg**
John Lennon	**Brian Epstein**
Viv Richards	**Ian Botham**
Tommy Steele	**Lionel Bart**
Jimmy Mulville	**Rory McGrath**
Martin Clunes	**Neil Morrissey**
David Seaman	**Bob Wilson**
Trevor Phillips	**Peter Mandelson**

BUNGEE JUMPERS

Davina McCall (over the Grand Canyon), Leonardo DiCaprio, Zara Phillips, Pat Rafter, Abs Breen, Andre Agassi, Ian Wright, Jeremy Guscott, Julian Lennon, Anna Walker, Chris Eubank, Debbie Harry, Jonathan Davies, Renny Harlin, Stuart Barnes, Joe McGann

VINEYARD OWNERS

Sir Cliff Richard, Mick Hucknall, Sir Peter Ustinov, Francis Coppola, Gerard Depardieu, Jean Tigana, Sir Chay Blyth, Michel Roux, Sam Neill, The Dalai Lama

ACTORS AND THE ROLES THEY TURNED DOWN

Vin Diesel turned down Ben Affleck's role in *Daredevil*

Debra Winger turned down Glenn Close's role in *Fatal Attraction*

Diane Lane turned down Renée Zellweger's role in *Chicago*

John Travolta turned down Richard Gere's role in *Chicago*

Kevin Costner turned down Matthew Broderick's role in *War Games* (he did it to appear in *The Big Chill* but his role in that was left on the cutting-room floor)

George Segal turned down Dudley Moore's role in *10*

Robert Redford turned down Dustin Hoffman's role in *The Graduate*

Lee Marvin turned down George C. Scott's role in *Patton*

Sylvester Stallone turned down Eddie Murphy's role in *Beverly Hills Cop*

George Raft turned down Humphrey Bogart's role in *The Maltese Falcon*

Marlon Brando turned down Robert Redford's role in *Butch Cassidy And The Sundance Kid*

Eddie Cantor turned down Al Jolson's role in *The Jazz Singer*

Henry Fonda turned down Peter Finch's role in *Network*

Elvis Presley turned down Kris Kristofferson's role in *A Star Is Born*

Julia Roberts turned down Sharon Stone's role in *Basic Instinct*

Robert De Niro turned down Willem Dafoe's role in *The Last Temptation of Christ*

Richard Gere turned down Bruce Willis's role in *Die Hard*

ALL THE BREEDS THAT HAVE BEEN BEST IN SHOW AT CRUFTS

2003: Pekingese

2002: Standard Poodle

2001: Basenji

2000: Kerry Blue Terrier

1999: Irish Setter

1998: Welsh Terrier

1997: Yorkshire Terrier

1996: Cocker Spaniel

1995: Irish Setter

1994: Welsh Terrier

1993: Irish Setter

1992: Whippet

1991: Clumber Spaniel

1990: West Highland White Terrier

1989: Bearded Collie

1988: English Setter

1987: Afghan Hound

1986: Airedale Terrier

1985: Standard Poodle

1984: Lhasa Apso

1983: Afghan Hound

1982: Toy Poodle

1981: Irish Setter

1980: Retriever (Flat Coated)

1979: Kerry Blue Terrier

1978: Wire Fox Terrier

1977: English Setter

1976: West Highland White Terrier

1975: Wire Fox Terrier

1974: St Bernard

1973: Cavalier King Charles Spaniel

1972: Bull Terrier

1971: German Shepherd

1970: Pyrenean Mountain

1969: Alsatian

1968: Dalmatian

1967: Lakeland Terrier

1966: Toy Poodle

1965: Alsatian

1964: English Setter

1963: Lakeland Terrier

1962: Wire Fox Terrier

1961: Airedale Terrier

1960: Irish Wolfhound

1959: Welsh Terrier

1958: Pointer

1957: Keeshond

1956: Greyhound

1955: Standard Poodle

1954: show cancelled

1953: Great Dane

1952: Bulldog

1951: Welsh Terrier

1950: Cocker Spaniel

1949: no show

1948: Cocker Spaniel

1940–1947: no shows

1939: Cocker Spaniel

1938: Cocker Spaniel

1937: Retriever (Labrador)

1936: Chow Chow

1935: Pointer

1934: Greyhound

1933: Retriever (Labrador)

1932: Retriever (Labrador)

1931: Cocker Spaniel

1930: Cocker Spaniel

1929: Scottish Terrier

1928: Greyhound

CRICKET – AS EXPLAINED TO A FOREIGNER

You have two sides, one out in the field and one in.

Each man that's in the side that's in goes out, and when he's out he comes in and the next man goes in until he's out.

When a man goes out to go in, the men who are out try to get him out, and when he is out he goes in and the next man in goes out and goes in.

When they are all out, the side that's out comes in and the side that's been in goes out and tries to get those coming in, out.

Sometimes, there are men still in and not out.

There are two men called umpires who stay all out all the time and they decide when the men who are in are out.

When both sides have been in and all the men are out (including those who are not out) then the game is finished.

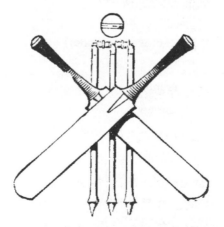

ALL THE HOLDERS OF THE MISS WORLD TITLE

2002: Azra Akin (Turkey)

2001: Agbani Darego (Nigeria)

2000: Priyanka Chopra (India)

1999: Yukta Mookhey (India)

1998: Linor Abargil (Israel)

1997: Diana Hayden (India)

1996: Irene Skliva (Greece)

1995: Jacqueline Aquilera (Venezuela)

1994: Aishwarya Rai (India)

1993: Lisa Hanna (Jamaica)

1992: Julia Kourotchkina (Russia)

1991: Ninibeth Jiminez (Venezuela)

1990: Gina Marie Tolleson (USA)

1989: Aneta Kreglicka (Poland)

1988: Linda Petursdottir (Iceland)

1987: Ulla Weigerstorfer (Austria)

1986: Giselle Laronde (Trinidad)

1985: Hofi Karlsdottir (Iceland)

1984: Astrid Herrera (Venezuela)

1983: Sarah-Jane Hutt (United Kingdom)

1982: Mariasela Lebron (Dominican Republic)

1981: Pilin Leon (Venezuela)

1980: Kimberley Santos (Guam – after Gabriella Brum of Germany resigned)

1979: Gina Swainson (Bermuda)

1978: Silvana Suarez (Argentina)

1977: Mary Stavin (Sweden)

1976: Cindy Breakspeare (Jamaica)

1975: Winelia Merced (Puerto Rico)

1974: Anneline Kriel (South Africa – after Helen Morgan of the United Kingdom resigned)

1973: Marjorie Wallace (USA)

1972: Belinda Green (Australia)

1971: Lucia Petterle (Brazil)

1970: Jennifer Hosten (Grenada)

1969: Eva Reuber Staier (Austria)

1968: Penelope Plummer (Australia)

1967: Madeleine Hartog Bell (Peru)

1966: Reita Faria (India)

1965: Lesley Langley (United Kingdom)

1964: Ann Sidney (United Kingdom)

1963: Carole Crawford (Jamaica)

1962: Catharina Lodders (Holland)

1961: Rosemarie Frankland (United Kingdom)

1960: Norma Cappagli (Argentina)

1959: Corine Rottschafer (Holland)

1958: Penelope Coelen (South Africa)

1957: Marita Lindahl (Finland)

1956: Petra Schurmann (Germany)

1955: Carmen Zubillaga (Venezuela)

1954: Antigone Costanda (Egypt)

1953: Denise Perrier (France)

1952: May Louise Flodin (Sweden)

1951: Kiki Haakonson (Sweden)

ALL THE CLUBS THAT HAVE LEFT THE FOOTBALL LEAGUE (WITHOUT BEING READMITTED)

Aberdare Athletic (1927)

Accrington Stanley (1962)

Aldershot (1992)

Ashington (1929)

Barnet (2001)

Barrow (1972)

Bootle (1893)

Bradford Park Avenue (1970)

Burton United (1907)

Chester City (2000)

Darwen (1899)

Durham City (1928)

Exeter City (2003)

Gainsborough Trinity (1912)

Gateshead (1960)

Glossop (1915)

Halifax Town (2002)

Hereford United (1997)

Leeds City (1919)

Loughborough (1900)

Maidstone United (1992)

Merthyr Town (1930)

Middlesbrough Ironopolis (1894)

Nelson (1931)

New Brighton (1951)

New Brighton Tower (1901)

Newport County (1988)

Northwich Victoria (1894)

Scarborough (1999)

Shrewsbury Town (2003)

Stalybridge Celtic (1923)

Thames (1932)

Wigan Borough (1931)

Workington (1977)

ALL THE WINNERS OF FIFA WORLD PLAYER OF THE YEAR

2002: Ronaldo

2001: Luis Figo

2000: Zinedine Zidane

1999: Rivaldo

1998: Zinedine Zidane

1997: Ronaldo

1996: Ronaldo

1995: George Weah

1994: Romario

1993: Roberto Baggio

1992: Marco Van Basten

1991: Lothar Matthaus

ALL THE FOOTBALL WRITERS' ASSOCIATION'S WINNERS OF FOOTBALLER OF THE YEAR

2003: Thierry Henry (Arsenal)

2002: Robert Pires (Arsenal)

2001: Teddy Sheringham (Manchester United)

2000: Roy Keane (Manchester United)

1999: David Ginola (Tottenham Hotspur)

1998: Dennis Bergkamp (Arsenal)

1997: Gianfranco Zola (Chelsea)

1996: Eric Cantona (Manchester United)

1995: Jürgen Klinsmann (Tottenham Hotspur)

1994: Alan Shearer (Blackburn Rovers)

1993: Chris Waddle (Sheffield Wednesday)

1992: Gary Lineker (Tottenham Hotspur)

1991: Gordon Strachan (Leeds United)

1990: John Barnes (Liverpool)

1989: Steve Nicol (Liverpool)

1988: John Barnes (Liverpool)

1987: Clive Allen (Tottenham Hotspur)

1986: Gary Lineker (Everton)

1985: Neville Southall (Everton)

1984: Ian Rush (Liverpool)

1983: Kenny Dalglish (Liverpool)

1982: Steve Perryman (Tottenham Hotspur)

1981: Frans Thijssen (Ipswich Town)

1980: Terry McDermott (Liverpool)

1979: Kenny Dalglish (Liverpool)

1978: Kenny Burns (Nottingham Forest)

1977: Emlyn Hughes (Liverpool)

1976: Kevin Keegan (Liverpool)

1975: Alan Mullery (Fulham)

1974: Ian Callaghan (Liverpool)

1973: Pat Jennings (Tottenham Hotspur)

1972: Gordon Banks (Stoke City)

1971: Frank McLintock (Arsenal)

1970: Billy Bremner (Leeds United)

1969: Tony Book (Manchester City) and
Dave Mackay (Derby County)

1968: George Best (Manchester United)

1967: Jack Charlton (Leeds United)

1966: Sir Bobby Charlton (Manchester United)

1965: Bobby Collins (Leeds United)

1964: Bobby Moore (West Ham United)

1963: Sir Stanley Matthews (Stoke City)

1962: Jimmy Adamson (Burnley)

1961: Danny Blanchflower (Tottenham Hotspur)

1960: Bill Slater (Wolverhampton Wanderers)

1959: Syd Owen (Luton Town)

1958: Danny Blanchflower (Tottenham Hotspur)

1957: Sir Tom Finney (Preston North End)

1956: Bert Trautmann (Manchester City)

1955: Don Revie (Manchester City)

1954: Sir Tom Finney (Preston North End)

1953: Nat Lofthouse (Bolton Wanderers)

1952: Billy Wright (Wolverhampton Wanderers)

1951: Harry Johnston (Blackpool)

1950: Joe Mercer (Arsenal)

1949: Johnny Carey (Manchester United)

1948: Sir Stanley Matthews (Blackpool)

ALL THE PROFESSIONAL FOOTBALLERS' ASSOCIATION'S WINNERS OF FOOTBALLER OF THE YEAR

2003: Thierry Henry (Arsenal)

2002: Ruud van Nistelrooy (Manchester United)

2001: Teddy Sheringham (Manchester United)

2000: Roy Keane (Manchester United)

1999: David Ginola (Tottenham Hotspur)

1998: Dennis Bergkamp (Arsenal)

1997: Alan Shearer (Newcastle United)

1996: Les Ferdinand (Newcastle United)

1995: Alan Shearer (Blackburn Rovers)

1994: Eric Cantona (Manchester United)

1993: Paul McGrath (Aston Villa)

1992: Gary Pallister (Manchester United)

1991: Mark Hughes (Manchester United)

1990: David Platt (Aston Villa)

1989: Mark Hughes (Manchester United)

1988: John Barnes (Liverpool)

1987: Clive Allen (Tottenham Hotspur)

1986: Gary Lineker (Everton)

1985: Peter Reid (Everton)

1984: Ian Rush (Liverpool)

1983: Kenny Dalglish (Liverpool)

1982: Kevin Keegan (Southampton)

1981: John Wark (Ipswich Town)

1980: Terry McDermott (Liverpool)

1979: Liam Brady (Arsenal)

1978: Peter Shilton (Nottingham Forest)

1977: Andy Gray (Aston Villa)

1976: Pat Jennings (Tottenham Hotspur)

1975: Colin Todd (Derby County)

1974: Norman Hunter (Leeds United)

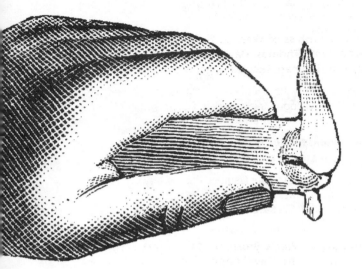

PEOPLE WHO HAVE BEEN IMMORTALIZED IN WAX AT MADAME TUSSAUD'S SINCE 1990

2003: Madonna (new model), Tara Palmer-Tomkinson, Jennifer Lopez, Julia Roberts, Brad Pitt (new model), The Hulk, Simon Cowell, Britney Spears, Justin Timberlake

2002: David Beckham, Sven Goran Eriksson, Kylie Minogue (new model), The Queen (new model), Geri Halliwell, Ant & Dec, Sarah Michelle Gellar

2001: Jerry Springer, Chris Tarrant, Alan Titchmarsh, George W. Bush, Gerhard Schroeder, Jackie Chan, Elle Macpherson, Susan Sarandon, Vladimir Putin, Penelope Cruz, Graham Norton, Tony Blair (new model), Ken Livingstone (new model)

2000: Barbara Windsor, Jane Horrocks, Patrick Stewart, Whoopi Goldberg, Samuel L. Jackson, Morgan Freeman, Jiang Zemin, Billy Connolly, Amitabh Bachchan, Charles Kennedy

1999: Sophie, Countess of Wessex, Fidel Castro, Jonah Lomu, Shane Warne, Iwan Thomas, David Jason, Dame Shirley Bassey, Tom Jones, Tim Henman, Nicolas Cage, Robert Carlyle

1998: Sir Sean Connery, Baroness Betty Boothroyd, Martina Hingis, Gary Lineker, Kylie Minogue (new model), Prince Andrew (new model)

1997: Oscar Wilde, Mary, Queen of Scots, Darcey Bussell, Brad Pitt, Pele, Jesse Owens, William Hague

1996: Jacques Santer, Jean-Paul Gaultier, Eric Cantona, Naomi Campbell, Jacques Chirac, King Baudouin of Belgium, Helen Sharman, Jayne Torvill, Christopher Dean, Olga Korbut, Daley Thompson

1995: Ayrton Senna, Pierce Brosnan, Mel Gibson, Jürgen Klinsmann, Hugh Grant, David Copperfield, Terry Venables, Linford Christie, Brian Lara, Tony Blair, Stephen Hawking, Oprah Winfrey, Henry Moore

1994: Chris Evans, Joanna Lumley, Paul Keating, Mary Robinson, Keith Floyd, Kenneth Clarke

1993: Bill Clinton, Boris Yoltsin, Sir Anthony Hopkins, John Smith, Saddam Hussein, Nigel Mansell, Gerard Depardieu, The Dalai Lama, Yitzhak Rabin, Harrison Ford

1992: Sir David Attenborough, Sir Patrick Moore, Nigel Kennedy, François Mitterrand, George Bush, F.W. de Klerk, Will Carling, Arnold Schwarzenegger, Madonna

1991: Paul Gascoigne, John Major, Nelson Mandela, Nick Faldo, Neil Kinnock, Paddy Ashdown, Dr George Carey

1990: Luciano Pavarotti, Jane Seymour, Dudley Moore, Sir Jimmy Savile, Yasser Arafat, Phillip Schofield

PEOPLE WHOSE WAXWORKS HAVE BEEN REMOVED FROM MADAME TUSSAUD'S SINCE 1990

Note: The waxworks are not melted down and so they can be put back into the exhibition if the person concerned is in the news again or if there is a one-off special display of a category – say, former prime ministers – which includes them

2003: Eric Cantona, Frank Bruno, Shane Warne, John Major, Robert Carlyle

2002: King Juan Carlos, Sir David Attenborough, Mikhail Gorbachev, Boris Yeltsin, Ian Botham, Jacques Santer, George Bush, F.W. de Klerk, King Baudouin of Belgium, Linford Christie, Nick Faldo, Jiang Zemin, Baroness Betty Boothroyd, Jürgen Klinsmann, David Copperfield, Brian Lara, Henry Moore, Neil Kinnock

2001: Paul Gascoigne, Jonah Lomu, Chris Evans, Mary Robinson, Dudley Moore, Keith Floyd, Iwan Thomas, Martina Hingis, Jayne Torvill, Christopher Dean, Nigel Mansell, Olga Korbut, Daley Thompson, Pele, William Hague

2000: Will Carling, Bob Hoskins, Nigel Kennedy, Paddy Ashdown

1999: Phillip Schofield, Michael Crawford, Sir Jimmy Savile

1998: Paul Hogan, Boris Becker

1997: Steve Davis, Anneka Rice

1996: Sarah, Duchess of York, Arthur Scargill, Brian Mulroney, François Mitterrand, Paul Keating

1995: Peter Shilton

1994: Michael Foot, Terry Wogan, Roy Hattersley, Bob Hawke, Lord Carrington, John Smith

1993: Charles Dance, Jane Seymour

1992: Lord Geoffrey Howe, Lord Nigel Lawson, Sir Robert Menzies, Nastassja Kinski, Lord Michael Heseltine, Lord Norman Tebbit

1991: Lord David Owen

1990: Benny Hill, Fatima Whitbread, John McEnroe

ALL THE BRITISH NEW TOWNS SINCE WORLD WAR TWO – AND WHEN THEY WERE NEW

Stevenage (1946)

Crawley (1947)

East Kilbride (1947)

Harlow (1947)

Hemel Hempstead (1947)

Newton Aycliffe (1947)

Glenrothes (1948)

Hatfield (1948)

Peterlee (1948)

Welwyn Garden City (1948)

Basildon (1949)

Bracknell (1949)

Cwmbran (1949)

Corby (1950)

Cumbernauld (1955)

Skelmersdale (1961)

Livingston (1962)

Redditch (1964)

Runcorn (1964)

Washington (1964)

Irvine (1966)

Milton Keynes (1967)

Newtown (1967)

Peterborough (1967)

Northampton (1968)

Telford (1968: known as Dawley from 1963 to 1968)

Warrington (1968)

Central Lancashire (1970 – based on Preston and Leyland)

Stonehouse (1973 – scrapped in 1976)

DISHES FROM AROUND THE WORLD

Pig's Organs In Blood Sauce (Philippines)

Baked Bat (Samoa)

Crispy Roasted Termites (Swaziland)

Roast Field Mice (Mexico)

Weaver Moths In Their Nests (Zaire)

Parrot Pie (actually twelve budgerigars) (Australia)

Bee Grubs In Coconut Cream (Thailand)

Guinea Pig In A Creole Style (Peru)

Queen White Ants (South Africa)

Calf Udder Croquettes (France)

Coconut Cream-marinated Dog (Indonesia)

Mice In Cream (Arctic)

Starling Stew With Olives (Turkey)

Stewed Cane Rat (Ghana)

Water Beetle Cocktail Sauce (Laos)

Turtle Ragout (Mexico)

Stuffed Bear's Paw (Romania)

Red Ant Chutney (India)

Baked Muskrat (Canada)

Raw Octopus (Hawaii)

Calf's Lung And Heart In A Paprika Sauce (Hungary)

Fox Tongues (Japan)

Pig's Face (Ireland)

Silkworm Pupae Soup (Vietnam)

Cajun Squirrel Ravioli (US)

Turtle Casserole (Fiji)

Lambs' Tails And Honey (Morocco)

Sun-dried Maggots (China)

PALLBEARERS FOR FAMOUS PEOPLE

Phil Everly, for Buddy Holly

Donald Dewar, for John Smith

Ben Crenshaw, for Harvey Penick

Jack Lemmon, for Rosalind Russell

John McEnroe, for Vitas Gerulaitis

Emerson Fittipaldi, for Ayrton Senna

James Stewart, for Clark Gable

Hubert de Givenchy, for Audrey Hepburn

Ian Botham, for Colin Milburn

Tom Mix, for Wyatt Earp

Joe Louis, for Sonny Liston

King Edward VII, for William Gladstone

Kenny Rogers, for Vincente Minnelli

Sir Bobby Charlton, Sir Tom Finney and Nat Lofthouse, for Sir Stanley Matthews

Tony Mortimer, for Reggie Kray

Rock Hudson, Frank Sinatra, Laurence Olivier, Gregory Peck, David Niven, Fred Astaire and Elia Kazan, for Natalie Wood

LIST OF LISTS

All the Professional Footballers' Association's winners of **Footballer of the Year** 370

All the **Rears of the Year** 67

All the winners of FIFA **World Player of the Year** 367

All the winners of the **Lifetime Achievement** award at the British comedy awards 150

Americans and their **classmates' ratings** 281

Anagrams 199

Animals 33

Around the **world** 30

Auditioned unsuccessfully for the **Monkees** 321

Banned books 92

BBC's only female **Sports Personalities of the Year** 179

Beatles songs and who or what inspired them 103

Beds and **sleep** 72

Birds etc 37

Book titles and their **literary origins** 217

British Association of Toy Retailers' **Toy of the Year** 64

Bungee jumpers 357

Celebrities and **toilets** 333

Famous novels originally **rejected** by publishers 215

Famous people and the ages at which they lost their **virginity** 229

Famous people and their **allergies** 355

Famous people **born on the very same day** as other famous people 242

Famous people **born on the very same day** as other famous people died 185

Famous people who are **vegans** 190

Famous people who bought **houses** that had belonged to other famous people 340

Famous people who use their **middle names** as first names 287

Famous people who were **adopted** 222

Famous people with famous **ancestors** 241

Famous people with famous **godparents** 179

Famous relatives of **Olympic competitors** 163

Famous women born with the first name **Mary** 286

Famous women who **adopted** children 222

Fathers 11

Fathers of **triplets** 255

Fears and **phobias** 338

Film gaffes 282

First 10 **castaways** on *Desert Island Discs* 159

First 10 **commercials** broadcast on British TV 169

First 10 **songs** played on Radio 1 261

First 10 **songs** played on *Top of The Pops* 261

First European countries to have **McDonald's** 113

Non-professional golfers who scored **holes-in-one** in golf 246

Number-one records at the time of all **General Elections** since record charts began 96

Odds against various eventualities 54

Only **children** 223

Only countries to have won the **Wimbledon** men's singles title 151

Opera 284

Oscar onlys 170

Other medical expressions used in **hospitals** 79

Other people and their fears and **phobias** 339

Pairs of famous people who **died** on precisely the same day 192

Pallbearers for famous people 380

Parents of **twins** 255

People and the instruments they 'played' on the **Bonzo Dog Band's** 'The Intro And The Outro' 226

People and the **instruments** they can play 342

People and the names they gave their **pets** 335

People and the **sports** they played 305

People and their **nicknames** from schooldays 276

People and their **tattoos** 213

People **named after** someone/something famous 287

People who appeared in **advertisements** when they were children 303

People who appeared in British **soaps** as themselves 246

People who are fluent in **foreign languages** 155

People who attended the **same schools** 268

People who came from **large families** 257

People who changed their **names** 293

People who committed **bigamy** 117

People who died on their **birthdays** 224

People who **dropped out** of college 280

People who endowed **scholarships** at their old schools 281

People who entered competitions to imitate or **impersonate** themselves and lost 165

People who experienced bad **stage fright** 343

People who got **firsts** at university 280

People who got **thirds** at university 280

People who **guested** in the Batman TV series 182

People who **guested** on records 3 PI

People who had bad adolescent **acne** 155

People who had **hips** replaced 158

People who have been immortalized in **wax** at Madame Tussaud's since 1990 372

People who have been pestered for **autographs** in toilets 334

People who have switched on the **Blackpool illuminations** 153

People who have switched on the **Oxford Street lights** 152

People who have/had famous **fathers-in-law** 258

People who have/had famous **mothers-in-law** 259

People who insured parts of their **body** 252

People who launched their own **fragrances** 250

People who launched their own **products** 250

People who lived in their **cars** 325

People who made **guest appearances** in situation comedies 247

People who married at the age of **13** 123

People who married at the age of **14** 123

People who married at the age of **15** 123

People who married at the age of **16** 123

People who married **eight** times 119

People who married **five** times 119

People who married **four** times 120

People who married **nine** times 119

People who married **seven** times 119

People who married **six** times 119

People who married their **cousin** 115

People who married their **ex-spouse's relation** 130

People who **never married** 118

People who overcame **stammers** 260

People who play/played in **bands** 312

People who played for – or had trials with – **football clubs** 310

People who read their own **obituaries** 156

People who survived **plane crashes** 158

People who turn **25** in 2004 51

People who turn **30** in 2004 50

People who turn **40** in 2004 47

People who turn **50** in 2004 46

People who turn **60** in 2004 43

People who turn **70** in 2004 41

People who turn **80** in 2004 40

People who went to **finishing school** 281

People who were **betrothed** very quickly 115

People who were born on **significant days** in history 144

People who were **bullied** at school 273

People who were **bullies** (self-confessed) at school 275

People who were **educated at home** 275

People who were **expelled** from school 278

People who would have turned **100** in 2004 39

People whose names are used in **Cockney rhyming slang** 289

People whose **waxworks** have been removed from Madame Tussaud's since 1990 374

People with a **twin** brother/sister 255

People with famous **aunts** 254

People with famous **uncles** 254

People with four **initials** 299

People with **roses** named after them 234

Personalized car number plates 327

Proof that **hell** is exothermic 168

Proverbs that are clearly **not true** 144

Qualified **pilots** 328

Real people mentioned in **Beatles** songs 234

Real **people** who appeared in *The Beano* 248

Royals on the **throne** 330

Sardines 299

Science 29

Scrabble 100

Screen **kisses** 349

Served in the **Israeli** army 321

Acknowledgements

For the past twenty years, I've been collecting weird and wonderful facts which I've been storing on bits of paper and, more recently, on my computer. Every few years, I'll use some of it in a book or a newspaper series, but it's always been my ambition to be able to put together the most fascinating, extraordinary facts I had – or could find – in one volume. A sort of director's cut, if you like, of my whole career. The difficult part was not what to put in but what to take out.

Consequently, most of what you will read has been acquired organically. However, I would also like to acknowledge material culled from the internet: particularly Proof That Hell Is Exothermic and The World's Greatest Urban Myth. I have tried to source these wonderful items but to no avail. However, I'm sure that their original authors would appreciate this wider audience.

Meanwhile, I am continuing to mine the seams of trivia – in the fervent hope that *That Book* will become an annual publication. To that end, if you have any interesting facts (along the lines of the ones in this book) or come across something you think might work in a future edition, please send them to me at: thatbook@mail.com

This book – or, rather, *That Book* – couldn't have seen the light of day without the extraordinary foresight, imagination and diligence of (in alphabetical order): Hugh Adams, Luigi Bonomi, Penny Chorlton, Patrick Janson-Smith, Mari Roberts and Doug Young. I would like to thank the following people for their help, contributions and/or support (moral or otherwise): Gilly Adams, Russell Ash, Paul Ashford, Jeremy Beadle, Marcus Berkmann, Paul Donnelley, Steve Elson, Chris Ewins, Jonathan Fingerhut, Jenny Garrison, Bill Hagerty, Simon Hinde, Peter James, Brian Johnson, Andy Kay, John Koski, Richard Littlejohn, Linda Marks, Tricia Martin, Emanuel Mond, William Mulcahy, Rex Newman, Dave Nicholson, Nicholas Ridge, Simon Rose, Ian Stern, Louise Symons, Chris Tarrant, David Thomas, Roy Wells and Rob Woolley.

I would also like to take this opportunity to pay tribute to David Wallechinsky. It was the pioneering work done by him and his family on the seminal Books of Lists that originally excited my interest in this sort of work.

If I've missed anyone out, then please know that – as with any mistakes in the book – it's entirely down to my own stupidity: forgive me.

She frowned and called him Mr.

Because in sport he kr.

And so in spite

That very night

This Mr. kr. sr.

(Anon.)